THE POVERTY
OF PRIVACY RIGHTS

THE POVERTY
OF PRIVACY RIGHTS

Khiara M. Bridges

STANFORD LAW BOOKS
An Imprint of Stanford University Press
Stanford, California

Stanford University Press
Stanford, California

Printed in the United States of America on acid-free, archival-quality paper

Library of Congress Cataloging-in-Publication Data

Names: Bridges, Khiara M., author.
Title: The poverty of privacy rights / Khiara M. Bridges.
Description: Stanford, California : Stanford Law Books, an imprint of
    Stanford University Press, 2017. | Includes bibliographical references and index.
Identifiers: LCCN 2016057430 (print) | LCCN 2016057999 (ebook) |
    ISBN 9780804795456 (cloth : alk. paper) | ISBN 9781503602267 (pbk. : alk. paper) |
    ISBN 9781503602304 (e-book)
Subjects: LCSH: Privacy, Right of—United States. | Low-income mothers—Legal
    status, laws, etc.—United States. | Low-income mothers—Civil rights—United States. |
    Poverty—Moral and ethical aspects—United States.
Classification: LCC KF1262 .B753 2017 (print) | LCC KF1262 (ebook) |
    DDC 342.7308/58086942—dc23
LC record available at https://lccn.loc.gov/2016057430

Cover design: Michael Vrana | Black Eye Design
Typeset by Bruce Lundquist in 10/14 Minion

This book is dedicated to the late E. Allan Farnsworth,
who called me "the cat's pajamas" on more than one occasion.

Table of Contents

Acknowledgments

This book began many years ago, way back when I was a graduate student endeavoring to investigate the lives of poor, pregnant women who were struggling to maintain their dignity as they received state-subsidized prenatal care. I first want to thank those women who shared their stories with me.

Over the past couple of years, I have presented portions of this book to audiences at a number of different venues—including conferences, faculty workshops, and speaking engagements at Harvard Law School, University of Toronto Faculty of Law, University of Maryland School of Law, Case Western Reserve University School of Law, New York University School of Law, Suffolk University Law School, University of Chicago Law School, Boston University School of Law, and Yale Law School. I thank all the participants at these various gatherings for offering helpful comments, suggestions, challenges, and insights.

I am particularly thankful for my wonderful colleagues at BU Law for engaging with this project—particularly Gerry Leonard, Tracey Maclin, David Seipp, Sarah Sherman-Stokes, Larry Yackle, and Kathy Zeiler. A special debt of gratitude is owed to David Lyons, who read several chapters several times and who so generously helped me with my moral theorizing. I am especially thankful for Linda McClain and Jim Fleming, who helped me to conceptualize what exactly I wanted to argue in this book and then encouraged me to actually write it. Thanks as well to the wonderful scholars outside of BU Law who helped me think through important parts of this book, especially Danielle Citron, Simon Stern, and Jeff Vagle.

I am grateful to Jenna Fegreus, Ellen Minot Frentzen, Jennifer Robble, and Stefanie Weigmann in the BU Law Library, whose research support I simply could not live without. I am also grateful to Mike Garry, my trusty research assistant and birthday twin, who has improved my scholarship with his exceptional attention to detail. Thanks are also owed to Devante Walton and Michael Onah, who did some crucial RA work when Mike had the audacity to graduate and leave me behind. I am especially appreciative of my amazing dean, Maureen O'Rourke, for supporting my scholarship (with funds, no less!) and for granting me the teaching leave that allowed me to write significant portions of this project. Thanks to my students—my brilliant, passionate, inspiring students—for making me want to make them proud.

Thanks to Michelle Lipinski, my editor at Stanford University Press, for being so responsive, supportive, and simply awesome. Special thanks are owed to Jennifer Gong for introducing me to Michelle. Without Jennifer, this book simply would not exist.

I am indebted to the community of dancers in New York City for always awing me. I remain utterly humbled by their talent and commitment to their artistry. I am honored to (still!) train and perform beside them. A sincere thank-you to Leanh Nguyen for being so very good at her job. Thanks to my beautiful friends for filling my time outside of academia with laughter, love, and light.

I thank my parents, Clive R. Bridges and Deborah A. Bridges, for making all of the sacrifices that they made in order to give me such a charmed life. Thanks as well to my sister and brother, Algeria Bridges and Khari Bridges, for making their love for me constant and familiar—something that has been with me since I took my first breath of air. Thanks are also owed to my extended family for being so proud of me. A special thank-you to my Uncle J, James Bridges, for his endearing brand of love and encouragement. When I told him that I was working on my second book, he said, "Well, it's about time," making me laugh harder than I had laughed in recent memory. Thanks to Mams and Paps Reynaert for welcoming me into their lives with open arms (and Chokotoffs!).

And, finally, thank you to Gert Reynaert—my best friend, *mijn hartendief, mijn honing konijn*. I had no idea that life could be this sweet. Thank you for finding me.

THE POVERTY
OF PRIVACY RIGHTS

Introduction

"More and more often, we all make silent calculations about who is entitled to what rights, and who is not. It's not as simple as saying everyone is the same under the law anymore. We all know there's another layer to it now."

Matt Taibbi, The Divide: American Injustice in the Age of the Wealth Gap, p. xvii

A cursory glance at the California Code of Regulations hardly excites. Because it appears to be nothing but chapters upon chapters of rules upon rules that concern the banalities of bureaucracies, one might be tempted to describe the code as boring. Sure, there are moments of titillation: Title 17 regulates the Office of Problem and Pathological Gambling. (It includes a provision that requires casinos to make payments to the Gambling Addition Program Fund.) And then there is Title 26, which concerns "Toxics." (It contains a subtitle that governs the Board of Barbering and Cosmetology and includes a rule that, in no uncertain terms, prohibits an establishment or school from "knowingly permit[ting] a person afflicted with an infection or parasitic infestation capable of being transmitted to a patron to serve patrons or train in the establishment or school.") But, besides these brief flashes of the ironic and the foul, the California Code of Regulations seems utterly mundane and quite dull.

Yet, nestled within it is Title 22, which itemizes rules and regulations for the provision of social services in California. And nestled within that title is Section 51179.10, which delineates the services that pregnant women will receive when they, lacking both private health insurance and the means to pay for prenatal care out-of-pocket, look to the state's Medicaid program for assistance in acquiring medical care. The provision requires that, alongside the expected examinations designed to assess and manage a pregnant woman's physical health, prenatal care services administered in line with it must include assessments of women's "nutritional status," "health education status," and "psychosocial status." Notably, the health education assessment requires that a professional evaluate a woman's "formal education and reading level . . . , religious/cultural influences that impact upon perinatal health; and client and family or support person's motivation to participate in the educational plan." Additionally, the psychosocial assessment requires that a professional review a woman's "social support system; personal adjustment to pregnancy; history of previous pregnancies; patient's goals for herself in this pregnancy; general emotional status and history; wanted or unwanted pregnancy, acceptance of the pregnancy; substance use and abuse; housing/household; education/employment; and financial/material resources" (22 C.C.R. § 51348(e)(1)(A)).

New York's Medicaid prenatal care program mirrors California's insofar as it requires various assessments of poor pregnant women that exceed evaluations of their physical health (Bridges 2011a, 2011b). During eighteen months of ethnographic fieldwork in the obstetrics clinic of New York City's "Alpha Hospital," a large public hospital that serves the city's poor, I had the chance to observe a psychosocial assessment that a social worker, "Tina," administered to a patient, "Erica," as required by law. I had asked Tina to ask Erica, who was pregnant with her fourth child, if I could sit in during her consultation. Erica consented and allowed me to tape-record her session:

Tina ("T"): Are you working?

Erica ("E"): No—I'm in college still.

T: How are you supporting yourself?

E: [long pause] How could I forget what it's called. . . . Welfare! [laughs]

T: You receive public assistance?

E: Yes.

T: How much?

E: Um, 354. . . .

T: And does that include what they give you for your rent?

E: Yes. Well, I don't pay rent.

T: You don't pay rent?

E: I live in a shelter.

T: What shelter do you live in?

E: Beta Houses.

T: Who's your caseworker?

E: Ms. C.

T: Do you have the number?

E: Yeah—I have the number: 1-212-555-1212. She has an extension: 1212.

T: And how long have you been there?

E: Almost four months.

T: And can you tell me what the circumstances were that put you in shelter?

E: Domestic violence.

T: And how long did the domestic violence last?

E: Two months.

T: So, you were in a domestic violence relationship for about two months, and then you moved to a shelter.

E: Uh-huh.

T: And how long was your relationship?

E: It wasn't really a relationship. It was, like, I would say—three months.

T: I'm sorry?

E: Three months—it was, like, a three-month relationship.

T: It was a three-month relationship. And do you have a police report and an order of protection?

E: The police report, yes. Not the order of protection—still didn't get it.

T: Would you like to talk to someone about the domestic violence?

E: No. . . .

T: Who's the father of the baby?

E: Nathanial Thompson. [pseudonym]

T: Is the father of the baby living with you?

E: No.

T: How long have you been in a relationship with the father?

E: Ten years.

T: The father of the baby?

E: Uh-huh. Same father as all the rest of them.

T: How old is he?

E: How old? 34.

T: Can you identify the father?

E: Yes. . . .

T: What's his name?

E: Nathanial Thompson.

T: And how would you describe your relationship with the father?

E: Fine—now.

T: "Fine now"?

E: Uh-huh.

T: Does he intend to help when the baby comes?

E: Yes—he's my fiancé. I just didn't get my ring yet. He better hurry up.

T: Is he working?

E: Yes. No, he doesn't work. Sorry. He's in college.

T: How does he support himself?

E: I know that he's on public assistance, but I don't know what he gets or anything like that.

T: But, he's going to able to support you and your child?

E: Yes, he's going to get a job by the time—he's about to be done with college.

T: You feel that when he's done with school, he's going to be financially able to support the child?

E: He's going to be making 43,000 [dollars] a year.

T: You know that already?

E: Yes. His job is already set up.

T: What does he do?

E: He's a computer technician. I don't know how he does it. I hate computers.

T: You are in a better situation than a lot of our patients.

E: I just have to get up out this dag-gone shelter. Then, I'll be fine.[1]

Thus, a state actor engaged Erica in a conversation that touched on many highly sensitive topics, including her previous romantic relationship, which tragically involved violence severe enough to land her in a shelter; the healthiness of her relationship with the father of her children; her earnings capacity; and the earnings capacity of the father of her children. Tina went on to ask Erica about her history, if any, with tobacco and alcohol products, controlled substances, mental illness, sexual abuse and violence, and a host of other intimate issues.

It is paramount to recognize that the sole reason Erica was compelled to have this conversation with a state actor was because *she was pregnant and had presented herself to a public hospital with the hope of receiving state-assisted prenatal care.* It is also important to observe that this is a painfully personal conversation that privately insured pregnant women can and, absent unique circumstances, usually do avoid.

It is not hyperbole to describe the inquiries required by the Medicaid programs in California and New York as *extensive.* Because of the all-encompassing nature of the interrogation, many persons might find the bureaucratic apparatus that has been constructed and reserved for women without private health insurance to be troubling. And many of those persons might describe their disquietude in the language of *privacy*.[2] That is, the programs of public health-care in California and New York do not leave the women that it serves with much privacy.

If we conceptualize the family as a private entity that the government ought not to regulate (absent evidence of abuse or neglect of one of its members), then these programs invade poor women's privacy inasmuch as they allow the government to monitor and regulate the family unit for the duration of the pregnancy and possibly after. If we understand certain information about ourselves as private—like details about our marriages or romantic relationships, the healthiness of our eating habits, the frequency with which we exercise (or not), and our success at remaining gainfully employed (or not)—then these programs invade poor women's privacy inasmuch as they require women to divulge that information and inasmuch as they share that information, once collected, with third parties. And if we understand a woman's decision about whether or not to become a mother to be a private matter, then most states' Medicaid programs violate poor women's privacy in that they implicate themselves in this decision by using government largesse to direct poor women toward or away from motherhood.

The Medicaid programs for pregnant women seeking prenatal care in California and New York—which are typical of other states' Medicaid programs in their demands—demonstrate a simple reality: To be poor is to be subject to invasions of privacy that we might understand as demonstrations of the danger of government power without limits. Indeed, one would expect that if the Constitution contains individual rights and liberties that restrict state power, it would prevent precisely what poor women endure with respect to state intrusions into their private lives.

Moreover, if the state treated other persons who receive government benefits the same way that the state treats poor mothers who receive government benefits, there would be a general sense of outrage; people would claim, loudly and frequently, that the government was violating citizens' privacy. Imagine what would happen if the government required farmers to divulge information about their sexual, occupational, and social histories when they applied for farm subsidies, or if it gave them larger subsidies if they promised not to terminate any future pregnancies. After much outcry, these laws would likely be struck down as a violation of farmers' privacy rights.

Indeed, if a state or the federal government compelled *all* pregnant women—poor and non-poor alike—to be counseled about smoking and drinking alcohol, to undergo "treatment and intervention directed toward helping [them] understand the importance of . . . good nutrition during pregnancy," and to discuss with a state actor their "goals for [themselves] in this pregnancy" and their "general emotional status," one would expect an uproar about the privacy invasions visited upon pregnant women by a paternalistic and overreaching state. Nevertheless, courts have routinely upheld the constitutionality of the privacy invasions that Medicaid programs force upon poor women.

The Government Interest in Protecting Children

Some will not be disquieted at all by poor mothers' experiences with the state. They will insist that a poor mother's privacy may justifiably be invaded when the state seeks to ensure that a woman's child will be born into a healthful environment and that the woman will properly parent the child once born. Proponents of this view will assert that it is pursuant to this state interest that the state gathers and shares private information about the woman, monitors her and her existing family unit, and constrains her reproductive decisions. It is important to take this claim seriously.

For example, consider California's Medicaid program and its requirement that, during the assessment of a woman's psychosocial status, a social worker inquires into a woman's "housing/household" situation. Arguably, the idea is that, if the woman reveals that she is cohabiting with a man to whom she is not married, the state has an interest in continuing to monitor the woman and her family because statistics reveal that children living in unmarried-couple households are at higher risk for physical and sexual abuse (Sedlak et al. 2010). Similar arguments can be made about inquiries that, for example, confirm that a woman smokes cigarettes, drinks alcohol, or does not go to all of her scheduled prenatal care appointments.

Some will argue that this information may index a woman's neglect of her fetus—revealing that she is likely to be a neglectful parent. They will claim that if the encyclopedic inquisitive net that the state casts indicates a risk that a particular individual will fail her child, the state is justified in maintaining her within its regulatory apparatus in order to protect the child once it is born. Proponents of this view will argue that the exhaustiveness of the state's inquest—and the fact that it touches on information and areas of life that the woman, and society generally, consider private—is necessary because the goal is the protection of the child. The means to this end, the invasion of poor women's privacy, is argued to be an unfortunate, yet inevitable, consequence of pursuing this goal.

But, why is the state convinced that the children born (or to be born) to poor women are in need of protection? Why is the state so persuaded of this fact that it has erected an elaborate bureaucratic apparatus that meticulously and methodically audits the pregnant poor? Indeed, we must ask, *Why does the state presume that poor mothers are at risk of abusing and/or neglecting their children?*

The most salient characteristic shared by all women receiving Medicaid benefits during their pregnancies is their poverty. And we might conclude that it is this characteristic that casts suspicion over poor mothers' ability to adequately care for their children. That is, if we are feeling charitable, we may conclude that the state presumes that poor mothers are at risk of abusing and/or neglecting their children because a mother's poverty makes it more likely that she will be unable to meet the material needs of her child. This charitable interpretation posits that the state invades a poor woman's privacy and impinges on her privacy rights because the state assumes that she may not be able to provide the basics for her child: food, clothing, shelter, and healthcare.

However, if this benign interpretation were true, the questions asked of poor women throughout their prenatal care would concern, specifically, their ability to provide their children with food, clothing, shelter, and healthcare. If this interpretation were true, the ambit of the state's inquisition would focus on whether the woman's financial condition could support an expanded family. Instead, inquiries about women's sexual histories, experiences with substance use and abuse, histories of sexual and domestic violence, and strategies for preventing the conception and birth of more children far exceed the purview of concern about the material conditions in which newborn children will be placed.

Indeed, we need to adopt a less benign interpretation: The state presumes that the risk of poor mothers abusing and neglecting their children is high, and this presumption of high risk has very little to do with the fear that poor mothers will not be able to provide for their children's basic needs. Instead, in this book I argue that the presumption of high risk has everything to do with the *moral construction of poverty*—the idea that people are poor because they are lazy, irresponsible, averse to work, promiscuous, and so on. This individualist explanation of poverty is the simple idea that people are poor because there is something wrong with them. If personal failures are the presumptive cause of poverty, then poor *mothers* ought to be supervised closely, as their personal failures necessarily implicate children.

It is worth noting, early and often, that wealthier women engage in the same behaviors in which poor women engage. Wealthier women cohabit with men to whom they are not married. Wealthier women have had many sexual partners. Wealthier women have used and abused illicit drugs. They, too, miss prenatal care appointments. They, too, have histories of sexual and domestic violence. They, too, have unplanned pregnancies. They, too, find themselves pregnant after being in relatively short relationships with the fathers of their babies. They, too, ought to contemplate strategies for preventing the conception and birth of more children if they want to limit the size of their families.

Yet, no state has erected an extravagant bureaucratic tool with which it can take an accounting of every non-poor pregnant woman. This is telling. It suggests that the state is not really interested in protecting children from abuse and neglect. Instead, it is only interested in protecting *some* children from abuse and neglect. That is, the state assumes that only some children need to be protected from their mothers. And those children are the ones that are born to poor women.

Why does the state make this assumption about poor women? It cannot be because poor women uniquely engage in problematic behaviors and have problematic histories; wealthier women do, too. It has to be because of something else. The thrust of this book is that this "something else" is the individualist, moralizing explanation for poverty accepted by society, the architects of these laws, and the jurists that interpret these laws as consistent with the Constitution.

Justice Marshall articulated this argument in his dissent in *Wyman v. James* (400 U.S. 309 (1971)), in which the Court upheld suspicionless searches of the homes of poor mothers receiving welfare assistance:

> It is argued that the home visit is justified to protect dependent children from "abuse" and "exploitation." These are heinous crimes, but they are not confined to indigent households. Would the majority sanction, in the absence of probable cause, compulsory visits to all American homes for the purpose of discovering child abuse? Or is this Court prepared to hold as a matter of constitutional law that a mother, merely because she is poor, is substantially more likely to injure or exploit her children? Such a categorical approach to an entire class of citizens would be dangerously at odds with the tenets of our democracy. (341–42)

Justice Marshall is right: Such an approach *is* dangerously at odds with the tenets of our democracy. Nevertheless, it is an approach that the Court has sanctioned time and time again.

Thus, a woman's inability to thrive within a capitalist economy—and her failure to attach herself to a man who has—is taken to predict the likelihood that she will mistreat and/or exploit her child. Moreover, the mistreatment and exploitation of children is sufficiently probable that the endeavor to prevent it justifies dispossessing all poor mothers of freedom from state intervention in private matters. Questions are asked of a poor woman not because the child to whom she will give birth might be wounded or wronged in some way—by his mother's imperfect diet, the marijuana that she smoked years ago, or her inability to read beyond a tenth-grade level. Instead, this information is gathered because the patient's poverty is presumed to indicate a flawed character that might manifest in harm to her child.

Now, some may counter that poor mothers simply have exchanged their privacy rights for state assistance. This position contends that if the government exercises power in poor mothers' lives in ways that the Constitution would ordinarily prohibit, it is only because poor mothers have *traded* their rights to limit that power for a welfare benefit. While initially appealing, the argument ultimately reveals itself to be specious.

This argument, which Chapter 2 addresses in depth, is premised on the assumption that poor mothers would have effective privacy rights and meaningful privacy if they did not accept a government benefit. But, this simply is not true. We need only imagine what would happen if poor mothers *refused* government benefits: They likely would be investigated by child protective services (CPS) for child neglect.

To explain: The benefits that poor mothers accept—the assistance for which they purportedly exchange their ostensible privacy rights—enable beneficiaries to provide their children with basic necessities. Medicaid enables poor mothers to access healthcare. Temporary Assistance for Needy Families (TANF) enables poor mothers to provide food and clothing to their children. The Special Supplemental Nutrition Program for Women, Infants, and Children (WIC) and the Supplemental Nutrition Assistance Program (SNAP, formerly known as food stamps) enable mothers to meet their children's nutritional needs. Public housing enables poor mothers to provide their children with shelter.

If poor mothers refused these benefits, they would not be able to provide their children with the basics: food, clothing, shelter, and healthcare. And the failure to provide these basics is textbook child neglect (DePanfilis 2006).

Thus, if an indigent mother refused to exchange her ostensible privacy rights for a government benefit, she would certainly find herself under investigation by CPS. Moreover, the point of a CPS investigation is to divest the family and the members that constitute it of privacy so that they may become visible to the state, enabling the state to determine whether the parents are competent to raise their children without ongoing intervention and regulation.

Accordingly, poor mothers exist in a fraught situation: They lose their privacy if they accept government assistance (because safety net programs demand access to private areas of beneficiaries' lives); and they lose their privacy if they do not accept government assistance (because they will be unable to provide their children with basic necessities, thus making them vulnerable to a privacy-invading investigation by CPS). Thus, the legal and social condition of poor mothers is one that is devoid of privacy—one in which state power surrounds them at all times, without regard to whether they receive public benefits. Either way, receiving public assistance or not, *it is impossible for poor mothers to create a space free of state power.* As such, we can conclude that poor mothers' vulnerability to state power—their complete exposure to government regulation—is not at all contingent on their receipt of a welfare benefit.

The Moderate Claim and the Strong Claim

In this book I make two interventions into the conversation around poor mothers' experiences with state power. First, I seek to complement accounts of how the state regulates poor mothers through TANF by offering an account of how the state regulates poor mothers and mothers-to-be through Medicaid. The privacy invasions that the state demands when poor mothers receive benefits from TANF programs have been well documented (Gilliom 2001; Gustafson 2011). However, there is a gap in the literature due to the lack of scholarly attention to Medicaid, an important program on which many poor women rely. This book does not attempt to canvass all of the government programs on which poor people depend and to describe the privacy invasions demanded (or not demanded) by each; instead, I seek to illuminate the privacy invasions demanded of poor women by one frequently overlooked, yet highly utilized program.

Second, in this book I advance the claim that poor mothers have been deprived of privacy rights. There are two ways to understand this assertion:

1. One might understand the claim that "poor mothers have been deprived of privacy rights" to be a *rhetorical* argument. If the claim is rhetorical, then it asserts that these mothers do in fact *have* these rights; however, for all practical purposes, they lack them. Under this formulation, describing poor mothers as having "no privacy rights" is a rhetorical flourish—meant to underscore the impotence of the privacy rights that they do indeed possess. This is the book's moderate claim. It asserts that poor mothers have privacy rights, but these rights are incredibly weak. Essentially, poor mothers have no *effective* privacy rights.

2. One might understand the claim that "poor mothers have been deprived of privacy rights" to be an *analytical* argument. If the claim is analytical, then it asserts that poor mothers actually *do not* possess privacy rights. This is the book's strong claim. It contends that poor mothers have been dispossessed of privacy rights; they are not bearers of privacy rights.

Let's elaborate on the strong claim: It begins with the recognition that privacy rights are imagined to generate value. Over the years, many scholars have theorized about this value. One might divide these theories into two camps: There are those that concern themselves with the value of privacy to the individual, and there are those that concern themselves with the value of privacy to society more generally. Scholars writing in the former camp have often used the language of dignity, personhood, autonomy, and individuality when describing what privacy protects and what makes privacy so vital to the individual (Bloustein 1978).

Other scholars turn their attention to the value that privacy produces for society more generally (Cohen 2000). For example, legal philosopher Anita Allen (1988) has noted that while we "promote and protect privacy to show moral respect for individuals and to confer moral dignity," the moral value of privacy is *also* tied to the fact that privacy makes "individuals more fit for social participation and contribution," thus benefiting "group life" (48). Privacy scholar Daniel Solove (2008) has also championed privacy by looking to the value that it creates for society, encouraging his readers to understand "privacy as having a social value" and to appreciate "the benefits it confers on society by enhancing and protecting certain aspects of selfhood" (92).

So, privacy is imagined to generate value—either for the individual or for society. And realizing this value is the reason why we recognize privacy rights. However, we also recognize that privacy is not inevitably put to noble uses. As Allen (2000) notes, "privacy itself is not an unqualified good" (1195). Privacy is the cover that prevents sunlight from disinfecting, the shield that permits crimes to go undetected, the barrier that obstructs help from reaching the helpless.

Accordingly, if the individual enjoying privacy rights will not put them to good uses, her enjoyment of these rights will not produce the value that otherwise justifies their provision. Indeed, her enjoyment of privacy rights may actually produce a *negative* value, as it allows her to use privacy in ignoble ways.

Now, due to the moral construction of poverty, there is a presumption that poor mothers will not put privacy rights to good uses. Indeed, the moral construction of poverty asserts that the poor are behaviorally and/or ethically flawed. (Their poverty proves as much.) Further, because poor mothers are pregnant or parenting, their behavioral and ethical flaws will, as a matter of course, affect children. Accordingly, the strong claim contends that poor mothers are not given privacy rights because society, and thus the law, presumes that their enjoyment of privacy will realize no value or a negative value (Eubanks 2006, 90; Handler and Hasenfeld 1991).

Thus, the strong claim argues that wealth is a condition for privacy rights and that, lacking wealth, poor mothers do not have any privacy rights. Accordingly, the privacy invasions demanded by Medicaid (and TANF and WIC and public housing and the child protection system) do not violate the privacy rights of poor mothers because their socioeconomic status has already precluded their possession of any privacy rights that the state is obliged to respect.

One need not accept the strong claim in order to appreciate this book's exploration of poor mothers' experiences with the state. Indeed, all of the arguments that I advance in this book as to why poor mothers do not have privacy rights in the strong sense are relevant as to why they do not have privacy rights in the moderate sense. That is, if poor mothers have not been given privacy rights (in the strong sense) because they are imagined to be behaviorally or ethically flawed, their behavioral and ethical flaws would also explain why they have been given ineffective privacy rights (i.e., the moderate claim). And if poor mothers have not been given privacy rights (in the strong sense) because their behavioral or ethical flaws necessarily implicate children, these flaws would also explain why have been given ineffective privacy rights (i.e., the moderate claim). The moderate claim and the strong claim both produce the circumstance in which poor mothers find themselves: completely exposed to state power.

Nevertheless, the strong claim ought to be taken seriously. Not only does it alter the terms of the current conversation, but it may also explain why *positive rights are only an illusory solution to the predicament that poor mothers face*. Chapter 1 explores this possibility.

Additionally, the strong claim allows us to draw parallels between poor mothers and other groups that have been deprived of or otherwise disqualified from having a right or a set of rights. Consider that Chief Justice Taney declared in *Dred Scott* (Dred Scott v. Sandford, 60 U.S. 393, 407 (1856)) that the "negro . . . had no rights which the white man was bound to respect." Consider as well that, until the Court's decision in *Obergefell v. Hodges* (135 S.Ct. 2584 (2015)), sexual minorities did not have the right to marry, although the Constitution has long been interpreted to bestow the right to their straight counterparts. Speaking about poor mothers as analogously not bearing a set of rights—privacy rights—encourages us to identify continuities between poor mothers and these other groups that have been deprived of certain legal protections. It allows us to think about the issue in new ways. And it allows us, perhaps, to imagine different solutions—possibilities that the Conclusion explores.

Finally, the strong claim permits us to consider the concept of *informal disenfranchisement*. Informal disenfranchisement refers to the process by which a group that has been formally bestowed with a right is stripped of that very right by techniques that the Court has held to be consistent with the Constitution. The best precedent for, and example of, informal disenfranchisement is black people's experience with voting rights. While the Fifteenth Amendment formally enfranchised black men, white supremacists in the South employed methods—poll taxes, literacy tests, residency requirements, and white primaries—that made it nearly impossible for black men (and after the passage of the Nineteenth Amendment, black women) to actually vote in the South for a century after their formal enfranchisement. Moreover, the Court held that these techniques of racial exclusion from the polls were constitutional.[3]

Central to the concept of informal disenfranchisement is the requirement that the mechanisms that function to deprive an individual of a right enjoy the Court's explicit approval. That is, in order for an individual to be informally disenfranchised of a right, the laws and practices that act to strip the individual of the right must be perfectly legal, with the Court having deemed them to be consistent with the demands of the Constitution. Thus, if poor mothers have been informally disenfranchised of their privacy rights, then the problem is not one of *noncompliance* with their rights, if we understand non-compliance as the failure to act in accordance with the command of a law. The problem that this book explores is not one involving state actors who disobey laws designed to protect poor mothers' privacy rights. Instead, the problem is one involving governments that disobey no laws at all—including, most importantly, the Constitution as interpreted by the Supreme Court. No laws are being broken when governments regulate poor families, extract and share personally identifiable and intimate information about indigent mothers, and coerce poor women into and out of motherhood. When governments install themselves in poor mothers' private lives—an installation that privacy rights are designed to disable—they act entirely in accordance with what the law demands. This is informal disenfranchisement: the *legal* deprivation of a right that has been formally bestowed.

. . .

The next section is a philosophical and political defense of the strong claim. It is my hope that readers who presently are skeptical of this claim will read the next section and walk away utterly convinced of the claim's propriety. Neverthe-less, if the reader remains skeptical, then she is invited to understand the rest of the book as an exploration of why, consistent with the moderate claim, poor mothers' extant privacy rights have been made ineffective. To this reader, the book will be an analysis of why poor mothers have been given meaningless rights and an exploration of what we can do to give those rights some teeth. However, those persuaded of the truth of the strong claim should understand the rest of the book as a study of the informal disenfranchisement of poor mothers and an interrogation of the changes that need to be achieved in order to bring this group within the class of persons to whom privacy rights are ascribed.

Defending the Strong Claim
Departing from Traditional Rights Discourse
To argue that poor women do not have privacy rights (in the strong sense) is inconsistent with how we are trained to conceptualize rights, especially con-stitutional rights. We are taught that once a constitutional right is recognized, everyone possesses that right equally. We understand that there were moments in our nation's history when groups of persons were denied rights altogether—during the days of chattel slavery, for example. And we understand that the

passage of the Reconstruction Amendments after the Civil War formally corrected this exclusion. We also understand that, throughout our history, groups have agitated for inclusion in the population of persons to whom rights would be ascribed—during the women's rights movement from the mid–nineteenth century into the early twentieth century, for example. And we also understand that groups have continued to agitate for the recognition of additional constitutional and non-constitutional rights that they believe will make their citizenship, their opportunities, or the rights that they already possess equal to those of other persons in the United States. The civil rights movement in the 1960s, the women's liberation movement in the 1960s and 1970s, and the movement for marriage equality for LGBT persons immediately come to mind.

We also learn that there are some classes of persons that do not possess the same rights as others—incompetent persons and minors, for example. However, we are told that these groups are exceptions to the general rule that once a constitutional right is recognized, everyone possesses the right equally. As such, the narrative that we have come to accept tells us that, for example, once the Supreme Court in *McDonald v. Chicago* interpreted the Second Amendment to provide individuals with the right to possess handguns in the home, the interpretation gave *everyone* the right to possess handguns in the home. According to this narrative, once the Supreme Court in *Roe v. Wade* interpreted the Due Process Clause to protect the right to an abortion, the interpretation gave *everyone* the right to an abortion.

We understand that there may be enduring questions about the right that the Court has found or recognized. (Does the right that the Court recognized in *McDonald* prohibit states from banning semiautomatic weapons? Does the right that the Court recognized in *Roe v. Wade* prohibit a state from attempting to dissuade a woman from undergoing an abortion by presenting her with the argument that the fetus is the moral equivalent of a baby?) However, we recognize that these questions pertain to the content and shape of the right that everyone possesses. How the Court answers these questions affects everyone equally insofar as everyone possesses the same right. This is what we are educated to believe.

We are also trained to understand that rights may be infringed when the government has good reasons for doing so. When the Court has found the right to be a fundamental one, the government's reasons for infringing it must be compelling. When the right is not fundamental, the government's reasons for infringing it need not be as urgent. As lawyers and members of the lay public, we become comfortable with that result because we are instructed to understand that rights are not absolute—that the government can override them if it demonstrates that the circumstances call for it. Our education tells us that what distinguishes a legitimate infringement of the right from an illegitimate violation of the right is whether the government's reasons for overriding it meet the burden of justification that the right demands.[4]

And this is how most have approached the question of the privacy rights of poor mothers. Consistent with the narrative that presupposes that everyone (who is not incompetent or a minor) possesses the same right once the right is recognized, most assume that poor mothers have privacy rights. But then, in the face of California's Section 51179.10 and similar state regulations, those who are disquieted by what these laws require argue that poor pregnant women's privacy rights are violated. For example, when the Ninth Circuit denied a petition for a rehearing en banc of a three-judge panel's decision to uphold a provision requiring that all beneficiaries of California's cash assistance program living in San Diego County submit to home visits by an investigator from the district attorney's office, the dissenters observed that no court would ever uphold the constitutionality of a similar provision applied against the wealthy. They argued that although the poor do not receive most government benefits, "this is the group we require to sacrifice their . . . right to privacy" (Sanchez v. County of San Diego, 483 F.3d 965, 969 (9th Cir. 2007, en banc)).

In stating that government programs violate poor mothers' privacy rights or demand that they be sacrificed or bartered, scholars and jurists are claiming that the government has overridden their rights without meeting its justificatory burden. Accordingly, they describe poor mothers' rights as weak or meaningless. They are weak because they invariably fail to stop the government from overriding them. They are meaningless because, in invariably failing to stop the government from overriding them, the government acts as it would act if poor mothers did not bear privacy rights at all.

This book's strong claim departs from the traditional account of poor mothers' privacy rights. The claim contends that the traditional narrative—presupposing that everyone who is competent and is not a minor possesses a right once it is recognized—is actually wrong. It declares that the reason the government can act as if poor mothers did not bear privacy rights is because *poor mothers do not bear privacy rights.*

Most have resisted this conclusion, even when they have acknowledged that poor people's purported rights function dramatically differently from the rights of their counterparts with class privilege. For example, when contemplating the reality that poverty makes it quite difficult, and frequently impossible, for poor persons to exercise the rights that traditional rights discourse asserts that they possess, political theorist John Rawls (1971) refused to conclude that the practical inefficacy and irrelevance of poor persons' theoretical rights demonstrate that they actually do not possess those rights. He writes:

> The inability to take advantage of one's rights and opportunities as a result of poverty and ignorance, and a lack of means generally, is sometimes counted among the constraints definitive of liberty. I shall not, however, say this, but rather I shall think of these things as affecting the worth of liberty, the value to individuals of the rights that the first principle defines. (204)

Here, Rawls distinguishes between having rights and the worth of the rights that one has. While poverty may make rights less valuable insofar as poverty precludes the indigent rightsbearer from taking advantage of them, Rawls maintains here that they possess the rights in the first place. He does not arrive at the strong claim: The utter inefficacy of ostensible rights demonstrates the nonexistence of those rights.

Rawls is not alone. Political theorist Isaiah Berlin arrived at a similar conclusion. Berlin once asked, "For what are rights without the power to implement them?" (Waldron 1993, 6). Although the prompt was provocative, Berlin, like Rawls, answered the question by distinguishing the possession of rights from their worth: He was willing to allow that indigent persons could be in possession of meaningless rights. Legal philosopher Jeremy Waldron (1993) writes of Berlin, "And *still*, he said, from the analytical point of view, 'liberty is one thing, and the conditions for it are another'" (6).

Waldron, who has been a proponent of positive economic and other subsistence rights, disagrees with Rawls and Berlin, however. And in disagreeing with them, Waldron proposes a theory of rights that is consistent with the strong claim. Waldron quotes a fellow proponent of positive economic and subsistence rights, Henry Shue, as saying, "No one can fully, if at all, enjoy any right that is supposedly protected by society if he or she lacks the essentials for a reasonably healthy and active life." Waldron (1993) goes on:

> What enjoyment means is actually *having* the right, in the substantive sense in which the right is thought to be worth having. A person does not have the right to vote unless there is some reasonable prospect that he can cast his vote on election day and have it counted. He cannot be said to have or enjoy the right

in this sense if, for example, there are no polling places nearby or if there is no transportation available to get him to the polls. (9)

Here, Waldron articulates a conception of rights wherein some people have the right to vote while others do not. Wealthy Person, who lives near polling places or who has the ability to drive to them, *has* the right to vote; simultaneously, Poor Person, who does not live near a polling place and does not have a car or other means of transportation, does not *have* the right to vote. In Waldron's conception of rights, a constitution or a piece of legislation may have given the right to vote to all persons of a certain age. Accordingly, in a theoretical sense, both Wealthy Person and Poor Person, who are persons under the constitution or the legislation and who satisfy the age requirement, "have" voting rights. Rawls and Berlin would conclude as much. However, Waldron disagrees, contending that the impossibility of exercising the right renders the right nonexistent.

Waldron's formulation of rights is important because it suggests the possibility of a legal landscape wherein some classes of persons have a right and other classes of persons do not have that right *although a constitution or law might have bestowed the right universally on all persons.* In Waldron's hypothetical, a constitution or law might have bestowed a right to vote on everyone. However, the inability of some persons to actually cast a vote on Election Day means, to Waldron, that these persons do not actually *have* the right to vote.

Now, the situation within which poor mothers find themselves is distinct from the problem presented in Waldron's example. In that hypothetical, the recognition of a positive right to vote would resolve Poor Person's lack of the right to vote. However, the recognition of positive rights to privacy would not completely solve the problem that poor mothers face. Unlike Waldron's example of voting rights, the reason why poor mothers do not have privacy rights is not simply that they do not have the means to exercise these rights. If that were the case, a positive privacy right might solve the problem in its entirety. However, the government also violates poor mothers' ostensible negative rights. That is, the government acts when the negative privacy right demands inaction. Thus, the problem that poor mothers face is not *solely* that their indigence denies them the means to exercise their purported rights, but *also* that the state intrudes when their purported rights demand no intrusion.

Further, when the state acts despite the fact that poor mothers' ostensible rights demand inaction, the Court routinely upholds the act. The strong claim observes this fact and concludes that a regular, systemic, and *judicially sanctioned* violation of a purported right is evidence of the nonexistence of the right. Although the Constitution might have bestowed privacy rights on every-one, poor mothers do not actually *have* these rights.

Allen (1992) has reached a conclusion similar to the strong claim—that a common and judicially endorsed violation of a right demonstrates the right's nonexistence—when contemplating the status of legal rights for indigent people of color in the United States. After surveying the inefficacy of black people's apparent legal rights, she queries whether we misdescribe the legal landscape when we say that black people are possessors of rights, albeit feeble ones. She writes that contemporary rights theorists

> are quick to stipulate that all normal adult human beings are members of the class of paradigm moral and legal rightsholders. . . . [T]he easy assertion by mainstream philosophers that all normal adult human beings are paradigm rightsholders rings hollow against the background of American history, in which the opposite proposition has been quietly believed and loudly defended in the courts and legislatures to the detriment of nonwhites, women, and the unpropertied poor. (124)

Allen concludes her powerful critique of the evident disenfranchisement of poor black folks with an invitation to legal philosophers to construct a theory of rights ascription that competently reconciles the formal enfranchisement of *all* persons with the apparent disenfrachisement of *some* groups of persons. The next section offers a theory of rights ascription that achieves this reconciliation.

The Strong Claim and the Philosophy of Rights

The intellectual forefather of the strong claim may be legal realist Karl Llewellyn, who distinguished between "paper rights" and "real rights" (Llewellyn 1931). Paper rights exist on the level of doctrine; they are formally recognized and bestowed by an entity with the authority to do so. However, real rights exist on the ground. One knows that they exist not by looking to whether a constitution, statute, or court opinion has formally provided it, but rather by looking to whether the purported rightsbearer enjoys a remedy when the ostensible right is violated. According to Llewellyn, if there is no remedy, there is no right (1244). Following this insight, one would be justified in claiming that the judiciary's refusal to remedy the rights violation that poor mothers are forced to endure evidences the nonexistence of the right.

However, Llewellyn might be wrong. For example, philosopher Neil MacCormick (1976) argues that while the Latin maxim *Ubi jus, ibi remedium* suggests that where there is a right, there is a remedy, it does not necessarily follow that *whenever* there is a right, there will be a remedy. He writes, "So far from its being the case that the remedial provision is constitutive of the right, the fact is rather that recognition of the right justifies the imposition of the remedial provision" (79). Thus, while a system is justified in providing a remedy upon its recognition of a right, it need not do so. If so, the right may exist in the absence of the remedy.[5]

The disarticulation of rights from remedies means that there is the theoretical possibility that one can possess a right for which there is no remedy on the occasion of its violation. One might look to moral rights as evidence of this possibility. As moral theorist David Lyons (1984) explains, moral rights

> include the rights that are sometimes called "natural" or "human," but are not limited to them. Natural or human rights are rights we are all said to have (by those who believe we have them) just by virtue of our status as human beings. They are independent of particular circumstances and do not depend on any special conditions. (111)

Moral rights are distinct from legal rights, which "presuppose some sort of social recognition or enforcement, the clearest case being rights conferred by law, including constitutional rights" (Lyons 1984, 111).

Now, moral rights may be violated systematically and with impunity; however, that systematic violation does not extinguish the right. For example, assuming that there is a moral right to be free from slavery or any condition of involuntary servitude, this moral right was violated every day of the 250 years in which the institution of chattel slavery existed in the United States. However, the legally sanctioned violation of the moral right of persons to be free from slavery did not extinguish the right. Instead, the right existed and persisted despite its disregard. Certainly, with moral rights, there may be a right without a remedy.

However, the fact that individuals can possess a *moral* right that is systematically violated without remedy does not necessarily establish that individuals can possess a *legal* right that is systematically violated without remedy. In other words, what is true for moral rights is not necessarily true for legal rights—the rights that this book explores. This is simply because some moral rights, like human rights, are unconditional; the rightsbearer possesses them by virtue of her humanness, and they are in no way contingent on anything beyond her being human.

On the contrary, legal rights are not unconditional. Indeed, they can be conditioned on whatever the law prescribes. As Lyons (1984) instructs us, legal rights, in order to exist as legal rights, must be recognized and/or enforced. Thus, if the ontological status of legal rights as legal rights depends on their recognition and/or enforcement, it is the height of reason to conclude that legal rights cease to be legal rights when they are not recognized and/or enforced. That is, if poor mothers' legal privacy rights are not recognized and/or enforced, then we may comfortably conclude that their legal privacy rights have ceased. We might conclude, as the strong claim encourages us to conclude, that poor mothers do not possess legal privacy rights because, in the absence of their recognition and/or enforcement, they do not exist.

The strong claim is easier to swallow if one subscribes to legal positivism, which theorizes that individuals have legal rights only to the extent that a social practice, as opposed to a moral fact, has created these rights (Shapiro 2007). And just as a social practice can create a legal right, a social practice can extinguish a legal right. As such, we might argue that social practice has extinguished poor mothers' legal privacy rights.

One of the most prominent proponents of positivism, H. L. A. Hart, theorized that the statement that "X has a right" depends on there being a formal obligation for Y to abstain from an action (or, in the case of positive rights, to do an action). In *Definition and Theory in Jurisprudence*, Hart (1953) offered that the statement that "X has a right" is true if there is a legal system, if there is a rule or system of rules under which a person Y has an obligation to act or refrain from acting, and if X has the choice to compel Y to honor his obligation (215).

According to Hart's scheme, the statement that "poor mothers have privacy rights" does not depend on the efficacy of those privacy rights, which the legal realist right-as-remedy position requires. Instead, the statement "poor mothers have privacy rights" is true if a legal system exists, if there is a rule that obliges Y, the government, to do or abstain from an activity, and if poor mothers can elect to exercise that right and trigger the government's obligation.

Now, it is an error to say that the government has an obligation that correlates to any individual's right. This is because when obligations are disobeyed, the consequence is legal punishment (Wellman 1975). However, the government cannot be "punished" in any significant sense of the word. As a result, in the context of constitutional rights or other rights against the government, that which correlates with an individual's right is not a governmental obligation but rather a governmental *disability*—that is, the withdrawal of state power to enact certain laws (Lyons 1970).

That said, it is important to recognize that Hart's theory of rights should not be taken to require that Y, the government, actually act within the constraints of the disability. Instead, "X has a right" or "poor mothers have privacy rights" would remain true even when Y (the government, in the case of privacy rights) does not hold up its end of the bargain. Although the disability would be disregarded, it would nevertheless remain.

But, Hart does not specify the content of the system of rules that creates Y's disability with respect to X. The strong claim that this book makes depends on the possibility that the rules that are explicitly stated about who may bear rights do not comprise the entirety of the system of rules. That is, while there may be explicit rules declaring that all adult, competent persons are bearers of the privacy right and establishing the government's disability, there are implicit rules—both created and evidenced by social practice—that relieve the government of its disability vis-à-vis certain categories of persons (i.e., those who society has deemed to be behaviorally and/or ethically flawed). In the absence of a governmental disability, members of the latter category are dispossessed of the privacy right.

The analysis above builds on an observation that Allen makes about Hart's positivism. She observes that Hart "did not address the kinds of reasons by which courts have been and should be swayed to admit new classes of right-holders. . . . [His] theory provides mainly formal guidance" (Allen 1992, 122–23). The strong claim argues that, in practice, U.S. courts have taken the presumed behavioral and ethical flaws of poor mothers to be a reason to deny them admission to the class of holders of the privacy right.

We might now ask, What arguments can be made to convince those who reject positivism to accept the strong claim? Perhaps it would not take much to convince this group. Even legal philosopher Ronald Dworkin, who lobbed one of the most influential challenges to legal positivism, was willing to concede that there could be some degree of separation between moral rights and legal rights. Thus, a legal system could create a legal right that does not have a basis in morality. (For example, a legal system could recognize a *legal* right to know, although there is no corresponding *moral* right to know.[6]) And, more importantly, a legal system could refuse to recognize a moral right as a legal right.

Consider Dworkin's (1977) statement that "[i]f citizens have a moral right of free speech, then governments would do wrong to repeal the First Amendment that guarantees it" (231). Here, Dworkin argues that although it would be wrong for a legal system to refuse to enforce moral rights through its system of legal rights, a legal system just might do this wrong thing. Thus, if the right to privacy is a moral right—or if there is a moral right to equal concern and respect, which requires that a government give all persons in a legal system the same set of legal rights—Dworkin does not deny that a government may refuse to reflect these moral rights in its system of legal rights, although it would be wrong for it to do so.

An important place where Dworkin and positivists part company is on the question of hard cases. Dworkin explains his disagreement with positivism as follows:

> [Legal positivism provides that w]hen a particular lawsuit cannot be brought under a clear rule of law, laid down by some institution in advance, then the judge has, according to that theory, a "discretion" to decide the case either way. His opinion is written in language that seems to assume that one or the other party had a pre-existing right to win the suit, but the idea is only a fiction. In reality, he has legislated new legal rights, and then applied them retrospectively to the case at hand. . . . I shall argue that even when no settled rule disposes of the case, one party may nevertheless have a right to win. It remains the judge's duty, even in hard cases, to discover what the rights of the parties are, not to invent new rights retrospectively. (105)

Dworkin proposes that moral facts determine the law in these hard cases. It is the judge's duty to divine these moral facts in order to determine what the law is. Of course, the judge may get it wrong: She may create a legal rule that does not reflect what the moral facts declare the law to be. Nevertheless, the ostensible gaps in the law are filled with moral law, and it is the job of the judge to ascertain how the moral law has filled these apparent spaces in the explicitly established law. (Legal positivism disagrees, denying that judges *must* look to morality in order to ascertain law. Instead, positivism insists that law *can* be independent of morality, and social practice can determine the law in hard cases.)

Dworkin's theory of abstract rights and concrete rights may be relevant to the question of poor mothers' privacy rights. He defines an abstract right as a "general political aim the statement of which does not indicate how that general aim is to be weighed or compromised in particular circumstances against other political aims" (1977, 119). He describes abstract rights as the rights that are spoken about in political rhetoric, like the "right to free speech or dignity or equality." Concrete rights, in contrast, are more precisely defined than the abstract right that justifies them. While there may be an abstract right to free speech, the related concrete right will be narrower—like the "right to publish defense plans classified as secret provided the publication will not create an immediate physical danger to troops" (1977, 119).

As it relates to the present study, the right to privacy may be an abstract right, and it may support a plethora of concrete rights. Concrete rights supported by the abstract privacy right may include these: the right to bring one's injured or sick child to a provider of medical care without being subjected to a subsequent investigation by CPS, provided that the circumstances of the child's injury or sickness are not those that also would subject a wealthier family to a CPS investigation; the right to prevent the unnecessary disclosure to third parties of one's status as a beneficiary of a state program that subsidizes childcare costs when the rightsbearer picks up or drops off the child at the childcare facility; the right to prevent state actors from searching areas of one's home that are not in plain view absent a warrant or exigent circumstances, even when one is a TANF beneficiary.

While the Court has held that poor mothers lack these particular concrete rights, there remain questions about other concrete rights that have not been litigated. Do poor mothers have a right to prevent the unnecessary disclosure to third parties of one's status as a beneficiary of WIC when receiving food from the program? Do poor mothers have a right to prevent state actors from searching areas of their *cars* that are not in plain view absent a warrant or exigent circumstances, even when they are TANF beneficiaries? For Dworkin, these are hard cases, "when no settled rule dictates a decision either way" (1977, 83). Although no settled rule clearly establishes that there is or is not a right in these cases, Dworkin proposes that there is a "right" answer, and it "remains the judge's duty, even in hard cases, to discover what the rights of the parties are, not to invent rights retrospectively" (108). It just may be that poor mothers *do* have these specific concrete rights. Of course, a judge or the Court may decide the case incorrectly and establish an explicit law that is "wrong." But, prior to the Court's decision, Dworkin may argue that poor mothers have these concrete privacy rights. And if they do, then it would be incorrect to argue, as the strong claim does, that they lack privacy rights.

The response to this challenge is to look to Dworkin's theory of how we are to know whether or not a concrete right exists prior to the explicit establishment of the right. Dworkin theorizes that we are to look to the "community's moral traditions . . . ,at least as these are captured in the whole institutional record" (153). When deciding hard cases, judges must be guided by the laws and institutions of the society and determine whether they suggest the existence of a right. These laws and institutions reflect the community's morality, which, indeed, is "decisive of legal issues" (154).

Here we have our reply to the suggestion that poor mothers might have concrete privacy rights prior to the establishment of an explicit rule: They do not. The community's morality, as reflected in this country's institutional record, makes it fairly patent that poor mothers lack these rights. An examination of this morality, which Chapter 1 undertakes, reveals clearly that poor mothers have been conceptualized as proper subjects of state regulation—the very thing that privacy rights are designed to prevent. Indeed, if a judge were to decide a hard case in way that establishes a concrete privacy right for poor mothers, that decision would represent a departure from the thrust of past precedents. And, Dworkin counsels, judges must decide cases such that there is "articulate consistency" (112). Articulate consistency in any case concerning the question of poor mothers' privacy rights would require a finding of their absence. This means that poor mothers lack privacy rights even prior to the final decisions in hard cases.

There is one last challenge to which the strong claim may need to respond. This is the challenge of someone who insists that the Constitution provides poor mothers with privacy rights—because the Fourth Amendment and/or the Due Process Clause of the Fourteenth Amendment protects them, and the Equal Protection Clause requires that they be bestowed on every person, rich and poor, equally. This challenger would insist that the Court's decisions cannot deprive a rightsbearer of a right that the Constitution provides her. Because the Court's decisions cannot dispossess a rightsbearer of a right that the Constitution recognizes, these decisions only allow for the violation of the right—not a revocation of the right. Thus, the argument is that poor mothers possess the privacy rights that the Constitution provides. The Court's decisions surrounding them merely allow for their violation.

Implicit in this challenge is the distinction between the Constitution and constitutional law. The former is the 6,000-word document that was ratified over two centuries ago. The latter is something different. It is the

> body of law that has resulted from the Supreme Court's adjudications involving disputes over constitutional provisions or doctrines. To put it a bit more simply, constitutional law is what the Supreme Court says about the Constitution in its decisions resolving the cases and controversies that come before it. (Meese 1986, 982)

The last challenge to the strong claim would say the following: To the extent that the constitutional law around poor mothers' privacy rights allows governments to act as if the privacy rights that the Constitution recognizes do not exist, then the constitutional law is getting the Constitution, the supreme law of the land, wrong. Constitutional law cannot change the meaning of the Constitution. Thus, if the Constitution provides privacy rights to poor mothers, then the Court's interpretation of the Constitution cannot repeal them.

However, this challenge assumes that there is a meaning to the Constitution that exists independent of the Court's interpretation. It assumes that the Fourteenth Amendment and the Fourth Amendment definitively recognize the privacy rights of poor mothers and, importantly, that this recognition does not at all depend on what the Court believes those amendments to mean. However, this is implausible. It seems doubtful that the commands in those amendments—that the "right of the people to be secure in their persons, houses, papers, and effects, against unreasonable searches and seizures, shall not be violated" and that states cannot deprive persons of equal protection of laws nor of life, liberty, or property without due process of law—simply *mean* that poor mothers have privacy rights. It is more likely that, if these amendments mean that poor mothers, or anyone at all, have privacy rights, it is because the Court has interpreted them to mean as much.

Constitutional law scholar Burt Neuborne (1986) has explained this position incisively, noting that the challenge to this position

> depends on viewing the "true" meaning of the ambiguous text of the Constitution as if it were an objective, external reality that exists independently of the will of . . . the judiciary. . . . The flaw in [this] reasoning is that there is no such thing as an objectively knowable, "true" Constitution just waiting to be discovered. (997)

To believe that Neuborne is correct is not necessarily to believe, in the famous words of Chief Justice Hughes, "the Constitution is what judges say it is" (Hughes 1908, 139). However, it is to say that when *ambiguous* provisions of the Constitution are involved—as is true in the case of privacy rights—the meaning of those provisions likely depends on what judges say it is.

If the above is correct, the meaning of the Fourth and Fourteenth Amendments depends on the Court's interpretation of that meaning. And while the Court may interpret these amendments to provide privacy rights to poor mothers, it may also interpret them to deny those same rights. The concept of informal disenfranchisement declares that while the Court has interpreted the Constitution to bestow poor mothers with formal rights, it has simultaneously interpreted the Constitution to strip poor mothers of the rights that have been bestowed formally. Thus, the Court's decisions do not allow poor mothers' rights to be "violated"; instead, those decisions deprive them of the rights that the Court is empowered to give and to take away.

A Legal Landscape Dotted with Conditional Rights

The strong claim might also be formulated in the language of conditional rights. We might understand it to claim that poor mothers do not have privacy rights because these rights are conditioned on the rightsbearer being presumed to possess a good moral character and to engage in good behaviors. Because poor pregnant women are not presumed to have this character or to engage in these behaviors, these rights are not ascribed to them.

Skeptics of the strong claim may resist the idea that the privacy right—a constitutional right with respect to family and reproductive privacy—may be conditional. Their instinct may be that constitutional rights are unconditional. The idea is that the Constitution bestows rights on "persons"; accordingly, all persons will bear any right that the Constitution bestows. There is no room within this understanding of constitutional rights for *conditional* constitutional rights.

However, this instinct is incorrect. The case of Puerto Rico demonstrates this. While the residents of Puerto Rico are U.S. citizens, those who reside on the island do not enjoy all of the constitutional rights that U.S. citizens on the mainland enjoy. Namely, in *Balzac v. Puerto Rico* (258 U.S. 298 (1922)), the Court held that Puerto Ricans on the island do not possess a Sixth Amendment right to trial by jury. Thus, although the Sixth Amendment right to a jury trial is a constitutional right, it is conditioned on the rightsbearer being within the borders of the continental United States (or in Hawaii and Alaska). The lesson of Puerto Rico is quite clear: Constitutional rights can be conditional.

Although some may admit that the case of Puerto Rico demonstrates that there are conditional constitutional rights, these persons may balk at the suggestion that constitutional rights may be conditioned on *moral character*. This notion—that the country would allow an appraisal of the moral character of the would-be rightsbearer to determine whether or not she will be given a right—contradicts the particular brand of constitutionalism embraced and practiced in the United States.

Nevertheless, the Immigration and Nationality Act, which sets forth the requirements that a person must fulfill if she would like to naturalize and become a U.S. citizen, explicitly requires an appraisal of the moral character of the applicant. The act requires that an applicant for naturalization "be of good moral character during the required residence period and up to the time of admission" (U.S. Code 8 (2006), § 1427(a)). Thus, in order to become a citizen, a person must demonstrate that he possesses a good moral character.[7]

Citizenship might be understood as a status that grants special rights. Indeed, Chief Justice Warren once described citizenship as "the right to have rights" (Perez v. Brownell, 356 U.S. 44, 64–65 (1958)). Further, some of the rights that citizenship bestows are *constitutional* rights—like Fourth Amendment rights against unreasonable search and seizure of property that one owns outside of the United States (United States v. Verdugo-Urquidez, 494 U.S. 259 (1990)). Accordingly, if citizenship means that a person is given certain constitutional rights, and if possession of good moral character is a condition of citizenship, then possession of good moral character is a condition of certain constitutional rights. This is the precise argument that the strong claim makes about privacy rights: Possession of good moral character is a condition of the privacy right. Because poor mothers are presumed not to have a good moral character, they are not given the privacy right.

One should also keep in mind that the right to informational privacy, which is one of the privacy rights that poor mothers are denied, has not yet been recognized as a constitutional right. The Court in *National Aeronautics and Space Administration v. Nelson* (562 U.S. 134 (2011) recently refused to hold that the Constitution protects a right to informational privacy. Accordingly, we might describe the right to informational privacy as one that does not rise to constitutional significance or, in shorthand, is non-constitutional. If, as this book suggests, the right to informational privacy is conditional, then it is in good company: There are a host of other non-constitutional rights that are conditional. Perhaps the most salient condition imposed on non-constitutional rights is not having been previously convicted of a felony. And the number of rights that bear this condition is substantial (Alexander 2010). The disenfranchisement of felons demonstrates that there is nothing exceptional about conditional non-constitutional rights.

The Politics of the Strong Claim

The strong claim offers an interpretation of how the privacy right—with respect to family, informational, and reproductive privacy—operates in the

United States today. Describing poor mothers as having been informally dis-enfranchised of privacy rights is offered as an interpretation of our existing legal landscape that is as plausible as the moderate claim, which describes poor mothers as in possession of privacy rights that are feeble, meaningless, easily surrendered, or violated. In offering an interpretation of privacy rights that is as plausible as the one that is consonant with traditional rights discourse, the strong claim simultaneously offers a challenge: It challenges us to think about why we have been seduced by a narrative about equal rights when everyday, lived reality suggests that nothing could be further from the truth.

Moreover, to describe poor mothers as bearing no privacy rights—as having been informally disenfranchised of these rights—changes the political project. It incites us to analogize poor mothers to other historically disenfranchised groups. It inspires us to recall the techniques that those groups used to win the rights that they claimed the Constitution promised them. And it reminds us that these groups did not acquire the rights that they desired by construing the Constitution in clever ways and encouraging the Court to do the same. Instead, these groups were bestowed with rights because they agitated for social, cultural, and political change. Describing poor mothers as like these formerly disenfran-chised groups shifts our political project from one that involves appealing to the Court to construe the Constitution differently to one that involves engaging in the messy work of forcing social, cultural, and political transformation.

Recognizing that it is a political move to interpret our legal present as one in which poor mothers have been deprived of privacy rights in the strong sense reveals that it is *also* a political move to interpret our legal present as one in which poor mothers have privacy rights, albeit feeble ones. *There is no apolitical interpretation of our legal present.* For those who insist that the moderate claim is the more accurate one, we ought to ask to what political end that position is being advanced.

Indeed, there is something pacifying about the moderate claim. It suggests that we are close to fashioning a society that is consistent with the principles contained in the nation's founding documents and the ideologies that the country purports to embrace and represent. The moderate claim suggests that we are "almost there"—that we just need to make a couple of small changes in order to bring our nation in line with the values to which we profess to be com-mitted. The moderate claim makes us self-satisfied, convinced that no great injustice is being wrought and that no radical transformations need to occur. The strong claim, on the other hand, might demand rebellion.

Now, there may be something counterintuitive about claiming that poor mothers do not have rights in the strong sense in order to advance the claim that they should be given these rights. This argument reverses what is usually done. Historically, advocates have claimed that persons possess rights, although they might not be legally recognized yet. The goal of the argument is to move society toward the legal recognition of the claimed right. Explains constitutional law scholar Richard Primus (1999),

> Consider a hypothetical suffragette who in 1910, before the extension of the franchise to women, declared, "Women have the right to vote." Her statement should not be understood to mean that women were able or permitted to vote. She was not offering a false description of society but making a prescriptive statement about the way in which society should operate. If told that no such right existed in American law, she would respond that American law was in moral error. . . . [T]he suffragette is making a claim about the way rights truly are, irrespective of positive law. (38)

Primus's suffragette claims rights that do not yet exist in law in order to "help call that state of affairs into existence" (39). The strong claim takes the opposite tack: It denies that rights that purportedly exist in law actually exist in order to call into existence a state of affairs in which they are actually provided.

Further, the usual approach is to contend that one has a right because, arguably, there is dignity, legitimacy, and virtue in claiming a right. As political scientist Stuart Scheingold (1974) writes, "How much more compelling to assert a right. You are claiming only what is due to you and what others have an obligation to fulfill" (58). Thus, there may appear to be something undignified, illegitimate, and not at all virtuous in arguing what the strong claim argues—that poor mothers do not have privacy rights.

Nevertheless, there is value in asserting the strong claim—simply because there is something profoundly disruptive about describing our legal order as one in which a group has been deprived of rights that have been provided to others. As Waldron (2000) explains,

> A theory of rights is not simply a list of demands: since Kant, it has been taken to imply that the demands can be organized into a vision of society, a *Rechtsstaat*, integrated around a concept of the person as the dominant single status of equality in moral and political life. If rights . . . are like a language, then it is a language with a grammar. (132)

To say that poor mothers have privacy rights that are violated, as the moderate claim asserts, is to describe our *Rechtsstaat* as one that is fundamentally just, yet in need of some improvement. To say that poor mothers lack privacy rights altogether, as the strong claim asserts, is to describe our *Rechtsstaat* as corrupt. It is to deny that it is one that is integrated around a concept of the person as "the dominant single status of equality in moral and political life." If the strong claim is true, then our *Rechtsstaat* is one in which being a person does not entitle one to equality, or it is one in which poor mothers are not considered persons.

If poor mothers do not have privacy rights, then it demands a radical reordering. Again, Waldron (2000) is helpful here. He writes that when individuals claim a right that has not yet been provided to them, the resultant task

> is to devise a *Rechtsstaat* that can accommodate all the claims of right that they propose to recognize; it is not their job to accommodate their demands to the claims or the systems that others have put forward. So when I said that a person asserting a new right has a responsibility to define a relational structure in which it can take its place, I did not mean that structure should be a comfortable or a familiar one. (133–34)

Thus, if poor mothers currently lack privacy rights in the strong sense, then actually bestowing them with these rights might force a restructuring of our entire society in order to accommodate this demand. This is the "radical reform or comprehensive social criticism" that Waldron suggests is possible.

In this book I advance the strong claim because I believe that it is much more of a comprehensive social criticism than the moderate claim. I advance it because I believe that it is much more likely to lead to radical reform than the moderate claim. I also advance the strong claim because I believe in the efficacy of rights, and I believe that privacy rights are valuable. If they are negative, they can constrain the government from acting in ways that offend our sensibilities. If they are positive, they can oblige the government to act in ways that ensure our dignity.

This should not be read to argue that privacy is beneficial always and in every case. Privacy, like everything else, is complex. As Allen (2000) writes,

> Privacy is often important, but there can be too much as well as too little privacy; subordinating as well as equalizing forms of privacy; fairly distributed, as well as unfairly distributed privacy; privacy used for good, as well as privacy used for evil; privacy that moves a people forward, and privacy that moves a people backwards. (1200)

Moreover, privacy is not everything. To say that poor mothers ought to be bestowed with privacy rights is not to say that this grant would solve all of their problems. Undeniably, other legal and social changes would need to be made in order for them to live lives with dignity. But, granting privacy rights would be a necessary, if not sufficient, step toward that end.

Further, I champion granting poor mothers privacy rights because a disturbing equality problem is created when they lack these rights. Our legal landscape is one in which wealthier women enjoy a right that, in its family and reproductive dimensions, has been recognized as fundamental. While wealthier women bear this fundamental right as a matter of course, their poor counterparts bear nothing.

And nothing justifies this result. As discussed above, the reason that is invariably given, by governments and legal scholars alike, for the state occupation of poor mothers' private lives is the state's interest in protecting children. Yet, even though wealthier women share the same histories and engage in the same behaviors as poor women, the government feels no need to occupy the lives of the wealthy in order to protect their children. Those of us interested in equality—in the simple truism that similar people ought to be treated similarly—will find such a result immensely disquieting.

Moreover, those of us interested in racial justice will also find deeply disturbing the legal landscape wherein wealthier women have privacy rights while poorer women do not. The lamentable truth is that race follows class closely in this country: There is an undeniable relationship between race privilege and class privilege, with the result being that racial minorities are disproportionately represented among the poor (Jones 2009). It follows, then, that racial minorities are disproportionately represented among those who have been dispossessed of their privacy rights. Those of us interested in racial justice will find this entirely unacceptable, reminiscent as it is of earlier moments in our country's history.

Critical thinkers of race will also pay attention to the way that racial discourses have functioned to produce a legal landscape wherein poor mothers are deprived of privacy rights. As noted above, and as explored more expansively in Chapter 1, one can presume that all poor mothers are ethically and/or behaviorally deficient only if one rejects explanations of poverty that locate its causes in macro structures, like a labor market that contains fewer middle-skill jobs that pay wages that can support a family. Explanations of poverty that locate its causes in individuals and their personal failings, and not in the structures in which they exist, have consistently enjoyed a certain degree of traction in the United States.

When one considers this fact along with the fact that racial minorities have always been disproportionately represented among the poor, one can begin to see a possible explanation for why large numbers of people in the United States believe that most poverty is caused by individual deficiencies: It is easy to moralize poverty when those who are disproportionately impoverished are racial Others. It is especially easy to moralize poverty when black people are the racial group that is most disproportionately represented among the poor, and the racial discourses that attach to that particular racial Other render them as lazy, sexually immoral, and labor averse. Thus, race plays an important role in explaining how we have arrived at a present wherein substantial numbers of people subscribe to the notion that individual shortcomings are responsible for most poverty. And race plays an important role in explaining why the country has been comfortable with denying privacy rights on the basis of the presumed shortcomings of the rightsbearer.

This is a species of an argument that legal theorist Dorothy Roberts has made quite cogently in her scholarship. She has argued that the Court's decision in *Rust v. Sullivan*—which upheld a law that prohibited doctors serving an indigent clientele from giving medically relevant information about abortion—was "politically acceptable" because of the race of the women affected. She writes, "Race may help to explain the government's willingness to exclude [the affected patients] from the privileges that other women enjoy. It may help to explain the Court's refusal to require that the government provide equal access to medical care" (Roberts 1993b, 597). Essentially, Roberts argues that race accounts for why the Court was comfortable denying some women reproductive privacy rights (as well as First Amendment rights to information and ideas).

More generally, Roberts has argued that privacy is something that, historically, the decision makers in this country have deemed black women unfit to possess. She has made this claim quite forcefully. "The state has always considered Black mothers, whether married or single, as needing public supervision and not entitled to privacy" (Roberts 1993a, 28 n.153). Again: "Because of racism, it is more likely that the government will interfere with [women of color's] reproductive decisions" (33). And again: "[T]he state is more willing to intrude upon the autonomy of Black mothers" (14).

While Roberts is correct insofar as poor mothers of color have been denied privacy and privacy rights throughout history, this book would add a slight gloss to her claim. Roberts appears to describe a form of racism that was most prevalent in the years that preceded the 1960s—old school racism—before the law prohibited explicit demonstrations of racism. She describes the government denying privacy and privacy rights to black women *because they are black women*. However, this book describes a racism that is more oblique—a new school racism. That is, age-old cultural discourses construct individuals racialized as black as pathological—as indolent, as sexually incontinent, as criminally inclined, and so forth. When those who comprise the poor are disproportionately black, then it is consistent with extant cultural discourses to suppose that the poor are poor because they are pathological—because they are indolent, sexually incontinent, criminally inclined, and so forth. Moreover, when those who are denied privacy rights on the basis of an ostensibly race-neutral criterion—presumed character—are disproportionately black, race explains why the country finds this result "politically acceptable."

Arguments that the Book Will *Not* Make

To recap, in this book I argue that poor mothers do not have family, informational, and reproductive privacy rights. I propose that the reason poor mothers are effectively (consistent with the moderate claim) or actually (consistent with the strong claim) deprived of these rights is that these individuals are not presumed to possess the character that justifies recognizing the rights in the first instance. This book explores family, informational, and reproductive privacy rights because the state most obviously regulates the areas of poor mothers' lives that these rights are designed to protect against state intervention. (There likely are other privacy rights—like the right to engage in consensual sexual relationships, recognized in *Lawrence v. Texas*—that poor mothers retain.) That said, it is important to articulate one argument that this book does *not* make: *This book does not make an argument about poor fathers' privacy rights.*

This book claims that poor mothers have been (effectively or actually) deprived of privacy rights because they are presumed to be ethically and/or behaviorally flawed; further, because their flaws necessarily implicate the children that they gestate and parent, they are deprived of the rights that might shield the state from supervising them, regulating them, and protecting their children. Because the justification for the deprivation of the right is the protection of children, one might be tempted to argue that poor *fathers* are similarly situated. One might be tempted to assume that when fathers have children in their charge, they too would be deprived of privacy rights, as the state would have an equal interest in protecting those children.

But, I cannot make that argument in this book. And this is entirely because I have not conducted research with poor fathers. The legal argument that this book makes about poor mothers' privacy rights is a product of the ethnographic research that I conducted with these mothers—research that culminated in *Reproducing Race: An Ethnography of Pregnancy as a Site of Racialization* (Bridges 2011b). After eighteen months of anthropological fieldwork with poor mothers, I got an excellent sense of their experiences with the state. *Reproducing Race* describes the omnipresence of the state in poor mothers' lives and investigates the cultural discourses that facilitate, normalize, and naturalize that omnipresence. The present book complements *Reproducing Race* because it offers a legal analysis of the issues that *Reproducing Race* explored ethnographically. This book offers a theory of privacy rights that can explain what *Reproducing Race* documented ethnographically.

However, this book cannot offer a theory of the privacy rights of poor fathers, simply because I do not know what their lives look like on the ground. I do not have ethnographic data concerning their experiences with the state. It could be that, as men, they have a greater ability than women to keep the state out of their lives. It is possible that when men are the heads of families, they can prevent the state's zealous surveillance and regulation of the unit. They might be able to retain informational privacy; they might be able to enjoy reproductive autonomy. Alternately, it is entirely possible that their gender affords them no privilege, and their experiences with the state mirror those of poor women. In the absence of data describing their lives, I cannot offer a theory of their rights.

It bears noting before continuing that while it is true that the state takes the protection of children to be a justification for depriving mothers of rights, and while it is true that women are made vulnerable to state power by their attachment to their children as their caregivers, it is not biology that attaches women to children as caregivers. *Social arrangements* attach women to children as caregivers. Thus, if mothers are overwhelmingly appended to children and are deprived of rights as a consequence thereof, it is society—not biology—that explains this vulnerability.

The Argument to Come

Chapter 1 documents the ubiquitous voices throughout history that have rejected structural explanations of poverty and, instead, have argued that poverty is the result of individual shortcomings. This chapter shows that the discursive link between poverty and immorality continues to the present day, as one need not listen too closely on any given day to hear a narrative in political or popular discourse that links poverty with behavioral or ethical deficiencies.

Chapter 2 explores the doctrine of unconstitutional conditions, a doctrine that provides that it is unconstitutional for a state to premise the conferral of a benefit on the beneficiary's surrender of a constitutional right. After analyzing the unconstitutional conditions cases, this chapter concludes that they reveal the justification for the state's denial (in both the moderate and strong sense) of privacy rights to poor mothers: The state denies individuals a right when it disbelieves that the individual will realize the value that the right is intended to generate.

Chapter 3 begins the exploration of the various facets of the privacy right, starting with the family privacy right. It examines various justifications for the right, concluding that the moral construction of poverty counsels in favor of dispossessing poor mothers of the right, in both the moderate and strong sense, because it suggests that poor mothers will not realize the value that the right is designed to yield.

Chapter 4 explores informational privacy in its various manifestations. This chapter examines the justification for the informational privacy right and concludes that poor mothers have been deprived of it, in both the moderate and strong sense, because of the belief that, as with family privacy rights, the right will not yield the value that it is designed to yield when poor mothers bear them.

Chapter 5 investigates reproductive privacy rights. It concludes that poor women have been deprived of these rights, both in the moderate and strong sense again, because society does not trust their ability to make competent, moral decisions about reproduction without state oversight.

The Conclusion proposes that poor mothers will only enjoy the positive or negative privacy rights that are formally bestowed to them when an individual's economic failure is no longer thought to indicate a flawed character. It examines other historical moments where disenfranchised groups struggled for rights that had been denied to them, focusing on black people's struggle for the right to vote and sexual minorities' struggle for the right to marry. The lesson of history is that poor mothers will only be granted actual and effective privacy rights when our culture unseats the moral construction of poverty from its present discursive throne.

1 The Moral Construction of Poverty

Voices throughout history have insisted that the poor person's poverty necessarily demonstrates his behavioral and ethical deficiencies. Some historians
trace this well-documented idea, the moral construction of poverty, in the
United States to the industrialization of the American economy. They contend
that, prior to the Civil War, it was not widely assumed that a compromised
character was responsible for an individual's indigence. However, around the
onset of the industrial revolution, "[a] new ideology arose . . . that attributed
moral character deficiencies to the poor" (Katz 1985, 252).[1]

Regardless of the precise moment in history when poverty and immorality
became linked discursively, our present society certainly is one in which the
relationship between the two concepts is firmly established. On any given day,
one need not listen especially closely in order to hear a narrative in political or
popular discourse that explains poverty in terms of the deficient character of
the people living that poverty. The examples really are quite ubiquitous.

Welfare Reform

We can start with Temporary Assistance for Needy Families (TANF), the federal program that partners with state governments to offer cash assistance to
indigent families. TANF was created in 1997 by the Personal Responsibility
and Work Opportunity Reconciliation Act (PRWORA)—a piece of legislation
that does not at all attempt to conceal its authors' conviction that the roots of
poverty are located in the individual and her bad behavior. Indeed, PRWORA

bears in its title the behaviorist explanation of poverty that motivates it: It is the *Personal Responsibility* and Work Opportunity Reconciliation Act. While there are several noteworthy features of TANF, the most relevant to the present discussion is the dual emphasis that TANF places on getting beneficiaries of the program into the wage labor market and into marriages.

With respect to getting beneficiaries into the wage labor market, TANF requires recipients to engage in any of a number of "work activities" for varying hours depending on the beneficiary's family structure (U.S. Code 42 (2006), § 607(c)). Should a beneficiary fail to meet the mandatory work requirements, the statute gives states the discretion to reduce her grant or to terminate it altogether (§ 607(e)).

Further, TANF also attempts to steer beneficiaries into marriages. When passing PRWORA, Congress presented the lack of marriage as the reason why there are so many problems in the United States. Indeed, in the congressional findings that open PRWORA, the first facts that Congress "found" were that "[m]arriage is the foundation of a successful society" and that "[m]arriage is an essential institution of a successful society which promotes the interests of children" (§ 601). Presumably, the parade of horribles that makes up the balance of PRWORA's congressional findings stems from the absence of marriage.

Congress tells us that children born "out-of-wedlock" are "3 times more likely to be on welfare when they grow up"; have compromised "school performance and peer adjustment"; have "lower cognitive scores, lower educational aspirations, and a greater likelihood of becoming teenage parents themselves"; are "3 times more likely to fail and repeat a year in grade school than are children from intact 2-parent families"; are "4 times more likely to be expelled or suspended from school"; are living in neighborhoods with "higher rates of violent crime"; and are overpopulating the "[s]tate juvenile justice system." Apparently, marriage is the solution to these social ills. Thus, the legislation lists a series of activities that may promote "healthy marriage," all of which states may fund with TANF monies (§ 603).

In this way, TANF presents the problem of poverty as stemming from individual bad behavior. In essence, TANF claims that if poor people would just get married and/or get a job, their poverty would go away. Sociologist Loïc Wacquant (2009) agrees with this reading, writing that TANF has

> powerfully reasserted the fiction according to which poverty is a matter of individual deed and will, and that it would suffice to stoke the matrimonial fire and zeal for work of those on assistance by means of material constraint and

moral suasion to defeat the culpable "dependency" they evince. . . . These moralistic stereotypes are tailor-made for legitimizing the new politics of poverty. (100–101)

Political Discourse

In 2014, then Speaker of the House John Boehner philosophized that the reason why large numbers of people remained unemployed after the official end of the Great Recession was not because the economy had transformed in ways that made jobs scarce for some segments of the population. Instead, he attributed enduring unemployment to the mindset of the unemployed: "I think this idea that has been born over the last—maybe out of the economy—over the last couple of years: 'You know I really don't have to work. I really don't want to do this. I think I'd just rather sit around.' This is a very sick idea for our country" (Cowan 2014). For Boehner, post-recession unemployment rates do no more than quantify and aggregate individuals' desires to avoid productive, valuable work. Should those individuals eventually find themselves in poverty, it will be due to their "sick" wish to avoid the paid labor force.

Also in 2014, Paul Ryan, who would become Speaker of the House following Boehner's resignation, articulated his sense that the problems of the "inner city"—the facially race-neutral signifier that, nevertheless, signifies a space populated by poor black and brown bodies—were attributable to "culture." He observed that "[w]e have got this tailspin of culture, in our inner cities in particular, of men not working and just generations of men not even thinking about working or learning the value and the culture of work. . . . There is a real culture problem here that has to be dealt with" (Delaney 2014). We can understand Ryan to be arguing that unemployment and poverty, particularly in the "inner city," can be explained in terms of a pathological worldview that misrecognizes the value of engaging in work in the paid labor market.

Pundits and Popular Discourse

On his tremendously popular television show, *The O'Reilly Factor*, television personality and bestselling author Bill O'Reilly has repeatedly articulated the view that poor people engage in imprudent, immoral behavior and that this behavior is responsible for their poverty. While some may be inclined to dismiss O'Reilly as a pundit among many pundits and his views as nothing more than perspectives that are palatable only to the radically conservative, his astonishing reach should not be underestimated. Fox News Channel, which airs

O'Reilly's show, has been the most watched cable news network for several years. Moreover, at the end of the third quarter in 2013, *The O'Reilly Factor* averaged 2.54 million viewers (Bibel 2013). Following the mid-term elections in 2014, *The O'Reilly Factor* had over *4 million* viewers (Mediaite 2014).

On November 13, 2014, *The O'Reilly Factor* invited journalist Bernard Goldberg to discuss race and poverty (Richter 2014). Goldberg began by citing statistics that purport to show that only 8 percent of people who finish high school, who avoid having children before they are married, and who avoid having children before they reach the age of 20 are in poverty. However, almost 80 percent of people who do not finish high school, who have children outside of marriage, and who have children while teenagers are in poverty. When O'Reilly questions Goldberg as to why "the left" does not acknowledge this, he responds,

> I think it's because it's an embarrassment. [Black elites] don't give dysfunctional behavior—and I think that's a fair description, if you drop out of high school, and you have babies when you're a teenager, it is dysfunctional behavior—they don't give that as a reason because it's embarrassing. They blame racism. Maybe once upon a time, when there were less opportunities for black people, racism might have been a legitimate reason. It isn't today.

O'Reilly concludes the segment with the statement, "Poverty is colorblind. And if you make mistakes in your life, and you dig yourself a hole where you're not educated and you gotta be on the dole to support your kids and you're dependent and all of that and you can't develop a career or a talent, you're done."

O'Reilly's sentiments in the November show echoed those that he had articulated earlier in the year. On January 9, 2014, he paused to reflect on President Lyndon Johnson's war on poverty, ultimately concluding that it was a misconceived effort (Fox News Insider 2014). He reached this conclusion because the social programs that Johnson passed in his effort to eliminate poverty in the country did not attempt to reach the true cause of destitution in O'Reilly's view: bad behavior. O'Reilly offered that "[m]aybe we should have a war against chaotic, irresponsible parents. But America will never launch that kind of war—because it's too judgmental and deeply affects the minority precincts. Therefore, cowardly politicians and race hustlers continue to bear witness that our economic system is at fault rather than bad personal decision making." He asserted that "[p]overty will not change until personal behavior does. Addictive behavior, laziness, [and] apathy all override social justice goals."

He described the nation as a meritocracy in which success and wealth are available to all who demonstrate sustained effort. He argued that

> [e]very child on this planet can learn. But, parents must drive the process by forcing the kids to perform in school. Every American can work hard. And if you do, you'll make money. Every American can practice self-respect, and if you do, people will hire you. But, if you're dishonest, embrace intoxicants, conceive children you can't support, act in a crude, self-disrespectful way, and generally believe that you are owed prosperity, poverty may well come knocking.

In short, O'Reilly placed immoral behavior at the foundation of poverty in the United States. When a guest on the show disputed this analysis, redirected attention to the dearth of available jobs that pay livable wages, and contended that "[w]e don't have a problem with workers who are too lazy to work for the jobs with good pay," O'Reilly was moved to cut him off. He interjected, "Yes, we do. We have an enormous underclass. . . . We have a problem of people who can't do the jobs that pay high wages. But, we also have an underclass that's in chaos. Go to Detroit if you don't believe me." When his guest countered that poor people cannot attain jobs that pay a livable wage because they have not been given the skills that they need, O'Reilly replied that poor people necessarily had been presented with the opportunity to acquire the requisite skills. The problem was that they had not *accepted* the skills. He concluded that "[t]he parents have to drive the kid in [to the schools]. And the irresponsible parents don't. You have to work hard to accept the education. And a number of Americans will not do that."

O'Reilly's views and his large viewership are worth discussing for two reasons. First, because millions of viewers watch his show every night, he enjoys a large platform from which to popularize the idea that immoral behavior—the refusal to accept education and job skills that have been offered, the failure to impress upon one's children the importance of going to school and working hard, having sex outside of marriage, having children outside of marriage, allowing oneself to become addicted to intoxicants, and simply being lazy—causes poverty.

Second, O'Reilly's large viewership is significant not only because of its effects—that is, he may convince those who are otherwise unconvinced that behavioral and ethical deficiencies cause poverty. His viewership also is significant because of its *causes*—that is, it may indicate that large numbers of people are *already* convinced that behavioral and ethical deficiencies cause poverty: Millions may watch the show because, in watching it, they can hear someone articulate the views that are already in line with their own.

. . .

Of course, structural explanations of poverty—which insist that macro forces and institutions cause poverty—have some degree of salience in the United States. Consider that in the early days of the campaign for the 2016 presidential election, Republican candidate Jeb Bush said that Americans needed to "work longer hours and through their productivity gain more income for their families" (O'Keefe 2015). This statement—which might be interpreted to argue that workers are not working hard enough if they are not earning enough income to support themselves and their families—is consistent with individualist explanations of poverty.

Indeed, economist and *New York Times* columnist Paul Krugman (2015) argues that to interpret Bush's remarks as motivated by the moral construction of poverty is consistent with Bush's professed intellectual inclinations. Krugman writes that Bush has expressed an affinity for conservative social analyst Charles Murray's scholarship. And in Murray's recent book *Coming Apart*, Murray has observed that "working-class white families are changing in much the same way that African-American families changed in the 1950s and 1960s, with declining rates of marriage and labor force participation" (quoted in Krugman 2015). Krugman continues:

> Some of us look at these changes and see them as consequences of an economy that no longer offers good jobs to ordinary workers. This happened to African-Americans first, as blue-collar jobs disappeared from inner cities, but has now become a much wider phenomenon thanks to soaring income inequality. Mr. Murray, however, sees the changes as the consequence of a mysterious decline in traditional values, enabled by government programs which mean that men no longer "need to work to survive." And Mr. Bush presumably shares that view. (Krugman 2015)

Bush eventually disputed this interpretation of his "work longer hours" remark. He stated that the remark was not an argument that workers who are having trouble supporting their families are lazy; instead, it was an indictment of the lack of full-time jobs available in the labor market (O'Keefe 2015). Bush stated that his comment was a measure of his concern for the "6.5 million part-time workers [who] want to work full-time" (O'Keefe 2015). Thus, Bush recognized the political inadvisability of blatantly individualist explanations of poverty and low income, and he instead embraced structural explanations of the phenomena—arguing that the country needed "high, sustained economic growth" in order to solve the problem of the evaporation of the livable wage (O'Keefe 2015).

Moreover, in recent years, studies that endeavor to show the precise structural mechanisms that produce poverty have been well received. For example, economist David Autor (2010) has documented in his scholarship the macro forces that have combined to produce poverty in the United States. In one well-cited paper, he notes that

> the structure of job opportunities in the United States has sharply polarized over the past two decades, with expanding job opportunities in both high-skill, high-wage occupations and low-skill, low-wage occupations, coupled with contracting opportunities in middle-wage, middle-skill white-collar and blue-collar jobs. . . . [J]ob opportunities are declining in both middle-skill, white-collar clerical, administrative, and sales occupations and in middle-skill, blue-collar production, craft, and operative occupations. The decline in middle-skill jobs has been detrimental to the earnings and labor force participation rates of workers without a four-year college education, and differentially so for males, who are increasingly concentrated in low-paying service occupations. (2010, 1)

Autor notes that middle-skill jobs likely have disappeared in the United States because they have been offshored or because technology has made it unnecessary to hire workers to perform the tasks that the job requires (2010, 4). Consequently, these jobs have rapidly vanished from the labor market in the United States.

The thrust of Autor's oeuvre is that the jobs that pay wages that can support middle-skill workers are simply not there. If these workers are poor, it is not because they are lazy, or promiscuous, or criminally inclined. It is because the market does not contain opportunities for them to be anything but poor. Notably, people and organizations from both sides of the political spectrum have frequently cited Autor's work (Sherk 2014; Stark and Zolt 2013).

Nevertheless, structural explanations of poverty have not deeply saturated the culture. In fact, a poll that the Pew Research Center conducted in January 2014 confirms that a majority of Americans believe that the poor are responsible for their poverty: 60 percent of respondents agreed with the proposition that "most people who want to get ahead can make it if they are willing to work hard" (Pew Research Center 2014).

Indeed, there is a substantial literature documenting that the most favored explanation of poverty in the United States is one that identifies individual behaviors as the root of indigence. In summarizing the literature, social psychologist Catherine Cozzarelli and her coauthors[2] write that

> most of these studies find that Americans believe that there are multiple determinants of poverty[,] but that individualistic or "internal" causes (e.g., lack of effort, being lazy, low in intelligence, being on drugs) tend to be more important than societal or "external" ones (e.g., being a victim of discrimination, low wages, being forced to attend bad schools). (Cozzarelli, Wilkinson, and Tagler 2001, 210)

We might wonder why individualist explanations of poverty are so readily accepted and believed in the United States. Indeed, many people with progressive politics subscribe to individualist explanations of poverty. Consider that the 2014 Pew poll discussed above notes that 76 percent of Republicans versus 49 percent of Democrats reported holding the belief that most can get ahead through hard work (Pew Research Center 2014). While those figures can be cited to show that people with conservative politics are more likely than those with liberal politics to believe that individual effort (and the lack thereof) produces economic success and failure, they can also be cited to show that *close to half of those with liberal politics believe that individual effort produces economic success and failure.*

The attraction of individualist explanations of poverty may be due to the fact that the alternative—structural explanations of poverty—strip those of us who are economically successful of the chance to claim those successes as entirely our own. That is, if the poor do not occupy that economic and social station because of their own efforts (or lack thereof), then those who are *not* poor do not occupy our own economic and social stations because of our own efforts. Stated differently, if structural forces contribute to and/or cause "their" failure, then structural forces likely contribute to and/or cause "our" success. That our achievements may not be entirely *earned*—but may have been gifted to us, in some important sense, by forces outside of our control—is a discomfiting reality that many people, even progressive ones, may reject.

The wide acceptance of individualist explanations of poverty may explain why programs that are designed to help the poor tend to be only slightly less harsh than the poverty that entraps them. Indeed, powerful cultural discourses assert that poor people who receive public assistance to help them cope with their poverty are even more morally impoverished than those who are poor but do not seek help from the state. Consider one philosopher's articulation of this notion:

> The welfare state seems to be corrupting some of our core moral principles. ... To be specific: The welfare state encourages people to ignore, to violate— even to pretend that it does not exist—the moral principle that it is wrong to live at other people's expense. ... Able-bodied adults who live at the unwilling expense of others degrade themselves even as they demean those forced to support them. ...
>
> [T]he welfare state seems to have clouded this central moral principle. Indeed, it seems it has entirely inverted it, even institutionalized its perversion. It has created a legal apparatus that allows, even encourages, some to live at others' expense, and this apparatus has given rise to the feeling among increasingly many people that they have the right—that they are "entitled," perhaps as a matter of "social justice"—to live at others' expense. (Otteson 2011)

The frequently punitive aspects of many public assistance programs might be understood as institutionalized responses to both the sense that the poor bear a bad moral character and the sense that the policies and programs that endeavor to help them are immoral because they allow the poor to benefit from the labor of others. As a result, many of the programs that are designed to relieve the poor of some of the most degrading aspects of poverty—like TANF and Medicaid—are themselves degrading, as they reflect the ideology that the programs are immoral endeavors to assist immoral people.

The Court and the Moral Construction of Poverty

In this book I assert that poor mothers have been (effectively or actually) deprived of privacy rights because, as poor people, they are presumed to suffer from behavioral and/or ethical deficiencies; moreover, because these deficiencies necessarily implicate children—as poor mothers are *mothers*, after all— they are not bestowed with (effective or actual) privacy rights that could constrain the government from regulating their private lives and protecting their children.

In order to establish this claim, it is not enough to show that ideologies linking poverty and immorality are popular. Instead, one also has to show that the jurists charged with interpreting the Constitution have come to accept these ideologies and to embody them in the cases that they decide; one has to show that the Court has constructed a jurisprudence that reflects the discursive link between poverty and immorality. When one looks in the corner of the Court's jurisprudence in which it has wrestled with the question of whether the government has any responsibility at all to its poorest citizens, one can see shadows of the moral construction of poverty.

There is *Dandridge v. Williams* (397 U.S. 471 (1970)), in which the Court upheld Maryland's policy of capping the size of AFDC (Aid to Families with Dependent Children) grants such that families consisting of seven or more persons were left with their needs unmet. After finding that rational basis review was the appropriate level of scrutiny for the law, the Court affirmed that the law was reasonably related to the state's goals of encouraging gainful employment and providing incentives for family planning. It is here that the Court reveals an underlying faith in the belief that people are impoverished because of their own character flaws. With respect to the state's goal of encouraging gainful employment by capping AFDC grants, the Court "invites the reader to make a series of associations that likely lead to the specter of the welfare recipient shirking employment—choosing to be a welfare recipient and not a wage earner—which is the most common contemporary version of the moral weakness of the poor" (Ross 1991, 1519).

Further, the trope of the *welfare queen* not so subtly lurks behind the state's goal of providing incentives for family planning. The statute is haunted by the specter of the woman who bears children for none of the myriad legitimate and honorable reasons that motivate women with class privilege to become mothers; instead, the welfare queen has children in large part because she knows that the state will finance them: "For these women, becoming pregnant is an act of moral weakness. The grant ceiling encourages them to do the right thing (have no more children), albeit for the wrong reason (in response to the state's financial incentive rather than as a matter of individual moral strength)" (Ross 1991, 1520).

There is also *Wyman v. James* (400 U.S. 309 (1971)), in which the Court upheld the constitutionality of New York's policy of requiring beneficiaries of AFDC to submit to home visits as a condition of eligibility. Justice Blackmun, writing for the majority, found the visits legitimate attempts by the state to protect children from exploitation. Indeed, there was some evidence that the named plaintiff who had challenged New York's policy had either been neglecting or abusing her son. The Court observes: "There are indications that all was not always well with the infant Maurice (skull fracture, a dent in the head, a possible rat bite). The picture is a sad and unhappy one" (Wyman v. James, 400 U.S. 309, 322 n.9 (1971)). However,

> [T]he issue in *Wyman* was whether the New York home visit regulations were constitutional, not whether Mrs. James had committed child abuse. The state had not premised its need to visit Mrs. James' home on any suspicion of child abuse. Thus, Blackmun's suggestion seems an irrelevant expression of his suspicion that she was physically abusing her son. But his suggestion of abuse becomes relevant to the constitutional issue the moment one plugs in the premise of moral weakness. The story of Mrs. James and the infant Maurice becomes a story of all AFDC mothers and their propensity, by virtue of their poverty, to abuse their children. Blackmun's suspicion then becomes relevant; it provides a state interest in home visits for the purpose of monitoring a group of parents especially prone to child abuse. (Ross 1991, 1524–25)

If the poor are likely to commit child abuse, then the state surely is justified in searching their homes for signs of that abuse. However, the only evidence that the Court marshals to support the proposition that the poor are likely to commit child abuse is their poverty. Their poverty can demonstrate this likelihood if one believes that poverty evidences some sort of moral degradation. *Wyman* embalms this understanding of poverty into the Constitution.

Yet, flowing in the jurisprudence, beside the undercurrent apparent in *Dandridge* and *Wyman* that links poverty with immorality, is a parallel stream asserting that poverty is an enduring feature of modern society. In some iterations of this stream, poverty is altogether incapable of eradication; other iterations propose that while it may be possible to eradicate poverty, it is impossible or inappropriate for the *judiciary* to achieve this feat. Other sections of the Court's opinion in *Dandridge v. Williams* provide a clear example of this parallel stream—what legal scholar Thomas Ross labels a "rhetoric of helplessness" (1991, 1522). After holding that Maryland's family cap policy did not violate the Equal Protection Clause, the majority concluded its opinion by professing that it was agnostic on the question of whether

> the Maryland regulation is wise, that it best fulfills the relevant social and economic objectives that Maryland might ideally espouse, or that a more just and humane system could not be devised. . . . *But the intractable economic, social, and even philosophical problems presented by public welfare assistance programs are not the business of this Court.* (Dandridge v. Williams, 397 U.S. 471, 487 (1970); emphasis added)

With this statement, the Court declares two things. First, it states that the institution of the judiciary is not well situated, or even empowered, to decide how best to redistribute income such that the least successful players in market capitalism are saved from the privation that comes with economic failure. Second, it states that the question of how to redistribute income in order to eliminate the cruelties endemic to poverty may be a question that *no* institution can solve. Indeed, for the Court, poverty is an "intractable" problem. In this way, the Court characterizes

> poverty as a product of a mix of abstract forces and ideas, beyond our practical control. Poverty is built into the basic structure of our society, it is a product of our history, traditions, philosophies, political structures, and economic structures. . . . [There is] no realistic solution or . . . [the solution] entails the loss of our most basic social structures. (Ross 1991, 1510)

Ross notes that there is a tension between the claim that the source of poverty is the immoral character of the poor and the claim that the causes of poverty are so hugely *macro* that even the judiciary is an impotent tool with which to address it. If the source of poverty is the poor person's moral lack, then the causes of poverty are not macro at all. Rather, they are intensely *micro*. And we only can eradicate poverty by repairing the broken moral compasses that erroneously guide the impoverished to their impoverishment. Ross reconciles the seeming contradiction with two observations. First, he notes that, even if the source of poverty is the poor's immorality and not structural imperfections, then the judiciary remains impotent to eradicate poverty. How can a court of law fix a person's character? Second, he notes that the two currents can be reconciled if a dichotomy is made between the undeserving and the deserving poor: The undeserving poor are those whose immorality has led to their poverty, while the deserving poor are those whose poverty is caused by powerful, uncompromising structural forces beyond anyone's and everyone's control.

The Deserving and Undeserving Poor

Thus, one must complicate the systematic relationship between poverty and moral lack. While it is true that "the culture of capitalism measures persons, as well as everything else, by their ability to produce wealth and by their success in earning it," and while it is true that this "leads to the moral condemnation of those who, for whatever reason, fail to contribute or to prosper," those who have failed to contribute or prosper are not equal subjects of moral condemnation (Katz 1989, 7). There are those who escape moral censure due to the fact that they cannot be blamed for their failure to contribute or prosper: the deserving poor. And then there are those who are the proper subjects of moral contempt, as they are to be blamed for their own failures: the undeserving poor. Poverty scholars Joel Handler and Yeheskel Hasenfeld (1991) explain it in terms of which categories of people are morally excused from work. The deserving poor enjoy this moral excuse; the undeserving poor do not.

While the line that demarcates the deserving from the undeserving poor has shifted throughout the nation's history, the blind, the deaf and mute, the insane, and others who are mentally or physically incapable of working have always been conceptualized as the deserving poor. Their poverty has never invited assumptions of personal shortcomings. Their disabilities have always rendered them morally excused from work.

However, other groups have varyingly existed on either side of the line that separates the deserving and the undeserving poor. The elderly are one example. At present, very few would argue that an indigent elderly person ought to be blamed for her poverty. For the most part, we conceptualize such individuals as too old to work—as having graduated out of the population of people who belong within the pool of available labor (Brodkin 1993, 658). As such, the indigent elderly are morally excused from work; they are the deserving poor.

Yet, the indigent elderly have not always been considered rightful members of the deserving poor. Prior to the New Deal, the elderly poor were more morally ambiguous. Discourses circulated in which the elderly poor were imagined to be those who had not worked hard during their youth (Handler and Hasenfeld 1991). They were those who had not engaged in the morally valuable activities of living thriftily and of saving one's earnings. They were those who had engaged in the morally corrupt activities of profligate spending and extravagant consumption.

Moreover, even if an aged person was poor despite his having lived morally during his youth, the fact of his poverty revealed the immorality of another group of persons: his children. If an older person was poor, then his able-bodied children, who bore the responsibility for caring for him in his dotage, were morally blameworthy. Thus, the figure of the poor aged body carried suggestions of immorality. As such, it was situated on the undeserving side of the deserving/undeserving poor binary. Cultural shifts would cause it to be moved to the deserving side, where it currently, and uncontroversially, resides.

Poor mothers also have existed on both sides of the deserving and unde-serving poor binary throughout history. In the colonial period, women with children, along with everyone else, were expected to labor (Padavic and Reskin 2002). Motherhood did not provide a moral excuse from work. If a mother was poor because she could not work or was poor despite the fact that she did work, she did not escape moral censure.

Culture shifted, however. By the early nineteenth century, discourses had developed that declared that the proper location for a mother was not the workforce but rather the home (Cahn 2000). In fact, the working-as-moral and not-working-as-immoral schema reversed itself. Not only did motherhood provide a moral excuse from work, thereby making the decision not to work outside of the home an imminently moral one, but it became morally inexcus-able for mothers to work outside of the home.

Powerful voices argued that working women were morally suspect because the workplace was an environment that cultivated and sanctioned the corrup-tion of morals (Handler and Hasenfeld 1991). Working women's "associations with men, impulsive spending, immodest dress, and profane language inevita-bly led to moral laxity. . . . Running through all of the debates was deep concern about the effects of women's working on morality" (55). Women in the labor force also threatened the moral fabric of society because they "depressed wages, depriving men of the ability to marry" (55). Further, *mothers* who worked out-side of the home were castigated twice over because their time spent in the morally debasing workplace was time spent away from their children. Cultural discourses constructed this as child neglect—the height of morally condem-nable behavior. Insofar as working mothers knowingly exposed themselves to the corrupting forces found in the labor market, they were moral failures as *women*. Insofar as working mothers needed to be absent from the home during their workdays and had to leave their children in the care of others, they were moral failures as *mothers*.

Poor mothers who worked were also condemned by the assumption that they needed to work because they were "unfit" to receive financial support from social programs designed to relieve mothers from the necessity of working outside the home. These programs had policies of excluding women who were thought to have behaved immorally; they made women who had engaged in premarital sex and childbearing, had divorced, or had been deserted by their husbands ineligible for benefits (McClain 1996). The fact that a mother worked was taken to mean that she had been excluded from these programs, and the fact of her exclusion from these programs was taken to mean that she had engaged in immoral behavior. Thus, working mothers' immorality could be assumed.

But, culture shifted once again. By the 1960s, this shift had reestablished the working-as-moral and not-working-as-immoral schema that had reigned at the dawn of the nation. One might explain this shift as a function of the insistence with which women entered the workforce. Female labor force participation skyrocketed despite powerful cultural discourses that declared that the appropriate place for them was the home.

Perhaps because women insisted upon working outside the home, the narratives that were told about working women transformed. And the more moral it became to work as a mother, the more immoral it became *not* to work as a mother. "The respectability of working married mothers only heightened the perceived deviance and moral depravity of single mothers, especially those with children born out of wedlock, who are on welfare rather than working" (Handler and Hasenfeld 1991, 137). This is the current culture within which we live: one in which all (except the wealthiest) mothers are expected to work. As such, those mothers who are poor and not working are firmly situated on the undeserving side of the binary, enjoying no moral excuse from work.[3]

Race and the Undeservingness of the Nonworking Poor Mother

Yet, explanations of the morality of the working mother that overlook race are radically incomplete. Race—that social force that both obviously and obliquely shapes the nation—must be considered in any analysis of how the working mother became moral and the nonworking mother became immoral. When one folds race into the story, one sees that it has operated to both naturalize and justify changes in the ethics of working motherhood.

When cultural discourses attached a badge of immorality to mothers who worked outside of the home, the fact that many of those mothers were black—indeed, the fact that *most* black mothers worked outside the home—validated this judgment. Certainly, the exclusion of black mothers from the home facilitated its construction as the "proper" site for mothers.

Part of the reason why many black women had been pushed out of the home and into the labor market is that the welfare programs that were designed to shield mothers from that very phenomenon systematically excluded black women (Huda 2001). In the 1960s, black women began agitating for access to these public assistance programs that historically had refused to serve them. Their efforts were quite successful on many fronts (Huda 2001). In contrast to the 1930s, when the beneficiaries of cash assistance programs for mothers were predominately white, by 1975 black women made up 44 percent of the beneficiaries of the then-existing cash assistance program for mothers, Aid for Families with Dependent Children (AFDC); white women constituted only 40 percent of the program's beneficiaries that year.[4] Access to AFDC meant that black mothers could now stay in the home and raise their children—a privilege that had only been available to white mothers for much of the nation's history.

However, although black women gained access to the home as a site of labor—a place that, up until then, had been understood as the "proper" moral site for mothers—they nevertheless remained incapable of accessing discourses that affirmed them as moral individuals. The justification for their continued exclusion from these discourses centers on the reasons why they did not have a male wage on which to depend: They were divorced, had been deserted by their husbands, or were never married to the fathers of their children (Huda 2001).

To be fair, divorce, desertion, and reproduction outside of marriage always had been understood as morally problematic behaviors. Prior to black women's agitation in the 1960s for access to welfare programs that benefited poor mothers, being divorced, deserted, or an unwed mother served as a moral disqualification from these programs. Interestingly, however, when divorce, desertion, and reproduction outside of marriage described the circumstances under which white women became single mothers, it was understood as a problem of patriarchy. White women's "single motherhood was viewed as evidence of their failure to abide by the sex-gender system's conventions governing marriage and the traditional two-parent family. Their anti-patriarchal conduct rendered them morally responsible for their poverty and justified the government's refusal to provide them with assistance" (Crooms 1995, 620).

However, when divorce, desertion, and never marrying described the circumstances under which black women became single mothers, it was understood as something bigger than a problem of patriarchy. It became a "tangle of pathology" (Moynihan 1965): If it was not generative of all of the social ills that plagued black people in the United States, then it certainly was responsible for most of them. Politician and sociologist Daniel Patrick Moynihan (1965) notoriously theorized problematic black motherhood in his 1965 report "The Negro Family." He observed that almost 25 percent of "urban Negro marriages" were dissolved, almost 25 percent of "Negro births" were "illegitimate," and almost 25 percent of "Negro families" were female-headed households (6). He noted that a fundamental fact of Negro American family life is the often reversed roles of husband and wife" (30). And he lamented the emasculation that black women visited upon their male partners:

> Consider the fact that relief investigators or case workers are normally women and deal with the housewife. Already suffering a loss in prestige and authority in the family because of his failure to be the chief breadwinner, the male head of the family feels deeply this obvious transfer of planning for the family's wellbeing to two women, one of them an outsider. His role is reduced to that of errand boy to and from the relief office. (19)

If patriarchy is a moral order, then black mothers—in their insistence upon assuming the roles that belonged to men, in their banishing of men to the roles that women occupied in years past, and in their creation of the conditions that invited men to abandon their families altogether—were agents of immorality.

This might explain why the home became understood as an improper, immoral place for mothers to be just as soon as black mothers could remain there to raise their children. As immorality attached to the space where black mothers could be found, the workforce became the site of moral righteousness. The poor black mothers who no longer needed to labor there were moral failures.

The racialized figure of the welfare queen is worth mentioning here. This caricature of indigent black motherhood can be described as

> a poor, black mother who first became pregnant as a teenager. Her sexual irresponsibility resulted in her dropping out of school and joining the AFDC rolls. Rather than marry the child's father and make the best of the situation, she chose to remain single, to collect AFDC and to have more children by different fathers. Her choices were driven by an AFDC program which rewarded her for remaining promiscuous, single, and prolific. Her sexual irresponsibility placed her at the beginning of a chain which ultimately ended with an impoverished and dysfunctional community. (Crooms 1995, 622)

We can credit President Ronald Reagan with giving birth to the mythos of the welfare queen (Cammett 2014). He tactically deployed her in an effort to gain popular and political support for his goal of reducing the size of "extreme" redistributive policies and social welfare programs. She came to stand for "big government." The more that he could get the public to fear and loathe her, the more that he could get the public to fear and loathe big government. Thus, Reagan often told the story of a Chicago woman who had "'80 names, 30 addresses,

12 Social Security cards and tax-free income over $150,000'" (Edsall and Edsall 1991, 148). And he asked the public to believe that this woman—who, in actuality, was "not a garden-variety cheat, but . . . rather a full-fledge[d] psychopath and con artist . . . whose other possible crimes include murder and kidnapping" (Cammett 2014, 244 n.66)—represented all AFDC recipients.

Reagan also told the tale of a "housing project in New York City in which a slum dweller . . . can get an apartment with 11-foot ceilings, with a 20-foot balcony, a swimming pool and a gymnasium, laundry room and play room, and the rent begins at $113.20 and that includes utilities" (Cammett 2014, 245). He asked the public to believe that this housing project, which was actually part of a larger development designed to serve 200,000 residents in the community, represented the housing that was generally available to any poor person who asked for state assistance.

However, simply because the fables Reagan wove were empirically false, it does not mean that they were untrue. That is, in a culture wherein black people have been constructed as sexually lascivious and intractably indolent since the dawn of the nation, the stories Reagan told made complete sense. And importantly, they were attractive to wealthier individuals inasmuch as the more that poor people could be understood as morally depraved, the more that they, the non-poor, could be understood as morally righteous.

The welfare queen merits discussion for two reasons. First, Reagan and others claimed that liberal welfare policies that generously and indiscriminately provided cash and other relief to the poor were responsible for the welfare queen's existence. Thus, the disgust that the public felt for the welfare queen could be productively channeled toward those policies, with AFDC being the primary target. In this way, the welfare queen created, or simply supported and strengthened, a popular and political climate within which the replacement of AFDC was possible. Essentially, the road to TANF winds by the welfare queen's luxury condominium.

Second, the welfare queen merits discussion because she is the apotheosis of immorality. If one is immoral because one has sex and has children outside of marriage, then the welfare queen is immoral for that reason. If one is immoral because one fails to engage in the morally valuable activity of laboring in the market, then the welfare queen is immoral for that reason. If one is immoral because one receives public assistance and, as such, lives at another's expense, then the welfare queen is immoral for that reason. Further, if one's immorality at living at another's expense is made more corrupt by living *lavishly* at another's expense, then the welfare queen is immoral for that reason. She is immoral four times over.

.   .   .

Political scientist Evelyn Brodkin has argued that current welfare policies treat the poor as enemies of the nation—as villains. She notes that *Webster's Dictionary* defines "villain" as "one who is capable of gross wickedness or crimes; a vile wretch; a scoundrel" (Brodkin 1993, 654). She then offers an instructive etymology of the word "villain," writing that the word

> has its origins in the obsolete French word "villein," a farm servant. By the 13th century, English peasants working feudal estates under the terms of villeinage were nominally regarded as "freemen" yet remained economically and socially subjects of their lord. This paradoxical condition of formal freedom coexisting within a system of economic and social subjugation might well be said to describe the status of the poor in postmodern America, where legal equality remains at considerable remove from one's social and economic status. Under these conditions, the social citizenship of the poor may be limited both by the "moral construction of poverty" and the material requirements for political influence. (Brodkin 1993, 654–55)

It is edifying that Brodkin describes the poor's status in terms of "citizenship," arguing that attributing impoverished people's poverty to their own bad behavior functions to limit this citizenship. Some scholars have described citizenship as the status whereby a person is granted a baseline set of rights bestowed by the relevant government. For example, legal scholar Kevin Lapp (2012) notes the argument that "to be a citizen means you possess a particular or minimum set of rights and privileges." Accordingly, if an individual does not possess that baseline set of rights—if she has been deprived of a right—then she is not a full citizen; she is a "second-class or semicitizen" (Lapp 2012, 1576).

This book serves to buttress Brodkin's intuition that the belief that poor mothers' immorality has caused their poverty limits their citizenship. To be precise, the conviction that moral deficiencies cause poverty serves to justify depriving poor mothers, either in the moderate or strong sense, of their family, informational, and reproductive privacy rights. As a result, they do not possess the full set of legal rights that the government bestows to citizens. Their citizenship is partial. They are second-class or semicitizens.

The Failure of the Positive Rights Solution

After taking an accounting of the dismal state of poor mothers' privacy—and the impotence of their ostensible privacy rights—some scholars have been moved to argue that the reason poor mothers are subject to indignities that wealthier mothers never have to endure is that the Constitution has been interpreted to be a charter of negative rights. That is, the Court has declared that the rights that the Constitution protects are those that simply immunize protected activities from government intervention and regulation (Appleton 1981). Advocates for poor mothers argue that this interpretation of the Constitution is at the root of the humiliations that poor women are obliged to suffer. What is needed, they contend, is an alternate interpretation—one in which the Constitution confers positive rights. Positive rights, unlike negative rights, "would compel affirmative governmental involvement—the official provision or facilitation of the activity or good protected by the right" (Appleton 1981, 735).

The Court unambiguously declared that the Constitution primarily protects negative rights in *DeShaney v. Winnebago County* (489 U.S. 189, 195–97 (1989)). In *DeShaney*, the Court denied that the Due Process Clause provided Joshua DeShaney with a right to the competent provision of services by his jurisdiction's child protection agency, which had returned him to the home of his father even though several state actors knew that Joshua's father was abusive. Eventually, Joshua's father beat Joshua so viciously that he suffered permanent brain damage. In holding that the Due Process Clause did not provide Joshua with the positive right to protection by the state, the Court argued that the clause

> is phrased as a limitation on the State's power to act, not as a guarantee of certain minimal levels of safety and security. It forbids the State itself to deprive individuals of life, liberty, or property without "due process of law," but its language cannot fairly be extended to impose an affirmative obligation on the State to ensure that those interests do not come to harm through other means. . . . Consistent with these principles, our cases have recognized that the Due Process Clauses generally confer no affirmative right to governmental aid. . . . If the Due Process Clause does not require the State to provide its citizens with particular protective services, it follows that the State cannot be held liable under the Clause for injuries that could have been averted had it chosen to provide them. (DeShaney v. Winnebago County Department of Social Services, 489 U.S. 189, 195–97 (1989))

For scholars concerned about poor mothers, the Court's decisions in *Maher v. Roe* (432 U.S. 464 (1977)) and *Harris v. McRae* (448 U.S. 297, 318 (1980)) underscore the problem posed by interpreting the Constitution to be a document that protects only negative rights. In *Maher* and *Harris*, the Court upheld the constitutionality of prohibitions on the use of Medicaid funds to pay the costs of indigent beneficiaries' abortions. The Court reasoned that the abortion right that it recognized in *Roe v. Wade* (410 U.S. 113 (1973)) did no more than prohibit governments from erecting obstacles in women's path to abortion; that is, the right *constrained* the government. The indigent plaintiffs in *Maher* and *Harris* who sought Medicaid coverage for their abortions wanted to compel the government to act—to oblige the government to facilitate their access to abortion. The *Harris* Court thought that this was a fantastical proposition, one that would "mark a drastic change in our understanding of the Constitution" (318). It claimed that while "the liberty protected by the Due Process Clause affords protection against unwarranted government interference with freedom of choice in the context of certain personal decisions, it does not confer an entitlement to such funds as may be necessary to realize all the advantages of that freedom" (317–18).

Indeed, the suggestion that the government could be obliged to facilitate poor women's abortions was deeply disturbing to the Court. "To translate the limitation on governmental power implicit in the Due Process Clause into an affirmative funding obligation would require Congress to subsidize the medically necessary abortion of an indigent woman even if Congress had not enacted a Medicaid program to subsidize other medically necessary services" (318). To a majority of the Court, this interpretation of the Constitution was simply implausible.

Scholars interested in poor mothers thought that *Maher* and *Harris* exemplified the danger of limiting the Constitution to be one that recognizes only negative rights (Appleton 1981; Soohoo 2012). To these scholars, the decisions demonstrated just how desperately poor women required positive rights. Wealthier women needed *negative* rights, they argued; they needed entities that would constrain the government from interfering with their ability to access the goods and services that they wanted, and could afford, to purchase in the market. Poorer women, on the other hand, needed *positive* rights; they needed entities that would enable them to access the goods and services in the market that their indigence rendered unavailable to them (Appleton 1981). For many indigent women, their lack of funds means that *Roe v. Wade* might just as well have never been decided.

Many have advocated for the recognition of positive privacy rights beyond the context of abortion, arguing that negative privacy rights alone do not enable poor mothers to be autonomous agents of their reproductive bodies. For example, legal theorist Dorothy Roberts (1995) has interrogated the Court's failure to invoke the unconstitutional conditions doctrine to strike down conditions on welfare benefits that burden poor mothers' ostensible privacy rights (931). As explored more expansively in the following chapter, the unconstitutional conditions doctrine prohibits the government from conditioning a benefit on the beneficiary's surrender of a constitutional right, even when the government is not obliged to provide the benefit in the first instance. The Court might have used the doctrine to strike down laws and policies that require poor mothers to surrender their theoretical privacy rights in order to receive a welfare benefit. The Court has refused to do so.

Roberts acknowledges that poor mothers' attempts to claim *privacy* while receiving *public* benefits produces an obvious tension. Yet, she writes that the unconstitutional conditions doctrine does not resolve that tension because it does no more than attempt "to preserve poor people's liberty within a constitutional framework designed to protect only property owners" (931).[5] Roberts argues that the unconstitutional conditions doctrine is weak for that very reason: It does not try to shift the constitutional framework from one that protects property owners to one that *also* protects the propertyless. Instead, it tries only to "minimize the harm to those who fall at the bottom (or completely out of bounds), without changing the basic order of things" (940). For Roberts, the solution is to actually transform the constitutional framework. She observes that

> [i]f the government were required to subsidize the activities at issue, and if reliance on public assistance therefore did not constitute a waiver of privacy, there would be no place for a special doctrine to prohibit government conditions that threaten these activities. It is our inability to defend poor women's reproductive liberty in terms of traditional constitutional discourse that forces us the rely on this weak-kneed doctrine. (939)

Essentially, Roberts imagines that the solution is positive privacy rights.

We can begin a response to the claim that positive rights will resolve poor mothers' predicament by recalling the basic legal realist insight that positive rights and negative rights are not analytically distinct entities. That is, every right to be free of government action entails some form of government action. Even Judge Posner (1996), a proponent of the belief that it is useful to distinguish positive and negative rights, acknowledges the analytical indistinctiveness between the two. He notes that the right to property commonly is understood as a negative right: The government may not take actions that deprive individuals of their property. However, an individual's right to government inaction with respect to her property requires extensive government action to protect that same property:

> The rights of property and of personal safety, which are negative liberties enforced by criminal and tort laws, imply a public machinery of rights protection and enforcement, a machinery that includes police, prosecutors, judges, and even publicly employed or subsidized lawyers for criminal defendants who cannot afford to hire their own lawyer. . . . [I]t is difficult to believe that negative liberties could be made meaningful without intervention by the public sector. (Posner 1996, 3)

Moreover, many negative rights can be reframed as positive rights, and vice versa. For example, the state was sued in *White v. Rochford* (592 F.2d 381 (7th Cir. 1979)) after police arrested an adult who was driving a car and, after making the arrest, left the children who were also riding in the car on the side of the road without adult supervision or any means of getting help. The court found that the state could be liable for damages, as it had acted when it "abandoned" the children and "deprived" them of adult protection (382). The dissent disagreed, arguing that the state had not acted at all; it had merely failed to bring the children to a safe place—an affirmative act that the dissent felt the Constitution did not impose.

Analogously, the state was sued in *Bowers v. De Vito* (686 F.2d 616 (7th Cir. 1982)) after it released from a state psychiatric institution a mentally ill patient who subsequently stabbed a woman to death. The court held that the state had no liability toward the decedent's family because the state had not affirmatively acted: "[The state] simply failed adequately to protect her, as a member of the public, from a dangerous man" (618). However, we can easily reformulate into affirmative terms that which the state did: It *deinstitutionalized* the patient and *released* him into society.

Nevertheless, even if we assume that there is a principle that can definitively distinguish between government action and inaction (and in so doing, definitively distinguish between when a claim is being made for a positive right or negative right),[6] we must confront the fact that many of the examples of poor mothers' lack of privacy that this book explores are actually *interventions* into their lives as a consequence of government action—not *deprivations* that are occasioned as a result of government inaction. When the government demands intimate information from a pregnant woman, when it shares that same information, when it enters a poor mother's home to investigate claims of child neglect, when it removes a child from her family and places her in foster care, and when it funds the costs of childbirth but not the costs of abortion, the government is actively *invading* the private lives of poor mothers. In these instances, the government is not sitting idly by as poor mothers endure the consequences of their propertyless condition. A reformulation of privacy rights into positive rights will not stop the government from actively intervening in poor mothers' private lives. Instead, actual *negative* rights—the rights that the Constitution has been interpreted to protect—would prevent the government from intruding into poor mothers' lives.[7] In this way, positive rights are not the solution to all of the problems that this book identifies; instead, *effective* negative rights are an important solution.

Nevertheless, it is true that positive rights may remedy some privacy deprivations. For example, if the right to abortion were understood as a positive right, then poor mothers would enjoy privacy in the sense that they would have tangible access to abortion. Thus, we ought not to dismiss positive rights simply because they will not remedy *all* of the privacy invasions that poor mothers experience; positive rights may still be valuable insofar as they can provide poor mothers with some protection from the deprivations that are concomitant to poverty. Such positive rights, coupled with effective negative rights, may be what poor mothers need to enjoy a life and a relationship with the state that resembles the life and relationship with the state that their counterparts with class privilege enjoy.

However, there is a very real danger that, despite a reformulation of rights, poor mothers would find themselves in the same predicament in which they are now: deprived of privacy rights in either the moderate or strong sense. That is, just as poor mothers have been (effectively or actually) deprived of negative privacy rights, they may be (effectively or actually) deprived of positive privacy rights.

In this book I contend that the moral construction of poverty counsels that privacy rights will not generate the value that otherwise justifies their recognition when poor mothers enjoy them. Hence, they have been effectively (consistent with the moderate claim) or actually (consistent with the strong claim) stripped of them. I have also described this in terms of a condition being put on the negative privacy rights that the Constitution has been interpreted to recognize. That is, if one is pregnant or parenting, one must be presumed to be sound—behaviorally and ethically—in order to bear an effective or actual right to compel state nonintervention with respect to the various arenas of life that the privacy right protects.

The question, then, is this: Will positive privacy rights be imagined to generate the value that otherwise justifies them when poor mothers bear them? If there is a condition on extant negative privacy rights, can we rest assured that a similar condition would not be imposed on positive privacy rights if they came to be recognized? Will the recognition of positive privacy rights entail reimagining the causes of poverty?

We have no assurances that the answer to these questions will be in the affirmative. The Court may interpret the Constitution to provide positive privacy rights without necessarily being committed to the proposition that better explanations of poverty can be found by looking to structural forces and not individual moral shortcomings. If there is an enduring belief that individual bad behavior lies at the root of poverty, then poor mothers would be presumed to be the immoral agents of their own misfortune—even in a legal landscape that recognizes positive privacy rights. Poor mothers may find themselves deprived of positive privacy rights just as they have been deprived of negative privacy rights.

Some may claim that positive privacy rights would not be conditioned on the presumed moral character of the rightsbearer because positive rights, unlike negative privacy rights, are unconditional. They may assert that once a positive right is recognized, the state is obliged to provide to everyone, without condition, whatever good or service to which the right pertains. However, this claim is incorrect. Positive rights, like negative rights, are legal rights. And, as explained in the Introduction, legal rights can be conditioned on whatever the institution that recognizes or enforces them prescribes. Stated another way, positive rights are not natural or human rights, which are unconditional. As such, if the state that recognizes positive rights decides to impose a condition on them, then they will be so conditioned. Further, the example that the Introduction gives of a conditional constitutional right—the Sixth Amendment right to jury trial, which is conditioned on the rightsbearer being within the borders of the continental United States, Hawaii, or Alaska—is a positive right in the sense that it imposes an obligation on the state to provide a jury trial before it punishes an individual for a crime.[8] The case of Puerto Rico demonstrates that positive constitutional rights, like their negative counterparts, can be conditional.

A more compelling argument in favor of the positive rights solution is that a Court that is moved to interpret the Constitution to contain positive rights that would provide for individuals' well-being would also be a Court that does not subscribe to the moral construction of poverty. That is, the belief that the Constitution ought to be interpreted to provide positive rights may be described as a politically liberal one. (Indeed, the political liberals on the Court—Justices Blackmun, Brennan, and Marshall—dissented from *DeShaney v. Winnebago County*'s holding that the Due Process Clause did not provide a child with a right to compel the state to protect him from his abusive father.) Moreover, the belief that macro forces, and not individual moral failings, cause poverty is also one that may be described as a liberal one.

Indeed, a wealth of studies document that political liberals, more so than political conservatives, tend to favor explanations of poverty that locate its causes in the societal structures in which individuals exist as opposed to the individuals themselves (Griffin and Oheneba-Sakyi 1993). For example, legal scholars Adam Benforado and Jon Hanson condense the literature into this summary:

> [C]onservatives tend to believe that "people are poor because they are lazy, do not improve themselves, cannot manage money, and abuse drugs or alcohol. Less conservative beliefs correlate with situational attributions: perceiving societal causes. . . . In this view, people are poor because of prejudice and discrimination, inadequate education, exploitation by the rich, and low wages." (2008, 383–84)

If these convictions—that the Constitution is properly interpreted to provide positive rights and that there is no causal link between poverty and immorality—are both liberal views, then it is unlikely that a majority of the Court would act liberally by recognizing positive privacy rights but then turn around and act conservatively by disqualifying the poor from possessing them.

It is mostly true that the Court acts liberally when a majority of the justices sitting on the Court are political liberals and acts conservatively when a majority are political conservatives.[9] However, the composition of the Court changes over time. And culture, which the Court's jurisprudence eventually reflects, shifts over time—a position that the Conclusion defends. Accordingly, the

Court that interprets the Constitution to contain positive privacy rights need not be the same Court that imposes a moral condition on those rights. And the dominant cultural discourses that counsel the Court to interpret the Constitution to contain positive rights need not retain their dominance; they may be replaced by cultural discourses that counsel the Court to impose a moral condition on those rights. Essentially, we could have a Constitution that contains positive privacy rights while also disqualifying poor mothers from possessing those rights. Positive rights, alone, are not the solution. Positive rights without a simultaneous rejection of the ideology that holds that the poor are morally responsible for their own poverty will leave poor mothers in the same situation in which they currently find themselves—disenfranchised.

What this discussion suggests is that the solution to poor mothers' predicament lies not in a reformulation of rights. The answer is not to change law. Instead, the answer is to change cultural discourses. If explanations of poverty in terms of individual moral shortcomings were pushed to the margins—if these explanations of poverty were understood to be no more than empirically false theories—then we would exist in a society that would support bestowing the privacy right to all persons equally. And even if moral conditions still were imposed on privacy rights, we would exist in a society that did not assume that poor mothers did not satisfy the condition.

If cultural discourses shifted, the jurisprudence that reflects those discourses would embody the sense that privacy rights, be they positive or negative, are valuable in the hands of poor mothers. It would embody the sense that it is as valuable to enable the poor to remain unstandardized by the state as it is to enable the wealthier. It would echo the conviction that the beliefs and values that the poor will inculcate in their children will contribute as wonderfully to our pluralist society as do the beliefs and values that the wealthier inculcate in their children. It would reflect a culture that believes that enabling poor mothers to make the decisions that are central to their ideas of personhood and parenthood is as valuable as allowing wealthier persons to make those decisions. In essence, privacy rights may be less valuable when individuals with problematic or nonexistent moral compasses possess them. But, if cultural discourses shifted, we would exist in a society that rejects the idea that we can make assumptions about the quality of an individual's moral compass based on her socioeconomic status.

Further, in a transformed society, we likely would not tolerate a jurisprudence that is built on the notion that there would be no value or negative value realized from poor mothers bearing privacy rights. The law would not assume that poor mothers would be more likely to abuse or neglect their children than their wealthier counterparts. It would not assume that poor mothers would be more likely to use their privacy rights to shield their bad decisions and bad behaviors from a state that is interested in protecting children. We would be a society that rejects the idea that we can make assumptions about the likelihood of a mother harming her child based on nothing more than that mother's socioeconomic status.

Finally, if cultural discourses shifted, jurists would be more likely to give poor mothers' interests in preserving their dignity the same deference that they give to wealthier mothers. We would live in a society that understands that an individual's poverty does not diminish her humanity. We would understand that an individual's poverty does not make her less deserving of having her desires respected.

Essentially, if culture and law exist in a dialectical relationship, a change in one term will be met with a change in the other term. As such, if our culture transformed into one in which the poor are considered moral equals to the wealthy, then the law would transform into one that treated the poor and the wealthy equally.

2 The Unconstitutional Conditions Doctrine

Revealing, Yet Misleading

In the United States, traditional rights discourse has captured the imagination of most people, layperson and lawyer alike. As discussed in the Introduction, this discourse describes our constitutional order as one in which all persons possess the same set of rights. While an individual or group may be formally disenfranchised and thereby denied a right or set of rights, all persons (excluding minors and the incompetent) who have escaped formal disenfranchisement are imagined to possess an equal set of rights. This is the story that traditional rights discourse tells us.

Accordingly, we struggle to reconcile this narrative with the fact that, although the Court has interpreted the Constitution to contain privacy rights, poor mothers do not enjoy privacy in any real sense of the word. While wealthier mothers can successfully use their privacy rights to shield themselves from governmental regulation,[1] most poor mothers cannot; the government is all around them—it is all over (Sarat 1990). We have trouble understanding why poor mothers' privacy rights seem to function differently than the privacy rights that wealthier mothers enjoy.

Observers attempt to reconcile this dissonance in various ways. Some claim that the government systematically *violates* the privacy rights that traditional rights discourse tells us that poor mothers invariably possess. In describing the government as violating poor mothers' privacy rights, these observers claim that the government acts illegitimately—that it invades poor mothers' privacy unjustifiably, wrongly, and unconstitutionally. This is in line with this book's moderate claim, which asserts that poor mothers have been deprived of effective privacy rights.

Other observers explain poor mothers' lack of privacy despite their purported possession of privacy rights in terms of the government's interest in protecting children. These observers argue that the state legitimately infringes on poor mothers' privacy rights in the pursuit of protecting children. They point out that rights are not absolute and that the government may legitimately overwhelm them if it uses its power to pursue a sufficiently justifiable end. The interest in protecting children is sufficiently justifiable, they say. Thus, they argue, the reason why poor mothers' privacy rights appear to be incapable of actually shielding them from government intervention is because the government overwhelms these rights in order to ensure that the women will not abuse or neglect their children. (Of course, we need to ask why the government systematically overwhelms poor mothers' purported privacy rights to protect children while refusing to do the same with wealthier mothers. The answer, this book proposes, is the moral construction of poverty, explored in Chapter 3.)

Yet another tack taken to reconcile traditional rights discourse with poor mothers' evident lack of privacy is to argue that poor mothers, like everyone else, initially bear privacy rights; however, they exchange these rights for government benefits. In essence, the argument is that the government conditions a benefit—like Medicaid or cash assistance in the form of TANF—on the beneficiary's relinquishment of her privacy rights. Accordingly, poor mothers who have health insurance provided through the government or who receive cash assistance from the state do not have privacy rights because they have accepted the deal: They have traded their privacy rights for the benefit.

This rendering of the issue is attractive for several reasons. First, it assumes that poor mothers and wealthier mothers at least *start off* with the same set of rights. As such, it is consistent with traditional rights discourse. Second, it appears to be in line with the Court's jurisprudence. The doctrine of unconstitutional conditions provides that the government cannot grant a benefit on the condition that the beneficiary surrender a constitutional right, even when the government is under no obligation to provide the benefit in the first place. The Court could invoke this doctrine and hold that it forbids the government from requiring poor mothers to surrender their ostensible privacy rights in order to receive a benefit. Although some litigants have urged the Court to do just that, and although some justices have argued in dissent that the Court should do just that, the Court has not done so. Thus, one could describe poor mothers' apparent lack of privacy rights as a consequence of the Court's failure to use the unconstitutional conditions doctrine to protect them from having to make such exchanges.

This chapter rejects this description. It does so because the unconstitutional conditions doctrine leads us to narrow our focus to the moment that poor mothers turn to the government for assistance. As such, it discourages us from perceiving and contemplating the lives that poor mothers live outside of their request for help. It encourages us to divorce poor mothers from the social context in which they live their lives. However, if we properly contextualize poor mothers, we see that *they do not enjoy privacy even when they do not receive a welfare benefit.* Three realities demonstrate that poor mothers' lack of privacy and lack of privacy rights, either in the moderate or strong sense, are not at all functions of their reliance on government assistance.

First, the benefits for which poor mothers purportedly exchange their privacy rights furnish basic necessities—food, clothing, shelter, and healthcare. Most states' child protective services (CPS) conceptualize a parent's failure to provide her child with these basic necessities as a species of child neglect. Accordingly, poor mothers who do not accept welfare benefits and, thus, who cannot provide their children with food, clothing, shelter, or healthcare tend to be subjected to privacy invasions visited upon them by CPS and the foster care system. The result is that poor mothers lack privacy *despite* (indeed, *because of*) their refusal of a welfare benefit.

Second, the poor have more state involvement in their lives due to their lack of resources, which compels them to consume public goods more often than their wealthier counterparts. This brings them into more frequent contact with state actors, which, in turn, makes them more vulnerable to state intervention—a result that is not at all dependent on their having accepted a welfare benefit.

Third, law enforcement heavily and relentlessly polices poor people. Further, this heavy and relentless policing impacts poor people more because Fourth Amendment rights have been narrowed by a jurisprudence that is inordinately sympathetic to the state's desire to catch and punish lawbreakers. Accordingly, poor people do not have privacy, even when they do not receive a welfare benefit, because they more frequently come into contact with a state that polices them with few constitutional limitations on the privacy invasions that it can force on those it is policing.

Contextualizing the privacy deprivations that poor mothers endure when receiving a welfare benefit in a broader experience of privacy deprivations that poor mothers must stomach by virtue of their being poor *people* demonstrates that the unconstitutional conditions doctrine only tells part of the story. It tells the part of the story where poor mothers lack privacy when they make requests from the state. It does not tell the other, quite revealing, part of the story where poor mothers lack privacy even when they have requested nothing from the state.

Although the unconstitutional conditions doctrine dissembles poor mothers' experience—leading us to believe that they enjoy privacy when they refuse state assistance—the unconstitutional conditions cases are helpful to analyze insofar as they reveal the justification for the state's denial, either in the moderate or strong sense, of privacy rights to poor mothers. That is, they reveal that the state denies individuals a right when it disbelieves that the individual will realize the value that the right is thought to generate. The next section sets out this argument.

The Unconstitutional Conditions Doctrine: Origins and Purposes

The unconstitutional conditions doctrine emerged due to the simple insight that, when it comes to the government burdening constitutional rights, there is more than one way to skin the proverbial cat.

The imposition of criminal and civil penalties on constitutionally protected activities represents an obvious, and timeworn, method for encumbering individual rights. However, the post–New Deal government—which spends, licenses, and employs at levels that its pre–New Deal antecedent did not even foreshadow—made ubiquitous a mechanism for burdening individual rights that, up until the expansion of government in the 1930s, had been rare: the imposition of conditions on government spending, licensing, and employment. Legal theorist Cass Sunstein (1990) traces the origins of the unconstitutional conditions doctrine to the *Lochner* era—that infamous period during which the Court fiercely protected the right to contract and, in so doing, struck down hundreds of state and federal statutes that attempted to regulate the excesses and economic injustices of the market. He notes that, during this time, it became apparent that if the government conditioned granting a license to an employer on the employer's adoption of a minimum wage, it produced the same result as that produced by the government's passage of a law that required that employer to adopt a minimum wage (1990). In light of this realization, proponents of laissez-faire government began to theorize the unconstitutional conditions doctrine, which functioned to forbid the government from doing indirectly what it could not do directly: If the *Lochner* era Court proscribed the government from interfering in contracts and redistributing wealth directly, the government could not achieve that interference and redistribution indirectly through conditions on licensing and the like.

Yet, while the *Lochner* era's interpretation of the Constitution as a document that prohibits wealth redistribution met its demise, the regulatory state did not. The question became this: Would the unconstitutional conditions doctrine persist along with the expanded, regulatory state? Or would it die along with the *Lochner* era's veneration of the right to contract? Justice Holmes, who was a staunch opponent of the *Lochner* view of the Constitution, thought the latter. He believed that the government ought to have wide discretion with respect to regulating and otherwise interfering in the market. Because the unconstitutional conditions doctrine would strip the government of that discretion, he rejected it (Sunstein 1990). Holmes's oft-cited theory was that the greater power not to grant a license, give a government job, or spend government funds includes the lesser power to impose conditions on the license, job, or funds. For Holmes, this was true even if the conditions burdened recognized individual rights.

There may be something intuitively appealing about Holmes's argument. Moreover, there is nothing explicit in the Constitution that restricts the government when it distributes benefits. Constitutional law scholar Philip Hamburger (2012) notes that the Constitution protects individuals' liberty by imposing limits on what the government can constrain. So, for example, the Constitution protects our liberty to speak freely by limiting government constraints on our speech. And the Constitution protects our liberty to have an abortion by limiting government constraints on abortion. However, "[b]ecause the Constitution typically protects liberty by limiting government constraints, not government benefits, the government seems largely unlimited when it places conditions on its benefits" (2012, 491–92).

However, the Constitution can also be read to restrict all government conduct—not just its constraints on liberty (Sunstein 1990). Thus, just as the Constitution limits the government when it imposes constraints, it limits the government when it grants benefits. Moreover, a world without the unconstitutional conditions doctrine—one in which the government could circumvent the limits that the Constitution imposes on it through its distribution of benefits—just seems like a world gone mad. As Sunstein observes, "If government could, for example, limit spending programs to those who speak favorably of the party in power, there would be a serious distortion of deliberative processes—one that creates precisely the same dangers, in terms of both purposes and effects, against which the first amendment was originally supposed to guard" (598). So, we need the unconstitutional conditions doctrine.

Although we need the unconstitutional conditions doctrine, the Court has no idea what that doctrine should look like and when it should come into play. As legal scholar Thomas Merrill (1995) puts it, "The Supreme Court has never offered a satisfactory rationale for this doctrine, or why it 'roams about constitutional law like Banquo's ghost, invoked in some cases, but not in others'" (859). Even Justice Stevens had to admit that the doctrine—for which he, as a member of the Court, has some degree of responsibility—has "long suffered from notoriously inconsistent application" (Dolan v. City of Tigard, 512 U.S. 374, 407 n.12 (1994)). Indeed, the consensus from observers is that the Court's use of the doctrine is unpredictable, untheorized, and unsatisfactory. Scholars have been able to cobble together some basic truths about the doctrine, however.

First, legal theorist Kathleen Sullivan (1989) has identified three areas of constitutional law where the unconstitutional conditions doctrine has been invoked: corporations' struggles against government regulation, states' struggles against federal regulation, and individuals' struggles to maintain their individual constitutional rights while receiving a governmental benefit. Further, although the entity claiming encroachment on rights may be an individual, corporation, or state, the analysis that the Court uses for evaluating the constitutionality of the encroachment ought to stay the same.

Second, the doctrine ought to come into play when the government offers a benefit with a condition that interferes with one (or more) of the beneficiary's constitutional rights (Sullivan 1989). Thus, if the government says that it will give Medicaid benefits only if the beneficiary pledges not to disparage the government in any public or private forum, then the unconstitutional conditions doctrine ought to come into play; the condition that the government imposes on the benefit interferes with the beneficiaries' free speech rights. The tension is that the post–*Lochner* Court usually reviews economic and social regulations—for example, government distribution of Medicaid benefits—with rational basis review; meanwhile, it reviews legislation that burdens constitutional rights with strict scrutiny (1989). Should the Court review the above hypothetical Medicaid condition with strict scrutiny or rational basis? The unconstitutional conditions doctrine would answer with strict scrutiny.

Third, the doctrine is irrelevant when the government has no discretion with respect to granting the benefit. "If government must provide a benefit unconditionally, it may not offer that benefit conditionally regardless of the content of the condition" (Sullivan 1989, 1423). Sullivan identifies at least two types of benefits that the government is not obliged to provide: exemptions from regulation and taxation and provisions of governmental largesse.

Fourth and finally, the doctrine is only relevant when the individual right that is burdened by the exemption from regulation and taxation or the provision of largesse is a "preferred" right. This means that the right, if directly burdened, would be protected with strict scrutiny (Sullivan 1989).[2]

Although it is possible to sketch out these four basic truths about the unconstitutional conditions doctrine, the Court has been utterly unsuccessful in spinning these truths into a coherent doctrine. As Sullivan (1989) describes, the doctrine is "riven with inconsistencies" (1416). This is not to say, however, that there is no thread that runs through the cases. Quite the contrary, there are *several* threads that run through the cases.

There is a thread in which the Court appears to be concerned about the importance of the benefit conditioned. Thus, in *Shapiro v. Thompson*, the Court struck down various state provisions requiring that an individual have resided in a jurisdiction for at least a year as a condition to receiving benefits under the Aid to Families with Dependent Children (AFDC) program. And in *Memorial Hospital v. Maricopa County*, the Court struck down an Arizona statute requiring an individual to have resided in a county for a least a year as a condition to receiving nonemergency care in a public hospital. In both of those cases, the opinion of the Court seemed concerned that individuals were being denied "the very means to subsist—food, shelter, and other necessities of life" (Shapiro v. Thompson, 394 U.S. 618, 627 (1969)). Indeed, as Justice Marshall, writing for the Court in *Memorial Hospital*, noted, "[G]overnmental privileges and benefits necessary to basic sustenance have often been viewed as being of greater constitutional significance than less essential forms of governmental entitlements" (415 U.S. 250, 259 (1974)). (Of course, this concern did not carry the day in *Wyman v. James*, in which the Court upheld a New York statute that conditioned AFDC benefits, the same benefits that the Court in *Shapiro* described as "the very means to subsist," on the beneficiary waiving her Fourth Amendment right to privacy in her physical home.)

In another thread, the Court is concerned about the "germaneness" of the condition. In this thread, the Court strikes down conditions on benefits that do not appear to be related to the reasons why the government might deny the benefit outright. For example, in *Nollan v. California Coastal Commission*, the Court struck down a zoning board's grant to homeowners of a permit to build a larger home on their beachfront property on condition that they allow the public an easement to pass across the property (483 U.S. 825, 836 (1987)). The Court said that the condition was not germane. It noted that the zoning board could have denied the permit altogether due to the fact that the newly constructed home would substantially reduce the public's view of the beach. However, the easement would not remedy that problem; it seemed to be completely unrelated to a concern about the public's ability to see the beach. Making plain that the seeming non-germaneness of the condition motivated the decision, Justice Scalia, writing for the Court, noted that had the zoning board conditioned the permit on the homeowners' granting the public a "viewing spot" from which to see the beach, the Court would have upheld the condition as constitutional:

> Although such a requirement, constituting a permanent grant of continuous access to the property, would have to be considered a taking if it were not attached to a development permit, the Commission's assumed power to forbid construction of the house in order to protect the public's view of the beach must surely include the power to condition construction upon some concession by the owner, even a concession of property rights, that serves the same end. (Nollan v. California Coastal Commission, 483 U.S. 825, 836 (1987))

However, the most obvious thread running through the unconstitutional conditions cases, especially those concerning individual rights, is the Court's language of "coercion," "deterrence," "penalties," and "nonsubsidies." The Court is clear that conditions that impose "penalties" on the exercise of rights are "coercive" and "deter" individuals from engaging in the activity protected by the right; consequently, these "penalties" are unconstitutional. On the other hand, conditions that simply amount to "nonsubsidies" of rights—that is, conditions that amount to a mere failure to fund the exercise of rights—are not coercive, do not deter, and, as such, are constitutional. However, the Court's criteria for distinguishing coercive, deterrent penalties from noncoercive, nondeterrent nonsubsidies are not at all apparent.

For example, in *Sherbert v. Verner* (374 U.S. 398 (1963)), the Court struck down a condition that South Carolina imposed on unemployment benefits requiring applicants to accept any job that was available to them, including jobs that required them to violate tenets of their religion. Pursuant to this condition, Adeil Sherbert, a member of the Seventh-Day Adventist Church, was denied unemployment benefits because she refused to accept jobs that required her to work on Saturdays, her religion's Sabbath. The Court struck down the condition as a coercive penalty on Sherbert's First Amendment free exercise rights, writing:

> Here, not only is it apparent that appellant's declared ineligibility for benefits derives solely from the practice of her religion, but the pressure upon her to forgo that practice is unmistakable. The ruling forces her to choose between following the precepts of her religion and forfeiting benefits, on the one hand, and abandoning one of the precepts of her religion in order to accept work, on the other hand. Governmental imposition of such a choice puts the same kind of burden upon the free exercise of religion as would a fine imposed against appellant for her Saturday worship. . . . [T]o condition the availability of benefits upon this appellant's willingness to violate a cardinal principle of her religious faith effectively penalizes the free exercise of her constitutional liberties. (404–406)

Contrast the Court's analysis in *Sherbert* with its analysis in *Harris v. McRae* (448 U.S. 297 (1980)). At issue in the case was the constitutionality of the Hyde Amendment, which prohibits the use of federal Medicaid funds to pay for abortions, except when the abortion is necessary to save the life of the woman or when the pregnancy results from rape or incest. This prohibition remains even when the abortion is "medically necessary"—even when continuing the pregnancy would seriously jeopardize the woman's physical health. As long as the pregnancy will only maim the woman, stopping just short of killing her, she cannot receive federal Medicaid funds for an abortion.

The Court rejected the opportunity to invoke the unconstitutional conditions doctrine and to use strict scrutiny when reviewing the Hyde Amendment in *Harris*, refusing to conceptualize the funding prohibition as conditioning the receipt of a Medicaid benefit on the beneficiary's surrender of her right to an abortion. Instead, the Court spoke in the language of unconstitutional "penalties" and constitutional "nonsubsidies," finding that the Hyde Amendment was the latter. It wrote, "[A] refusal to fund protected activity, without more, cannot be equated with the imposition of a 'penalty' on that activity" (317 n.19).

The discontinuity with *Sherbert* is striking. The Court in *Sherbert* could have easily characterized observing one's Sabbath as "protected activity."

Indeed, observing one's Sabbath *is* constitutionally protected activity. More-over, the Court could have reasoned, like it did in *Harris v. McRae*, that the denial of unemployment benefits to Sherbert because she would not take a job that forced her to work on her Sabbath was merely the "refusal to fund protected activity"—a constitutional nonsubsidy. It did not do this. Similarly, the Court's reasoning in *Sherbert* could have easily been adapted to the facts of *Harris*, which hypothetically might have declared:

> Here, not only is it apparent that appellant's declared ineligibility for benefits derives solely from [her desire to terminate her pregnancy], but the pressure upon her to forgo that practice is unmistakable. The ruling forces her to choose between [engaging in constitutionally protected activity] and forfeiting ben-efits, on the one hand, and abandoning [her constitutionally protected interests in safeguarding her health, decisional autonomy, and bodily integrity], on the other hand. Governmental imposition of such a choice puts the same kind of burden upon [the abortion right] as would a fine imposed against appellant for [terminating a pregnancy]. . . . [T]o condition the availability of benefits upon this appellant's willingness to [forgo terminating a dangerous pregnancy] ef-fectively penalizes the free exercise of her constitutional liberties.

The Court, of course, did not take this route.

We have to ask why. One might be tempted to argue that the distinction between *Sherbert* and *Harris* is that in the former, the Court was dealing with a venerated, enumerated right—a First Amendment right. In the latter, the Court was dealing with a problematic, textually suspect, unenumerated right—the abortion right. If this theory is correct, the Court's willingness to allow burdens on a right would turn on the right itself. Indeed, Merrill (1995) has noted the possibility that there may be a hierarchy of preferred rights in the context of the unconstitutional conditions doctrine. Writing of *Nollan* (and *Dolan*, in which the Court similarly struck down a condition on the grant of a building permit that required the beneficiary to surrender her right to just compensation subsequent to a governmental taking), Merrill observes that "it is unclear whether all provisions of the Bill of Rights (including, for example, the Second and Seventh Amendments) are entitled to equal status for purposes of the unconstitutional conditions doctrine, or, more narrowly, whether it is only the Takings Clause that must be elevated to a condition of parity with these other rights" (866). Even Justice Stevens has argued that there is a hierar-chy of preferred rights for unconstitutional conditions purposes, contending that the doctrine "has never been an overarching principle of constitutional law that operates with equal force regardless of the nature of the rights and powers in question" (Dolan v. City of Tigard, 512 U.S. 374, 407 n.12 (1994)).

Thus, one could argue that *Sherbert* and *Harris* can be reconciled because they concern different rights. One could argue that the jurisprudence can be read to establish that First Amendment rights, like Fifth Amendment rights against takings without just compensation, are vigorously protected, and the Court will be highly skeptical of the constitutionality of any condition that functions to burden them. Conversely, privacy rights are not as well protected, and the Court will be more tolerant of conditions that may burden them.

However, the Court's decision in *Rust v. Sullivan* gives the lie to this theory. In *Rust*, the Court upheld conditions on Title X monies (which fund family planning services for indigent communities) that functioned to burden the First Amendment rights of healthcare provider beneficiaries and their indigent clients. The conditions provided that programs receiving Title X funds could not "provide counseling concerning the use of abortion as a method of family planning or provide referral for abortion as a method of family planning" (Rust v. Sullivan, 500 U.S. 173, 179 (1991)). Indeed, programs receiving Title X funds were "expressly prohibited from referring a pregnant woman to an abortion provider, even upon specific request" (180). Thus, if a woman asked her provider about abortion, the provider was instructed to respond that the institution where she was receiving her care "does not consider abortion an appropriate method of family planning and therefore does not counsel or refer for abortion" (180). Despite the fact that the conditions raised serious First Amendment problems relating to compelled speech, coerced silence, and the right to receive information, the Court upheld them. Rejecting the argument that the conditions were coercive, presumptively unconstitutional penalties insofar as they imposed "viewpoint-discriminatory conditions on government subsidies and thus penalize speech funded with non-Title X monies" (192), the Court reasoned that they were merely noncoercive, presumptively constitutional nonsubsidies: "A legislature's decision not to subsidize a fundamental right does not infringe the right" (193). And it added a cherry on top, quoting its opinion in *Harris* for the proposition that "[a] refusal to fund protected activity, without more, cannot be equated with the imposition of a 'penalty' on that activity" (193).

The Court's willingness to uphold the constitutionality of conditions that burdened First Amendment rights in *Rust* indicates that one cannot reconcile

the results in *Sherbert* and *Harris* with the theory that the Court is more protective of First Amendment rights than privacy rights. Rather, it may suggest
that *the individuals whose rights are burdened by conditions may influence the
Court's use of the unconstitutional conditions doctrine.* That is, the Court may
be more inclined to use the doctrine to protect the rights of individuals whom
the Court finds to be sympathetic. Certainly, the conditions at issue in *Rust*
burdened the First Amendment rights of healthcare providers, who were essentially gagged and prohibited from engaging in conversation around abortion.
However, the conditions at issue in *Rust* substantially, and more profoundly,
burdened the First Amendment rights of *poor, pregnant women*—in need of
full information and incapable of receiving it from the only healthcare providers that their indigence made available to them.

Two recent cases concerning conditions that affected First Amendment
rights provide support for the claim that, when evaluating the constitutionality
of conditions, the Court is more influenced by the individuals whose rights are
burdened than it is by the right that is burdened. In *Christian Legal Society v.
Martinez* (561 U.S. 661, 670 (2010)), the Court *upheld* a condition that burdened
individuals' First Amendment speech and association rights. Meanwhile, in
Agency for International Development v. Alliance for Open Society International
(133 S.Ct. 2321 (2013)), the Court *struck down* a condition that burdened individuals' First Amendment speech rights.

Christian Legal Society concerned the titular Christian student group at the
University of California, Hastings College of the Law, which sought official recognition from the school and, concomitant to that recognition, access to facilities and a small pool of money that could subsidize its activities. However, the
school had imposed a condition on its recognition of student groups: In order
to be recognized, a student group had to open its membership to all students at
Hastings, without regard to their "race, color, religion, national origin, ancestry,
disability, age, sex or sexual orientation" (Christian Legal Society v. Martinez
2010, 670). The Christian Legal Society, which had adopted bylaws that prohibited non-Christians and those who engage in "unrepentant homosexual conduct" from becoming members of the student group, argued that the condition
burdened its speech and association rights. The Court disagreed.

Meanwhile, *Agency for International Development* concerned a policy that
prohibited federal funds from going to any nongovernmental organization
(NGO) engaged in global efforts to combat HIV/AIDS that had not adopted
"a policy explicitly opposing prostitution and sex trafficking" (Agency for In-

ternational Development v. Alliance for Open Society International, Inc. 2013, 2324). Several affected NGOs argued that the funding condition burdened their speech rights inasmuch as it required them to censor themselves "in publications, at conferences, and in other forums about how best to prevent the spread of HIV/AIDS among prostitutes" (2326). The Court agreed.

How does one reconcile these two cases? One could attempt to argue that the condition in *Christian Legal Society* was a nonsubsidy while the condition in *Agency for International Development* was a penalty. But, identifying one condition as a nonsubsidy and the other as a penalty is merely conclusory, failing to provide a theory for arriving at the conclusion. One could more convincingly assert, though, that the sympathetic (and unsympathetic) qualities of the actors who were burdened by the conditions at issue help to explain the cases. That is, the condition at issue in *Christian Legal Society* burdened a group that sought a license to discriminate. Moreover, the license to discriminate that they sought was directed at LGBT persons—a class that the Court has increasingly recognized as a vulnerable minority with a long, regrettable history of state-authorized and state-legitimated discrimination.

It is easy to find unsympathetic the actors whose rights were burdened in *Christian Legal Society*. One could conclude that, because the actors were unsympathetic, the Court deployed the unconstitutional conditions doctrine such that it tolerated burdens on their rights. Conversely, the condition at issue in *Agency for International Development* burdened the rights of NGOs seeking to save the lives of vulnerable, oftentimes exploited individuals around the world. It is easy to find them to be sympathetic. And one could conclude that, because these actors were sympathetic, the Court deployed the unconstitutional conditions doctrine such that it did not tolerate burdens on their rights.

But, an additional gloss on the theory is required. This is true especially in light of *Shapiro v. Thompson*, which, as discussed above, struck down several states' requirements that individuals reside in the state for a certain period of time before they could become eligible for AFDC benefits. The Court used the unconstitutional conditions doctrine in that case to protect the rights of poor mothers—a group that, as this book argues, the Court and society more generally finds to be highly unsympathetic. *Shapiro* and *Maricopa County*, in which the Court struck down a similar residency requirement for the use of public hospitals, together suggest that *the Court's use of the unconstitutional conditions doctrine is not solely a function of the Court's perception of the actors whose rights are burdened by a condition; rather, it is also a function of how the Court perceives the value of particular actors wielding the particular rights that are burdened.* If the Court believes that there is a value in the affected actors exercising the right that a condition burdens, then the Court will use the unconstitutional conditions doctrine to strike down the condition. The converse is also true: If the Court believes that there is no value, or a negative value, in the affected actors exercising the right that a condition burdens, the Court will use the doctrine to uphold the condition.

This theory explains the Court's unconstitutional conditions jurisprudence. Indeed, it explains why the doctrine has become a vigorous protector of property rights. In other words, the Court has not developed a robust critique of property rights—although these rights exist in a social context of disquieting poverty and inequality. Thus, the Court invariably is undisturbed by various actors' exercises of these rights. It sees a value—or, at least, it does not see a negative value—in actors' exercise of property rights. Accordingly, the Court tends to strike down conditions that burden them.

This theory also explains the Court's decision in *Sherbert,* which concerned an observant Christian who was interested in exercising her First Amendment rights and practicing her religion in a fairly staid fashion: All she wanted to do was observe her Sabbath. The Court perceived a value in this sympathetic actor's exercise of her First Amendment right and, accordingly, struck down the condition that would burden it.

This theory also explains the Court's decisions in *Christian Legal Society* and *Agency for International Development.* While the actors in *Christian Legal Society* were also observant Christians and, in that respect, sympathetic, they sought to exercise their First Amendment rights in a hurtful fashion: They sought to exclude and stigmatize sexual minorities. Because the Court not only did not see a value in this exercise, but likely also saw a *negative value* in it, the Court upheld the condition that would burden it. Conversely, the actors in *Agency for International Development* were sympathetic NGOs doing beneficial, constructive work, seeking to exercise their First Amendment rights to enable them to continue to do that work. The Court saw a value in this exercise and struck down the condition that would burden it.

A theory that understands the unconstitutional conditions doctrine to be a function of the Court's perception of the value produced by the burdened actors exercising the burdened right explains the result in *Shapiro,* in which the Court protected the right to travel of a maligned group: poor mothers. That is: in *Shapiro,* the Court used the unconstitutional conditions doctrine to strike down residency requirements that burdened the right to travel because it perceived a value—or, perhaps more precisely, it did not perceive a negative value—in poor mothers being mobile. Similarly, the Court used the doctrine in *Maricopa County* to strike down residency requirements for the use of public hospitals because it did not perceive a negative value in poor people's physical movement.

Now, if what this book argues is true, and if the Court believes that there is a futility, or a danger, in poor mothers bearing the ability to shield themselves from government intervention in their private lives, then one would expect the Court to wield the unconstitutional conditions doctrine such that it tolerates burdens on their ostensible privacy rights. And this is precisely what the jurisprudence yields: In case after case, the Court has upheld conditions that force poor mothers to surrender the privacy rights that traditional rights discourse claims that they have.

We can start with *Rust v. Sullivan*, discussed above. Prohibiting counseling that touches on abortion implicates not only healthcare providers' First Amendment speech rights and their indigent clients' First Amendment rights to information and ideas, but also their clients' reproductive privacy rights. A lack of information about the legality of abortion, the safety of abortion, and where one could obtain an abortion places a clear burden on the ability to actually acquire an abortion. If the right to abortion—a stick in the bundle of rights that is reproductive privacy—means the ability to access the procedure, then the gagging of providers produced by the funding conditions at issue in *Rust* certainly made the exercise of the abortion right much more difficult. Put simply, the funding conditions burdened that right. And the Court could not sympathize with the poor, pregnant women whose ostensible reproductive rights were burdened. The Court could not perceive a value in allowing these women the ability to engage in the emotional and moral calculations that may lead a woman to believe that abortion is in her best interests.

Given cultural discourses that counsel that poor mothers are behaviorally and ethically deficient—discourses discussed in Chapter 1—the Court was skeptical that the indigent women affected by the funding conditions in *Rust* could possess the circumspection needed when deciding whether to engage in a practice about which reasonable, intelligent minds have vehemently disagreed since time immemorial. *Rust v. Sullivan* came out the way that it did because the Court thought it better not to allow presumptively irresponsible, poor, pregnant women the ability to exercise a right as grave as the abortion right. The same analytic applies to *Harris v. McRae.*

We can also look at *Wyman v. James* (400 U.S. 309 (1971)), briefly mentioned above. In the case, the Court upheld the requirement that poor mothers waive their Fourth Amendment privacy rights in their physical homes as a condition to their receipt of AFDC. And if the theory that this chapter proposes is true, the Court decided the case in the way that it did because it did not see a value in allowing these women the ability to keep the government out of their homes. In fact, more probably, the Court saw a negative value in empowering poor mothers to keep the government out of their homes, as the right to shield their homes from inspection is the right to shield the children who reside there from inspection. These are women who, according to dominant cultural narratives, made the immoral choice to allow their poverty to intersect with their motherhood. The danger is that they could make immoral choices with respect to the children in their charge. Indeed, the perceived danger inherent in poor mothers' bearing the ability to shield their homes and, consequently, their children from state inspection was demonstrated by the condition of the plaintiff's son Maurice: "There are indications that all was not always well with the infant Maurice (skull fracture, a dent in the head, a possible rat bite). The picture is a sad and unhappy one" (322 n.9).

We can also look at *Dandridge v. Williams*, in which the Court upheld a Maryland "family cap" law that limited the size of indigent families' AFDC grants. While families with six or fewer persons received grants that covered their needs (per the state's calculation), families with seven or more persons did not. Framed in terms of the unconstitutional conditions doctrine, the law conditioned an AFDC grant that met the family's standard of need on the surrender of the beneficiary's right to bear a child and expand her family to one that includes more than six persons. An individual receiving a grant that barely covered her family's basic subsistence needs would be coerced into not expanding her family if she knew that the state would not increase the size of its grant accordingly. In this way, the family cap law made the exercise of beneficiaries' right to procreate, which the Court in *Skinner v. Oklahoma* (316 U.S. 535 (1942)) considered a fundamental right, a grossly improvident choice that could endanger the very survival of the family unit.

It would be naïve to believe that the Court could sympathize with the actors in this case: poor women who insist on their motherhood in a political and social landscape that denigrates it and constructs it as a social problem. And it would be naïve to believe that the Court could see a value in allowing these actors to be shielded from government intervention in their reproductive

decision making. It is more probable that the Court saw only negative consequences flowing from poor women's unregulated fertility. Hence, the Court
upheld a condition that would regulate it.

One should also keep in mind an analysis presented in Chapter 1: The facts
in *Dandridge* allowed the Court to conjure up the figure of the welfare queen:
she who represents the dangers of poor women's unregulated fertility, and she
who shirks labor market participation and, instead, has babies for the sole purpose of receiving increasingly larger checks from government cash assistance
programs. Indeed, the law at issue in *Dandridge* was framed as a pursuit of the
state's interest in "encouraging gainful employment" and in "providing incentives for family planning" (397 U.S. 471, 483–84 (1970)). These articulated interests suggest that the authors of the family cap, the lawyers who defended it, and
the Court that found the ends legitimate and the law a reasonable means for
accomplishing them had in mind the welfare queen—a woman who needs to
be incentivized to find gainful employment as much as she needs to be incentivized to engage in family planning.

The Court was left to imagine that the large families that found themselves
without a grant capable of covering their basic needs were ones headed by a
woman who had six or more children. The Court was free to disregard the fact
that many of the larger families that the law harmed were those that misfortune
had cobbled together—families consisting of grandmothers caring for their
children's children. The Court was free to ignore that some families injured by
the law already consisted of more than six individuals when economic hardship
struck, compelling them to turn to the government for help; that is, they had
been financially independent and were comprised of more than six people before it became necessary to seek AFDC assistance. The Court could suppose that
women who just needed to "get a job" headed the affected families; it could disregard its own acknowledgment that "no family members of any of the named
plaintiffs in the present case are employable" (Dandridge v. Williams 1970, 486
n.20). The Court could simply note that two of the named plaintiffs, Mrs. Williams and Mrs. Cary, had eight children apiece, and it could allow the mythol-
ogy of the welfare queen to provide the backstory of how it came to be that
these women found themselves with so many children and in need of welfare.

Indeed, the welfare queen is the social problem that results when poor
women are left with the means to shield the government from regulating
their reproductive decision making. She exists in the interstices of the Court's
opinion in *Dandridge*. And it is no wonder why the Court thought it best to

interpret the Constitution to tolerate a condition that would eliminate her. She informs the Court's choice to interpret the Constitution in a way that left the state with the ability to attempt to shape poor women's reproductive futures.

Many of the women who challenged conditions that burden their ostensible privacy rights might appear to a Court—steeped in and reflecting the moral construction of poverty—to be women who *ought* to have their fertility and private lives regulated. Consider *Harris v. McRae*. In dissent, Justice Stevens attempts to humanize the women who stand to be maimed by the federal government's refusal to fund even medically necessary abortions. He quotes the affidavit of a 25-year-old woman who stated that after the birth of her third child, she "developed a serious case of phlebitis from which [she has] not completely recovered. Carrying another pregnancy to term would greatly aggravate this condition and increase the risk of blood clots to the lung" (Harris v. McRae, 448 U.S. 297, 353 n.5 (1980)). However, she became pregnant again and delivered her fourth child. When she became pregnant with her fifth child, she went to a clinic to request an abortion after being informed that she "might suffer serious and permanent health problems" if she continued the pregnancy.

To a Court that is inclined to believe that poor women's fertility ought to be managed because they cannot be trusted with making decisions about whether and when to have a child, Justice Stevens's human example of the law's brutality might have worked against him. Indeed, this woman, who was facing her fifth pregnancy and who had been told two pregnancies prior that she ought not to get pregnant again, might have represented to the Court the consequence of leaving poor women unmonitored and unguided in their reproductive decision making. To a Court that subscribes to the moral construction of poverty, poor women will make poor decisions. Hence, it is best if the government monitors and guides them.

The same is true for another woman who submitted an affidavit during the litigation that culminated in *Harris v. McRae* (1980): "Jane Doe is 38 years old and has nine previous pregnancies" (353). A Court predisposed to believing that poor women should not be left alone with their reproductive capacities might stop there and note the seeming *excessiveness* of this woman's fertility. But, the affidavit goes on:

> She has a history of varicose veins and thrombophlebitis (blood clots) of the left leg. The varicose veins can be, and in her case were, caused by multiple pregnancies: the weight of the uterus on her pelvic veins increased the blood pressure in the veins of her lower extremities; those veins dilated and her circu-

lation was impaired, resulting in thrombophlebitis of her left leg. The varicosi-
ties of her lower extremities became so severe that they required partial surgical
removal in 1973. Given this medical history, Jane Doe's varicose veins are almost
certain to recur if she continues her pregnancy. (353)

A Court that subscribes to political and popular discourses that problematize poor women's reproduction might observe that this woman seemed to
have allowed her fertility to cripple her. Indeed, even after undergoing surgery
for a condition brought about and exacerbated by pregnancy, she became pregnant again. To the Court, she may represent why it is best for the government
to regulate poor women's fertility. Left to their own devices, they will likely
harm themselves and third parties—that is, the children that they birth and
inevitably the state coffers that must support the ever-expanding family.

It might be stating the obvious to note that wealthier women sometimes
choose to have several children. (Indeed, these large families are celebrated occasionally. The reality shows *19 Kids and Counting, United Bates of America,
The Willis Family*, and *Jon & Kate Plus 8* all featured extremely large, wealthy
families.) Wealthier women sometimes choose to become pregnant even after
suffering difficult prior pregnancies. Wealthier women sometimes decide to
terminate a pregnancy if the harm that it poses becomes especially threatening
to them. Wealthier women become pregnant even after doctors have informed
them that they should avoid subsequent pregnancies: That is to say, wealthier
women are just like poor women. The only difference is that wealthier women's
socioeconomic status allows them entrance into cultural discourses that affirm
that they know what is best for them—even when they err. They are allowed a
space to make mistakes and be countercultural and celebrate their capacity for
producing new life. Poor women are not.

In sum, the unconstitutional conditions cases can be explained by analyzing
whether the Court perceives a value in the particular actor bearing the particular right that a condition burdens. If the Court believes that there is a value, it
will strike down the condition; if it believes that there is no value or a negative
value in the actor wielding the burdened right, then it will uphold the condition. Accordingly, the Court invariably upholds conditions that burden poor
mothers' ostensible privacy rights, as the Court frequently believes that there is
no value or a negative value in poor mothers wielding the right to shield themselves from state intervention in their private lives.

·   ·   ·

However, the unconstitutional conditions cases are misleading. They dissemble the actual social, legal, political, and constitutional circumstances in which poor women exist. If we decontextualize poor women from the lives they lead—if we solely pay attention to them in the moment when they ask the government to help them meet their basic subsistence needs—then it appears that it is only in that moment and in that position of supplication that their ability to shield themselves from regulation is removed and their private lives are opened up for inspection and management. But, when we place them back in their lives as they live them, we see that their private lives are *always* opened up for inspection and management, even when they do not receive government benefits. That is, their inability to shield themselves from regulation is not a function of their receipt of a benefit, but rather is their existential condition in our current sociopolitical order. They have no privacy—and not because they have exchanged the rights that would provide them privacy for government assistance. Instead, they have no privacy because they are poor.

In other words, a poor mother lives her entire life under constant state surveillance. Thus, the unconstitutional conditions cases are misleading because they disguise a preexisting political and constitutional circumstance for a trade. Nevertheless, they are simultaneously instructive because they reveal the justification for the original deprivation. That is, the unconstitutional conditions cases pretend that poor women have been compelled to trade away extant privacy rights for benefits. Yet, the same reason why the Court would sanction a trade between privacy rights and government benefits—there is no value or a negative value in allowing poor, pregnant women and mothers the ability to shield themselves from government intervention in their private lives—justifies dispossessing (either in the moderate or strong sense) poor women of privacy rights altogether.

Living Without Privacy

The lives that poor mothers lead are ones that are, at all times, open to surveillance and intervention. This is due to the three realities discussed below.

Picking Poison: The State that Provides Welfare Benefits Versus the State that Protects Children

The argument that poor mothers exchange their privacy rights for welfare benefits presupposes that, if a poor mother did not accept a particular welfare benefit, she would retain her ostensible privacy rights and would enjoy the privacy that wealthier mothers enjoy. However, the benefits for which poor mothers supposedly trade their privacy rights do not grant them gratuitous or indulgent items. Quite the contrary, these benefits enable poor mothers to provide basic necessities that their children require. Medicaid allows poor mothers to access the healthcare that will enable them to have healthy pregnancies and to give birth to healthy babies. Temporary Assistance for Needy Families (TANF) provides them with the means with which they can purchase food and clothing for their children and the ability to meet housing costs. The benefits provided through the Supplemental Nutrition Program for Women, Infants, and Children (WIC), as well as those provided through the Supplemental Nutrition Assistance Program (SNAP, formerly known as food stamps), stave off food insecurity and enable poor mothers to feed their children. Public housing and Section 8 housing vouchers provided through the Department of Housing and Urban Development enable poor mothers to shelter their children.

As Chapter 3 on family privacy rights makes clear, a parent's failure to provide healthcare, food, clothing, or shelter has been defined to constitute child neglect. Accordingly, a parent's inability to provide her child with these basic necessities serves as a justification for the state, through its CPS department, to intervene in the family to protect the child (DePanfilis 2006). Indeed, the state frequently removes children from their homes and places them in foster care in order to protect them from this kind of poverty-induced neglect (Novoa 1999). And it grossly minimizes the situation to describe a mother who is being investigated by CPS or has been stripped of custody of her child as having been deprived of privacy.

The claim that poor mothers will be subjected to CPS investigations—and the real possibility of losing their children to the foster care system—if they do not accept welfare benefits assumes the unavailability of jobs that can pay poor mothers a sufficient wage to sustain a family. In fact, the unavailability of these types of jobs has been well documented. Sociologist Loic Wacquant (2009) observes that in 2002—a year marked by economic health and growth, well before the Great Recession devastated the economy—the jobs held by poor mothers who would otherwise rely on TANF for their families' subsistence needs were not the kinds of jobs that shield families from poverty. Far from it, Wacquant reports that the median wage that these mothers earned "was $8.06 per hour, barely above the hourly minimum and far below the wage needed to lift a family of three above the poverty line (around $11 per hour)" (96). Thus, laboring in the market typically does not enable a poor mother to provide her children with consistent food, clothing, shelter, and healthcare. Eschewing welfare benefits and becoming a wage laborer does not allow a poor mother to shield herself and her family from the child protective state.

We, as a society, have identified CPS and the foster care system as the solution to poor parents' inability to provide their children with the basic necessities that programs like Medicaid, TANF, WIC, SNAP benefits, public housing, and Section 8 housing vouchers furnish. Dorothy Roberts (2012) contends that the state "addresses family economic deprivation with child removal rather than services and financial resources" (1484). She notes that by using CPS and the foster care system to deal with poor mothers' inability to provide for their children, society has made "a political choice to investigate and blame mothers for the cause of startling rates of child poverty rather than to tackle poverty's societal roots" (1484). She concludes, "Instead of devoting adequate resources to support their families, the state increasingly shuffles family members into the punitive machinery of . . . child protection" (1491–92).

Thus, poor mothers lose their privacy if they accept welfare benefits. And they lose their privacy—and, all too often, their children—if they do not accept welfare benefits. In other words, poor mothers are stuck between the Scylla of receiving public assistance and the Charybdis of being an unskilled wage laborer. Importantly, both Scylla and Charybdis strip poor mothers of privacy—the first directly, the second ultimately. Thus, poor mothers' lack of privacy is not conditional at all. Instead, it is constant and certain (Wacquant 2009).[3]

Public Goods and Public Oversight

The claim that poor mothers, and poor people generally, have to rely on public goods more than wealthier people is not a claim that poor people have to turn to welfare programs, like TANF and Medicaid, more often than their wealthier counterparts. They do. But, the immediate claim is that poor people are unable to purchase the privatized versions of public goods. Thus, they take public buses and trains instead of driving cars. They live in public housing instead of private homes. They go to public hospitals or private hospitals that maintain close relationships with the state instead of private hospitals that have little state involvement (Appell 1997).

The result of the sheer visibility to the state actors that administer or are merely present in these public institutions is that poor people are simply more vulnerable to state intervention. One need not be steeped in Foucauldian theory to understand that visibility can be radically disempowering (Foucault 1995). And indeed, poor mothers are radically disempowered by their ability to be seen by the state (Appell 1997). This disempowerment manifests in various ways, one of the most relevant being that they are more likely to become the objects of child welfare investigations (Gilman 2012). We will look at this argument more expansively in Chapter 3.

The Pervasive Policing of the Poor

Most scholarship concerning social welfare within neoliberalism[4] has not closely interrogated the criminal justice system, as the two areas of law appear to be largely unrelated and to concern different populations of people. However, Wacquant (2009) has argued that one errs when one fails to study the welfare state and the penal state together (1). When one analyzes the biopolitical state that provides basic needs for its subjects alongside the punitive state that punishes its subjects for transgressing its norms, one will see that the state that assists and the state that penalizes are actually two sides of the same coin. Welfare provision and the criminal law are dual efforts to regulate the same "problem" population: the poor, who now exist within a transformed economy that no longer contains sufficient jobs that pay a wage that can support individuals and families. Wacquant observes that, together, the supportive state and the punitive state trap poor people

> in a *carceral-assistantial net* that aims either to render them "useful" by steering them onto the track of deskilled employment through moral retraining and material suasion . . . or in the penitentiaries. . . . These two domains of public action continue to be approached separately, in isolation from each other, by social scientists as well as by those, politicians, professionals, and activists, who wish to reform them, whereas in reality they already function in tandem at the bottom of the structure of classes and places. (12–13)

Welfare provision and the criminal law are analogous enterprises not only because they endeavor to manage the same "problem," but also because they are motivated by the same theory of human behavior. That is, both systems view personal shortcomings as explanations for how the populations that they regulate arrive within their jurisdictions. Individual irresponsibility explains why a person, eventually, must turn to the welfare state for assistance in meeting her subsistence needs. And individual irresponsibility explains why an individual transgresses a norm reflected in the criminal law and, eventually, why he finds himself within the criminal justice apparatus (Wacquant 2009). Wacquant summarizes that the welfare state's and the penal state's

> convergence onto the same populations trapped in dilapidated urban enclaves, their joint invocation of the ethics of individual responsibility and (de)merit, and their shared punitive ethos constitute powerful prima facie evidence that restrictive social welfare reforms and expansive criminal justice policies are twinned state responses to the generalization of social insecurity in the nether regions of US social space and that they must therefore be analyzed together. (2009, 69)

Wacquant's analysis is simultaneously devastating and convincing, and it should be taken to heart for that reason. However, he errs when he conceptualizes the welfare state as the governmental arm that manages women and the penal state as the governmental arm that manages men. Indeed, he describes it as a "sexual and institutional division in the regulation of the poor" (2009, 15). However, to understand the penal state as gendered in the way that he imagines allows him to miss the fact that women and girls are ensnared within criminal justice institutions at alarming rates.

Legal theorist Kimberlé Crenshaw (2012) offers a corrective to Wacquant's oversight. She notes that many studies of mass incarceration, which tend to level racial critiques against the practice, ignore the "hyperpresence of women of color in the system" (1427). The result is that there is "virtually no recognition or acknowledgment of the fact that the disciplinary projects against the Black community as a whole include policies and ideologies that function to regulate and punish Black women as well" (1432). The reality is that, while women of color are not *equally* burdened by the penal state relative to men of color, they are *proportionately* burdened by it. She writes that "within their respective gender groups, men and women of color face racialized risks of incarceration that are similar to their white counterparts. In other words, the increased risk of incarceration relative to race is virtually the same for Black men and women as for whites" (1436–37). Essentially, Crenshaw's point is that women of color are policed by the police, too.

Thus, if Wacquant is right that we must analyze the penal state if we are to understand how the state manages poor people in the age of neoliberalism, and if Crenshaw is right that women very much are implicated in that penal state, then a study that endeavors to describe poor women's experiences with privacy is incomplete if it does not analyze the penal state. Thus, the balance of this chapter examines the means by which the penal state manages the poor: an eviscerated Fourth Amendment and a dogged scrutiny of poor communities. While numerous studies have noted that the combination of these two facts deprives poor people of privacy and makes them vulnerable to state power, this chapter underscores that these studies are *also* describing the lives of poor women and *poor mothers*. And if, due to the hyperpolicing of their physical spaces, the residents of poor communities are stripped of privacy, then poor women and mothers are stripped of privacy. And this evacuation of their privacy is not at all contingent on their receipt of a welfare benefit.

With respect to the penal state, two steps accomplish the pervasive policing of poor bodies. The first step is a jurisprudence that interprets the Fourth Amendment in a painfully constrained manner, contracting the amendment and, in so doing, shrinking the zones of privacy that it protects. The Court has long established that the Fourth Amendment protects persons, not property; moreover, it has long used the language of privacy to describe this protection (Katz v. U.S., 389 U.S. 347, 353 (1967)). The result, then, of the contraction of the Fourth Amendment's privacy protections is that persons are made more public; more of an individual's life is made the stuff of legitimate public intervention.

The second step is the training of the state gaze on poor individuals and poor communities. In theory, the contracted Fourth Amendment fails to protect the privacy of both rich and poor alike. However, the Fourth Amendment's contraction is simply a much more relevant fact for poor individuals. That they do not have any claim to privacy is demonstrated time and time again—for some, on a daily basis. This is a reality that wealthier persons just do not share.

One might begin the story of how the Fourth Amendment became an anemic protector of privacy with the Court's decision in *Terry v. Ohio* (392 U.S. 1 (1968)). In *Terry*, the Court retreated from the principle developed in the then-existing case law that a police officer must have probable cause to believe that an individual had committed a crime before he could search or seize him without his consent. *Terry* held that a police officer could stop a person if he simply has "reasonable suspicion" that a crime had occurred or was about to occur; further, an officer could frisk the individual if the former had a reasonable belief that the latter had a weapon. The Court attempted to limit its holding so that it could not be read to give police officers free rein to stop and pat down anyone they encountered based on nothing more than a (frequently racialized) "hunch"; the decision required that the police officer must be able to articulate specific reasons for why he chose to stop any individual with reference to "the facts in light of his experience" (27). Nevertheless, one can easily see how *Terry* could become contorted such that it legitimates police stops and interrogations of any racially or socioeconomically marginalized person.

Moreover, bear in mind that the police practices that *Terry* authorizes implicate privacy not only in the sense that state agents are empowered to touch persons' physical bodies. They also implicate informational privacy—the interest in keeping one's personal information to oneself and, if that proves impossible or impracticable, in not having one's personal information aggregated and possibly shared with others. Legal scholar Kimberly Bailey (2014) notes that many jurisdictions have created gang databases and that the data that populate these databases are gathered from stop-and-frisks (1566). Moreover, one does not have to be in a gang to have one's information in the database; one need only to have been stopped after having made an officer "reasonably suspicious" (1566–67).

The Court continued to roll back the privacy protections that the Fourth Amendment provides in *Whren v. United States* (517 U.S. 806 (1996)). There, the Court held that, while police officers need probable cause to believe that an individual had committed a traffic violation before stopping his vehicle, the officer could use the violation as a pretext for investigating a crime that is unrelated to the initial stop. Criminal procedure expert William Stuntz (1999) describes *Whren* as effectively making traffic stops "unregulated," as violations of traffic laws are so commonplace that they are a banality, a normal fact of daily life (1271). Moreover, Stuntz argues that *Whren* simply extends the logic of *Terry*, which applies to persons traveling on foot, to persons traveling in cars. As *Terry* held that persons who are walking have a reduced claim to privacy, *Whren* held the same for persons who are driving:

> *Whren* shows how broad police authority over pedestrians is, for *Whren* does no more than narrow the gap between Fourth Amendment protection for drivers and the rules for police–pedestrian encounters. The police can, after all, already "stop" pedestrians without cause, given that every street encounter is functionally a stop. (1271–72)

The Court has narrowed even further the privacy protections that the Fourth Amendment affords by allowing the police to *thoroughly* investigate possible crimes that are unrelated to an initial traffic stop. In *Illinois v. Caballes* (543 U.S. 405 (2005)), the Court held that the police may use a drug-sniffing dog at a traffic stop, as the dog's sniff is not a "search" within the meaning of the Fourth Amendment and does not trigger its privacy protections.

Additionally, there is the issue of consent. Police officers do not need probable cause or reasonable suspicion to stop or search any individual if that person gives her consent to the police contact; the consent essentially amounts to a waiver of Fourth Amendment rights and the minimal privacy protections that they now afford.

The Court might have generated a robust jurisprudence around consent, holding that a person can only voluntarily consent to police interrogation and physical searches if she has been informed of her right *not to consent* to these public interventions. Moreover, the Court might have held that the voluntariness of any consent that has been given should be judged in light of the circumstances under which the police encountered the individual, which might include an inquiry into whether the individual's race and class made voluntary consent to police contact extremely unlikely.

The Court did not go this route. It has held that a police officer's failure to inform an individual of his right not to consent to police contact does not vitiate that individual's consent (Schneckloth v. Bustamonte, 412 U.S. 218, 231–32 (1973)). And it has required no inquiry into the actual voluntariness of an individual's consent despite the fact that "[m]ost individuals do not feel free *not* to give such consent, especially if they are poor or of color" (Bailey 2014, 1561). Further, the Court has held that what is good for pedestrians is good for motorists. Per *Ohio v. Robinette* (519 U.S. 33 (1996)), the police do not have to inform motorists of their right not to consent.

Perhaps the most thorough evacuation of poor people's privacy would come from a decision holding that mere presence in a high crime area (read: poor neighborhood) constitutes reasonable suspicion, thereby permitting the police to stop and frisk any person encountered there. Such a holding would essentially make poor bodies public, relinquishing the poor body of any privacy that it would otherwise possess. The Court has not gone this far, holding in *Illinois v. Wardlow* (528 U.S. 119 (2000)) that, "standing alone," presence in a poor neighborhood does not give rise to reasonable suspicion (124). However, the Court in that case also authorized the equation that "presence in a poor neighborhood" plus "anything that may be interpreted as an effort to avoid police interaction" equals "reasonable suspicion." Thus, if a person in a poor community appears to attempt to avoid police contact, then he may be subject to a stop-and-frisk and the privacy (and dignity) invasions that it entails. This is true—even though it may be the height of reason for a poor person to avoid the police in light of the police's monopoly on legitimate violence, vastly unchecked discretion, and history of illegal, illegitimate brutality.

There is also the fact that the Fourth Amendment only protects from the state that which is protected from private citizens. Thus, to the extent that individuals lack privacy vis-à-vis their neighbors and other people with whom they come into daily contact, then they lack privacy vis-à-vis the state. As Stuntz (1999) observes, "Privacy follows space, and people with money have more space than people without" (1270). With this in mind, the physical conditions in which many of the urban poor live—that they often live in close proximity to their neighbors and in ill-constructed buildings—means that they are more vulnerable to the state's power to observe and punish. The poor who live in apartments with shared common areas are much more vulnerable to constitutional government intrusion than are the wealthy who live in less densely populated areas or, in the alternative, in high-rises whose greater price point reflects the cost of the building's privacy-shielding features.

It is, in part, due to the fact that the poor live in closer quarters than their more affluent counterparts that they tend to live more of their lives outside of those quarters. Whereas wealthier individuals have homes that make it easy and enjoyable to entertain themselves, their families, and their friends—indeed, living in a home in which one can "entertain" is a mark of one's socioeconomic status, a legible sign that one "has arrived"—the poor are much more likely to find their entertainment outside of their homes. Stuntz (1999) writes that because the homes of the poor may not be physically comfortable, "it is natural to want to spend less time, and do less, in them. Other forms of entertainment are more costly than sitting on a front stoop or wandering the streets and talking to friends" (1271). The fact that the poor are in public more than the wealthy makes them more susceptible to being policed by the police.

Moreover, the jurisprudence has narrowed even further the amount of privacy that the poor already living in close quarters can enjoy, holding that an apartment adjoining another that is actually the subject of a warrant may be searched as long as they sufficiently and "objectively" resemble one another (Maryland v. Garrison, 480 U.S. 79, 88 (1987)). Of course, this is "something that would never happen with two freestanding houses or even most well-designed (i.e., more expensive) apartments" (Slobogin 2003, 403).

Wealth can also buy one egress from urban centers and access to the suburbs, the aesthetics of which (wooden fences and stately, bucolic lawns) function not only as techniques for demonstrating wealth but also as techniques for preventing intrusions into privacy. "[T]he extent to which one can afford accouterments of wealth such as a freestanding home, fences, lawns, heavy curtains, and vision- and sound-proof doors and walls" is the extent to which one can shield oneself and one's privacy from state power (Slobogin 2003, 401).

Stuntz (1999) observes that the privacy differential that exists between rich and poor is not reserved to living spaces; it also applies to work spaces. He writes:

> A police search of an enclosed office requires probable cause and a warrant. Consent of the employer is not enough. People who work on assembly lines or shop floors or hotel kitchens do not have offices; they share their work space with many others. When that space is open to the public, the police can see what it holds without justification. When that space is open only to employees, the police may need the consent of the employer, but not the consent of the suspected employee. In practice, probable cause and warrants are never needed. (1270–71)

Consider as well the fact that the poor tend to rely on public transportation more than the wealthy. And although the Fourth Amendment affords very little privacy protection to drivers in private cars, it affords them more protection than it does to passengers on public transportation. "Fourth Amendment law treats passengers on subways and buses no differently than pedestrians on the street. And pedestrians receive less Fourth Amendment protection than drivers" (Stuntz 1999, 1271).

In light of this jurisprudence, one is justified in concluding that the Fourth Amendment is a feeble protector of privacy. But, it gets worse: The state power that the Fourth Amendment authorizes—or rather, the state power that the Court's interpretation of the Fourth Amendment allows to go unlimited—is directed toward the poor at rates that dwarf their wealthier counterparts. Stated differently, the fact that the Fourth Amendment is quite narrow and protects individuals' privacy quite minimally is simply more relevant for the poor; it is implicated in their lives more substantially.

The state polices poor communities heavily—relatively speaking and absolutely. Thus, not only does the Fourth Amendment permit the police to exploit the lack of privacy that the poor have because of their poverty, but the police exacerbate the poor's lack of privacy by focusing its attention on poor communities. In other words, while the Fourth Amendment allows the state to see the poor, many states have decided to *focus* their gaze on poor communities.

Police departments give disproportionate attention to poor communities not simply because these communities tend to have higher rates of violent crime than non-poor communities (Slobogin 2003, 408). It is also, and perhaps more significantly, due to the fact that those with the power to determine policing priorities have decided that drugs are a social scourge, and efforts to eliminate or reduce drug crimes should be given precedence (Stuntz 1999, 1274). That is, society has made a *decision* to police drug possession and distribution vigorously.

Because the buying and selling of drugs in poor communities tend to occur in more easily policed public spaces, police direct their efforts there, as it is easier to *successfully* police drug possession and distribution there. Moreover, the financial incentives that the federal government provides make robust policing of the poor even more attractive. Writes Bailey (2014), "Given the financial stakes involved, drug offenders in poor, inner city communities arguably are the most logical targets of the war on drugs. If federal grant money incentivizes high arrest rates, then the police will focus on communities where they can increase their numbers with the lowest amount of effort" (1550).

Furthermore, a strong argument could be made that, even if it was just as difficult to successfully police drug possession and distribution in poor communities as it is to successfully police it in wealthier communities, police departments would nevertheless focus their resources and energies on poor communities. To the extent that racial minorities are disproportionately represented among the poor, policing of non-white (particularly black and brown) bodies is accomplished by policing the poor. Moreover, scholars of race have long observed that, in the country's cultural imagination, black people perpetrate society's drug problem (Bailey 2014). This has rendered invisible the reality that white people use illegal drugs at rates that match their non-white counterparts. In this way, one could understand how some believe (and implement policies pursuant to the belief) that society can only claim victory in the war on drugs when there are no more *black and Latinx* drug dealers and users. If so, police departments would wage their drug wars in poor communities where black and Latinx drug dealers and users can be found, even if policing these communities were as difficult as policing their wealthier, whiter counterparts.

One should also bear in mind Stuntz's argument that the state's gaze is zero sum; that is, the increase in attention that the police directs toward poor communities is met with a corresponding reduction in the attention that it pays to wealthier communities. He describes the differential in constitutional protection afforded to different spaces and activities in terms of costs (1999, 1274). As such, home and office searches, which generally require probable cause and a warrant, cost more than searches of pedestrians on the street, which *Terry* held require only reasonable suspicion. He notes that the wealthy are more likely to commit their crimes in spaces that require more expensive methods of policing, while the poor are more likely to commit their crimes in places that are "cheaper" to access. This pushes the ever-efficient state away from policing the wealthy and the crimes that they commit and toward policing the poor and the crimes that they commit.

Thus, reducing the privacy that the poor enjoy vis-à-vis the state actually purchases an increase in the privacy that the wealthy enjoy vis-à-vis the state. It also means that it is the height of efficiency for the police "to target the kinds of drug markets that prevail in poor black neighborhoods," as the Court's jurisprudence has lowered the relative cost of policing these markets (Stuntz 1999, 1266). When one pairs this efficiency with the country's "racial common sense" that counsels that criminality and racial minority are simultaneous, it creates a perfect storm of surveillance and punishment of poor communities of color.

New York City's infamous stop-and-frisk program is a dramatic demonstration of this fact. I discuss it here because, while the program was extreme, one can find more moderate versions of it in most poor communities in the nation. Indeed, *Terry* authorizes moderate versions of New York City's stop-and-frisk. Thus, to see what life was like under the program is to see the most important contours of what life currently is like for the urban poor.

Stop-and-frisks in New York City consisted of the aggressive policing of people residing in areas that exhibited signs of physical and social disorder. As sociologists Jeffrey Fagan and Garth Davies (2000) note, "These signs of disorder often are more prevalent in urban neighborhoods with elevated rates of poverty and social fragmentation" (461–62). Thus, poor people residing in poor neighborhoods were subjected to an oppressive police presence—a presence that randomly intercepted them as they engaged in the banalities of daily life. Notably, the effort was not very successful at actually intercepting drugs and weapons and at finding individuals with outstanding warrants. "Eighty-eight percent of these stops did not result in an arrest or a summons being given. Contraband was found in only 2% of these stops" (Bailey 2014, 1557). However, we should note that, in addition to its inefficiency as a crime-fighting technique, the program thoroughly eviscerated the privacy of regular, law-abiding, poor citizens.

If one listens to the voices of poor persons who were forced to live under New York City's stop-and-frisk program—what one might understand as a logical culmination of the *Terry* decision—one can clearly see that, when privacy is understood as freedom from public intervention, the urban poor clearly did not have it. Police interrogations and pat-downs are certainly public interventions. And poor persons, of both sexes, were subject to these interventions, these invasions of privacy, as a matter of daily life.

> If I'm in a group of people, you can't be in front of the building you live in. If you show the police officers your ID that says you live [there], they tell you to go in the house or walk somewhere else; you can't be here on the block. They want to kick you off the block. They want to kick you out the building. We can't be outside? . . . So what can we do? We want to go out. We don't want to be in the house 'cause there's probably nothing to do in the house. Police don't care about that. (Center for Constitutional Rights 2012, 19)

In order to retain some semblance of privacy, the poor were forced to avoid public spaces—to stay inside.

> You shouldn't be held up in your apartment, if you have one. You shouldn't be afraid to come outside and go to the store to get a soda for fear that the police are going to stop you, and you're either going to get a expensive, a high-cost summons or you're going to get arrested. (Center for Constitutional Rights 2012, 6)

It is essential to recognize these police practices as *privacy* invasions. Moreover, they were privacy invasions that women were forced to endure, as well. One woman described her and her sisters' encounter with the police as follows:

> [They] told us to stand up take off our shoes, socks, hoodies, and told everybody to take their top shirt off and leave only their undershirt or one shirt on. They told us to unbutton our pants and roll the waistband down. Three of us were in pajamas. They made us stand and wait with backs turned until a female officer came. She turned us around by our necks and frisked us. They were looking for weed. They found nothing, but took us to the precinct anyway, where our mother had to come get us. (Center for Constitutional Rights 2012, 13)

Some described their lives under this particularly constrained interpretation of the Fourth Amendment as an "occupation"—the term that legal theorist Jed Rubenfeld (1989) uses to describe political regimes in which the state has totally divested its subjects of privacy and privacy rights (784).

What is important to note here is that the privacy invasions that the urban poor endured as a matter of daily life under New York City's stop-and-frisk program were not contingent on their acceptance of a welfare benefit. One cannot describe their lack of privacy as a function of their having surrendered it for public assistance. Instead, they were subject to these invasions simply because they were poor and lived in poor communities. Indeed, the city's stop-and-frisk program was the "policing [of] poor people in poor places" (Fagan and Davies 2000, 457). Moreover, it was a program wherein women were very much the subjects of the state's gaze. The urban poor continue to live less dramatic, subtler versions of the program in cities across the nation.

New York City's stop-and-frisk policy was certainly a racialized, and racist, program: Fagan and Davies show that "police over-stopped black and Hispanic citizens relative to their crime participation, well in excess of their white neighbors" (2000, 482). This fact reminds us that any contemplation of the dramatically unconstrained power that the state has with regard to the poor, made possible by the Court's Fourth Amendment jurisprudence, is incomplete without a pointed discussion of race. That is, while the Fourth Amendment permits the state to see the poor (because their poverty makes it impossible for them to purchase access to the spaces that could buy them invisibility), and while jurisdictions decide to direct their gaze away from the rich and toward the poor, it is an empirically demonstrated truth that the state focuses its gaze most specifically on the bodies of people of color. In the words of Fourth Amendment expert Tracey Maclin (1998), "In America, police targeting of black people for excessive and disproportionate search and seizure is a practice older than the Republic itself" (333).

What results is that poor people of color lead lives that are the *most* devoid of privacy. Thus, while *Whren* authorizes pretextual stops of *all* vehicles, police departments more frequently use the privacy-invading power that the decision grants against people of color.[5] As such, black motorists enjoy less privacy than white motorists. Further, while *Terry* authorizes the police to stop *all* pedestrians if there is "reasonable suspicion that crime is afoot," the police undeniably use the power that *Terry* grants against black pedestrians more often. The unavoidable conclusion is that black, usually poor, pedestrians enjoy less privacy than white pedestrians of all socioeconomic statuses.

The Fourth Amendment facilitates the removal of the privacy of poor people of color not solely through its authorization of the detention and interrogation of their bodies, but also through its turning of a deaf ear toward the complaints that people of color have made. In *Whren*, the Court held that "the constitutional basis for objecting to intentionally discriminatory application of laws is the Equal Protection Clause, not the Fourth Amendment" (Whren v. United States, 517 U.S. 806, 813 (1996)). In other words, the Fourth Amendment authorizes the state to invade the privacy of people of color, and then it refuses to hear protests that the state power that it has authorized has been abused.

The Fourth Amendment also facilitates diminishing the privacy of poor people of color through its unsophisticated invocation of the "reasonableness" standard. Indeed, the demand for reasonableness is quite ubiquitous in Fourth Amendment doctrine. A search is only a search within the meaning of the Fourth Amendment if it infringes an individual's "reasonable expectation of privacy" (Katz v. United States, 389 U.S. 347, 360 (1967)). A police officer can only stop an individual pursuant to *Terry* if he has a "reasonable suspicion" that the individual is about to commit a crime; further, she can only pat down that individual to search for weapons if a "reasonably prudent man in the circumstances would be warranted in the belief that his safety or that of others was in danger" (Terry v. Ohio, 392 U.S. 1, 27 (1968)). A "stop" is only a stop within the meaning of the Fourth Amendment if a "reasonable person would have believed that he was not free to leave" (Michigan v. Chesternut, 486 U.S. 567, 573 (1988)).

It has almost become a truism within critical approaches to the law that reasonableness is a standard fraught with bias. Reasonableness masquerades as a "point of viewlessness"—pure objectivity (Raigrodski 2008, 215). However, in actuality, it reflects particular subject positions while simultaneously dissembling that reflection. Reasonableness "legitimates selective viewpoints . . . while not treating them as viewpoints at all" (Raigrodski 2008, 168). As to be expected, that which is reasonable usually reflects the particular subject positions of the people who are empowered to define it. With respect to the Fourth Amendment, this power presently resides in the Court, which fills the category of reasonableness with content through its decisions and, in so doing, instructs police departments and officers throughout the nation as to what is and is not reasonable. The jurisprudence has constructed a standard of reasonableness that "may bear only a tangential relationship to the lives of those more commonly subject to police investigations" (Raigrodski 2008, 165).

The Court demonstrated this disconnect in *Florida v. Bostick* (501 U.S. 429 (1991)) when it held that a young black man had not necessarily been subjected to a seizure within the meaning of the Fourth Amendment when police officers stood in the aisle next to where he was seated on a bus, effectively blocking his exit, and asked for permission to search his luggage for drugs. He had argued that a reasonable person would not have felt free to leave in such a situation; this was especially true given the fact that, had he successfully maneuvered his way around the officers and exited the bus, he would have been stranded in a strange city without his luggage when the bus eventually departed. The Court found that a reasonable person would have felt free to terminate the police encounter.

This raises the question: Who is this "reasonable person" that the Court has in mind? Who is this person who, when confronted by two police officers who had flashed their badges and announced their identity as narcotics officers while wearing bright green "raid" jackets and visible gun holsters, would have felt comfortable telling these officers to go away? Who would have thought it possible to squeeze past the officers, exit the bus, and deal with the consequences of being in an unfamiliar city without any obvious means of reaching one's destination *or* returning to one's origin?

It is possible that *no* real person would have felt that the options that the Court argued were available to Bostick were actually available to him. (In fact, it may be that only an *unreasonable* person would feel free to terminate such an encounter.) However, if a person does exist who would have behaved in the manner that the Court suggests the defendant might have behaved, this person is probably *not* a racial minority who has lived in a poor community in the nation. This person is probably *not* a poor black person, steeped in wisdom generated from centuries of encounters between police and civilians, who reasonably believes that the police are just as likely to act violently as they are to leave in peace. This is probably *not* a person who reasonably assumes that the police respect whatever ostensible rights an individual possesses as often as they violate them. This person probably does not understand that the line between legitimate violence sanctioned by law and illegitimate violence prohibited by law is a blurry one on the ground; this person likely does not realize that legitimate violence sanctioned by law and illegitimate violence prohibited by law actually *feel* the same when brought to bear on the bodies of individuals who disrespect any given police officer's authority. The reasonable person is *not* poor and a racial minority. This incongruity renders poor, racial minorities even more vulnerable to state intrusions into privacy.

. . .

In this chapter, I have endeavored to show that the unconstitutional conditions cases do no more than reveal the justification for denying (either in the moderate or strong sense) poor mothers privacy rights. Further, I have argued that if one subscribes to the tale that the unconstitutional conditions cases lead one to believe—the tale of poor mothers bearing privacy rights that they surrender in order to receive a welfare benefit—one has to also subscribe to the belief that poor mothers have (effective) privacy rights and privacy before they turn to the state for welfare assistance. The literatures documenting the use of CPS and the foster care system to manage the effects of childhood poverty, the public lives that poverty forces poor families to live, and the overpolicing of poor people who bear gutted Fourth Amendment rights belie the claim that poor mothers have—in any meaningful sense of the word—privacy before they receive a benefit from the state. Poor mothers' existence in this nation is one that is always already devoid of privacy, in no way conditioned on their decision to turn to the state for assistance.

3 Family Privacy

Like all rights, the right to family privacy—which, in this chapter, we understand as an individual's right to care for her child and to direct his upbringing[1]—is not absolute. The law has long established that, in certain situations, the state may override a parent's childrearing choices.

For example, in *Prince v. Massachusetts* (321 U.S. 158 (1944)), the Court held that the state may override a parent's choice to direct her child to engage in religious proselytizing on public streets. In *Troxel v. Granville* (530 U.S. 57 (2000)), the Court established that even a "fit" parent may have to allow a third party to have contact with her child if the contact is deemed to be in a child's best interest or necessary to avoid harm to the child, provided that the relevant statute gives sufficient weight to the parent's judgment. And other cases established that the state may override a parent's decisions regarding her child's education: The state may direct a parent to send her child to school, and, if the parent decides to homeschool a child, the state may mandate "minimum qualifications of the instructor, the curriculum, the number of days of instruction, the standardized tests that must be administered, and parental reporting obligations" (Rosenbury 2007, 873).

Perhaps the most spectacular demonstration of the fact that the right to family privacy is not absolute relates to the state's power to intervene in the family—even to the point of dissolving it altogether—in the case of child abuse or neglect. The common law birthed the doctrine of *parens patriae* ("parent of the nation"), which grants the state the authority to protect children. Thus, the state, in this role, may require parents to provide "proper food, clothing, shelter, and medical care to their children" and to refrain from engaging in abusive behavior toward them (Kindred 1996, 521). If the parent is neglectful or abusive, the state as parent of the nation may intervene in the parent–child relationship, regulate it, and terminate it, if need be.

The threshold for a finding that a parent is abusive or neglectful and, consequently, that the state is justified in impinging on a parent's right to family privacy, is, in theory, quite high. Explains family law scholar Annette Appell (2001), "The state . . . cannot intervene merely because it has a difference of opinion with the parent about what is best for the child" (704).

This raises some questions: Why have we as a nation decided to create a strong presumption against state intervention in a parent's relationship with her child? How can we justify the family privacy right? What is its value? What good is the right thought to produce? This chapter argues that poor mothers have been deprived, either in the moderate or strong sense, of their rights to family privacy. Understanding why the law has recognized the family privacy right might help us understand the reason for this deprivation.

Justifications of the Family Privacy Right
Instrumental Justifications
In *Meyer v. Nebraska* (262 U.S. 390 (1923)), the Court struck down a law prohibiting schools from teaching any language other than English to students in seventh grade and below. Passed in response to xenophobic fears of a large foreign-born population that "follow[ed] foreign leaders [and moved] in a foreign atmosphere," the Nebraska legislature designed the law as a public safety measure that would ensure that American children acquired "American ideals" through instruction in English to the exclusion of "foreign tongues" (401). While the Court sympathized with the motivations behind the law—it understood the "[t]he desire of the legislature to foster a homogeneous people with American ideals" when the memory of World War I was still fresh and antipathy toward German "truculent adversaries" was high—it nevertheless saw the dystopic qualities of the Nebraska law (402). The Court referred to Plato, who had envisioned a law mandating

> [t]hat the wives of our guardians are to be common, and their children are to be common, and no parent is to know his own child, nor any child his parent.
> . . . The proper officers will take the offspring of the good parents to the pen or fold, and there they will deposit them with certain nurses who dwell in a sepa-

rate quarter. . . . In order to submerge the individual and develop ideal citizens, Sparta assembled the males at seven into barracks and [e]ntrusted their subsequent education and training to official guardians. (401–402)

The Court wrote that, while Plato was a genius in many respects, his "ideas touching the relation between individual and State were wholly different from those upon which our institutions rest" (403). The Court believed that the Constitution prohibited the pursuit of these Platonic ideals.

Two years later in *Pierce v. Society of Sisters* (268 U.S. 510 (1925)), the Court struck down an Oregon law requiring children between the ages of 8 and 16 to attend a public school. The law had been passed in response to postwar desires to cultivate a common national culture and to steep children in it. The Court wrote that these desires were not compelling enough to override "the liberty of parents and guardians to direct the upbringing and education of children under their control" (534). The Court elaborated:

The fundamental theory of liberty upon which all governments in this Union repose excludes any general power of the State to standardize its children by forcing them to accept instruction from public teachers only. The child is not the mere creature of the State; those who nurture him and direct his destiny have the right, coupled with the high duty, to recognize and prepare him for additional obligations. (535)

Meyer and *Pierce* together stand for the proposition that the right of family privacy is valuable because it prevents the state from standardizing children. In a nation that purports to pride itself on its diversity, the family privacy right is important because it creates the conditions within which individual families can collectively generate a citizenry that has a plurality of thoughts, values, beliefs, and principles. This heterogeneity itself is good.

Scholars have elaborated on this justification for the family privacy right, with some focusing on the political significance of constraining the government's ability to standardize children. For example, legal scholars Anne Dailey (1993), Bruce Hafen (1983), and others have contended that it is good for democracy when children—who one day will be adults who participate in governing the nation—have a multiplicity of values and beliefs. Summarizing this perspective, Appell (2001) writes that children who have not been standardized by the state

enrich[] the government by creating citizens separate enough from the state to be capable of exercising their power to govern. In contrast, institutionalized or uniform child rearing values would presumably create citizens who would not question the state and who would not provide the diversity of opinions and values that can serve as a check on the government. (707)

If we shift our focus slightly and allow our gaze to settle on the state that would standardize children, we find another reason society might limit such a state: A standardizing state is absolutely terrifying. In essence, the state would become omnipresent: It would be *in* its subjects' values, beliefs, opinions, worldviews, politics, and so forth.

If the state is present in its subjects' minds and hearts—indeed, if the state *forms* its subjects' minds and hearts—the state, in very important ways, would form the institutions in civil society that individuals create: family, school, religion, the press, the market, and so on. And if the state forms the institutions in civil society, it would approximate absolute power. This is totalitarianism.

Justice Douglas articulated this danger in his dissent in *Poe v. Ullman* (367 U.S. 497 (1961)), which held that the plaintiffs lacked standing to challenge a Connecticut law banning the use of contraceptives—the same law that would be struck down a few years later in *Griswold v. Connecticut* (380 U.S. 939 (1965)). Referencing a regime that allowed the state unfettered control of decisions as personal to individuals as whether to start a family and how to raise their children, Douglas wrote,

> One of the earmarks of the totalitarian understanding of society is that it seeks to make all subcommunities—family, school, business, press, church—completely subject to control by the State. The State then is not one vital institution among others . . . [but] seeks to be coextensive with family and school, press, business community, and the Church, so that all of these component interest groups are . . . reduced to organs and agencies of the State. (Poe v. Ullman 1961, 521–22)

Legal theorist Jed Rubenfeld (1989) has expanded upon Justice Douglas's insight, inviting us not to focus on what the state would prohibit in the absence of the privacy right, but instead to focus on what the state would affirmatively require. If we accept Rubenfeld's invitation, we would see a state that requires parents to inculcate particular values in their children in particular ways at particular times. The family privacy right, and the privacy right in all of its various iterations, is important because it is a bulwark against this type of totalitarianism.

Pragmatic Justifications

Distinct from these instrumental justifications of the family privacy right is one that conceptualizes the right's value in very pragmatic terms. According to this view, parents should be allowed to raise their children as they see fit and without undue state interference and regulation because, comparatively speaking, they are best situated for the task of caring for their children and instilling in them the knowledge that they will need to become independent adults. Essentially,

> state actors cannot offer the quality and degree of human intimacy that children require to grow into secure and stable adults. . . . [E]ven if the state were to undertake the parenting role, there is the sense that parents provide something for their children that is beyond the reach of governmental expertise. (Brito 200, 244–45)

This pragmatic justification for the family privacy right sometimes rests on the supposition that parents have instinctual, "natural bonds of affection" for their children (233–45). This inherent love, coupled with a parent's unrivaled knowledge of her child, predisposes a parent to act in her child's best interest (Buss 2002; Gilles 1996). This view holds that we should assume, and we should create laws that assume, that the decisions that parents make for their children are, objectively speaking, those that are best for the children—absent, of course, compelling evidence suggesting otherwise. The Court articulated this justification for the family privacy right quite clearly in *Troxel v. Granville*, discussed briefly at the start of the chapter:

> [T]here is a presumption that fit parents act in the best interests of their children. . . . The law's concept of the family rests on a presumption that parents possess what a child lacks in maturity, experience, and capacity for judgment required for making life's difficult decisions. More important, historically it has recognized that natural bonds of affection lead parents to act in the best interests of their children. Accordingly, so long as a parent adequately cares for his or her children (i.e., is fit), there will normally be no reason for the State to inject itself into the private realm of the family to further question the ability of that parent to make the best decisions concerning the rearing of that parent's children. (530 U.S. 57, 68 (2000))

Noninstrumental Justifications

Many cases have built on the sense articulated in *Meyer* and *Pierce* that the family privacy right ought to be protected because it allows families to instill a variety of different values in children, thereby benefiting the nation. However, other cases can be read to argue that permitting families to instill diverse values in children is good *in and of itself*. Consider *Moore v. City of East Cleveland* (431 U.S. 494 (1977)), in which the Court struck down an ordinance that limited occupancy of a dwelling to a family, while defining "family" narrowly to include only nuclear families and certain forms of extended families.

In the course of holding that the ordinance violated a right to family privacy that could be located in the Due Process Clause, the Court gave a nod to the anti-standardization bent of *Meyer* and *Pierce*, writing that the "Constitution prevents East Cleveland from standardizing its children—and its adults—by forcing all to live in certain narrowly defined family patterns" (506). However, the Court goes on to suggest that while anti-standardization is good for the nation, anti-standardization is also good for the individual insofar as it allows individuals to impart the values that are most dear to them: "Our decisions establish that the Constitution protects the sanctity of the family precisely because the institution of the family is deeply rooted in this Nation's history and tradition. It is through the family that we inculcate and pass down many of our most cherished values, moral and cultural" (503–504).

Scholars have elaborated upon this justification of the family privacy right, noting that individuals benefit from imparting their values to their family members because the denial thereof functions to deny their capacity for moral autonomy,[2] which, according to Kant (1887), is the basis of human dignity. Legal scholar Peggy Cooper Davis (1994) offers a particularly compelling rendering of this argument.

Davis describes the violence committed against black families during the centuries of chattel slavery in the United States, noting that those who endeavored to exert total control over enslaved people understood that destroying families would further that end. She observes that the dominating class realized that devastating the black family through constant regulation, intervention, and physical separation—indeed, through completely denying it privacy and exposing it to the unconstrained power of both public and private actors—resulted in the inability of individual men and women to pass down their values to their children. This practice denied that enslaved parents were morally autonomous beings, and it denied their children the capacity to achieve moral autonomy.

Thus, Davis contends that it violates the dignity of individuals when they cannot share their most treasured values with their children and when their children cannot receive those values. Following this conceptualization, we ought to protect the right to family privacy not because it is good for democracy and not because it prevents the government from becoming too omnipresent—too totalitarian. We ought to protect this right not for pragmatic reasons—not because, most likely, the parent will be the entity that will best care for the child. Although these may be good reasons for protecting the family privacy right, Davis argues that we ought to protect this right because, insofar as it protects dignity, it is good in and of itself:

> The idea of civil freedom that grows out of the history of slavery, antislavery, and Reconstruction entails more than the right to continue one's genetic kind in private. It also entails a right of family that derives from a human right of intellectual and moral autonomy. It entails the right of every individual to affect the culture and embrace, act upon, and advocate privately chosen values. For parents and other guardians, civil freedom brings a right to choose and propagate values. For children, civil freedom brings nothing less than the right to grow to moral autonomy, because the child-citizen, like the child-slave, flowers to moral independence only under authority that is flexible in ways that states and masters cannot manage, and temporary in ways that states and masters cannot tolerate. (1371–72)

Family Privacy Rights that Yield No Value

Our next task is to reflect on these three justifications of the family privacy right in light of the moral construction of poverty—the idea that poor persons have only themselves to blame for their impoverishment. Consider the idea that people are poor because they are indolent, have no work ethic, are sexually intemperate, are predisposed toward criminality, are addicted to drugs and alcohol, make bad decisions, refuse to delay gratification, and engage in self-destructive and irresponsible behaviors. Consider the narrative about poor people that has circulated in cultural discourses since the birth of the nation, a narrative that describes the poor as "lazy, ignorant, unintelligent, impulsive, prone to gambling and drinking, irresponsible, and immoral" (Pelton 1999, 1479–80).

Consider specifically discourses about poor mothers, discourses that describe their fertility as accidental—as the result of ignorance, sexual incontinence, and the failure to think of consequences. Consider competing discourses that describe poor mothers' fertility as cunning and exploitative—not as an effort to manifest the best parts of themselves in their children, but as an effort to solidify their access to governmental largesse.

We can begin with instrumentalist theories of the family privacy right, which declare that the right is beneficial because it is good for the nation and democracy when children have received values from their parents with which they can challenge state power when they reach adulthood. If the kinds of values that the ethically and behaviorally flawed poor would instill in their children cannot be conceptualized as good for the nation—if the child who has been instilled with these values cannot be imagined to grow into an adult who will contribute positively to political discourse and the country more generally—then the value of the family privacy right will go unrealized. Thus, we can see an argument for dispossessing the immoral poor of these rights. Moreover, to the extent that, absent state oversight and regulation, presumptively deficient parents may instill values in their children that are dangerous and counterproductive to democracy, political discourse, and the nation, then family privacy rights may produce a *negative* value when wielded by the poor. The idea is that it may actually be safer for the nation if the state supervises poor parents as they go about inculcating values in their children. State presence in the family unit allows the state the capacity to endorse the transmission of "good" values through inaction and to disrupt the transmission of "bad" values through active intervention.

Consider as well that *Pierce* justified the family privacy right by arguing that parents, who nurture children and direct their destinies, are also charged with the duty to "prepare [them] for additional obligations" (268 U.S. 535 (1925)). If we view poor parents through a lens informed by the moral construction of poverty, what confidence could we have that a poor parent would prepare a child for additional obligations? What confidence could we have that a welfare-dependent parent, who is unable to support herself financially in a nation of abundance, has *herself* been prepared for additional obligations? Through their financial independence, wealthier parents would offer assurances of their own preparation and their ability to prepare a child. Meanwhile, the poor would fail in this regard.

Other instrumental justifications for the family privacy right locate its value in its prevention of our government from becoming totalitarian. Because this justification focuses on family privacy rights as public goods, it does not assume that the right's value depends on how the rightsbearer wields it. As such, one might argue that there is a value in bestowing the family privacy right even to those whom we believe to be ethically and behaviorally deficient because their bearing the right acts as a bulwark against totalitarianism. However, the possibility that a government can be totalitarian vis-à-vis some subjects and not totalitarian vis-à-vis others defeats this argument.

In truth, the government may occupy all corners of some of its subjects' lives, while simultaneously removing itself from those same corners of other subjects' lives. Framed as Rubenfeld (1989) invites us to do, the government can affirmatively require deeply personal things from some of its subjects while making no requirement of others. The state can command some parents to inculcate particular values in their children in particular ways at particular times while commanding nothing of other parents. Simply stated, a government does not have to be totalitarian to *all*; it may be selectively totalitarian.

And then there are the pragmatic justifications of the family privacy right, attesting that the right is valuable because parents are best situated to act in their children's best interests due to their instinctual bond with their children coupled with their superior knowledge of them. Here, as with instrumentalist justifications, the moral construction of poverty counsels that the value of the family privacy right will go unrealized when the poor wield it. Should we have any confidence that an individual who has let herself fall into poverty, and who has made the choice to remain there, will acquire competency regarding her child that will be superior to a state actor? According to the moral construction of poverty, the decision to reproduce while poor is an irrational, irresponsible one. Should we have any confidence that the decision-making capacity of a woman who has made the bad decision to allow her poverty to intersect with motherhood would somehow become rehabilitated after the birth of her child? Should we have any confidence that, once she has become a mother, she would begin to make responsible, wise decisions?

Because the stakes are so high—because the health and well-being of a child hangs in the balance—it is an assumption that the law has chosen not to make. In essence, pragmatic justifications for the family privacy right provide that, barring extenuating circumstances, the state should not second-guess the choices that parents make respecting their children because parents will make choices that are best for their children. Poor mothers live in those extenuating circumstances; they exist in that state of exception. By depriving poor mothers of effective (consistent with this book's moderate claim) or actual (consistent with its strong claim) family privacy rights, law and society contend that we ought not to assume that poor mothers should be trusted to raise their children expertly.

And what of noninstrumental justifications of the family privacy right? What of the idea that we respect an individual's dignity when we construct a space of nonintervention around her relationship with her child? Does that not counsel in favor of bestowing family privacy rights to poor mothers—even if, in keeping with the moral construction of poverty, we can presume that they engage in pathological conduct and have problematic values? There are two responses to this position.

First, we ought not to underestimate how discourses that blame individuals for their poverty function to diminish the humanity of the poor. The work that the moral construction of poverty does might be analogized to racial discourses,[3] which often make it possible to discount the humanity of the racialized subject (Omi and Winant 1994). While we may not deny that the poor are human, we may deny that they have a human dignity that is worth respecting and protecting. We may deny that their interest in moral autonomy and in seeing themselves reflected in their children is as compelling as our own.

Second, we ought not to lose sight that family privacy rights implicate the health and well-being of children. The more privacy that we give to the family unit, the more likely it is for child maltreatment to go undetected. Accordingly, we may decide that, while an individual's dignity interests are significant, the state's interest in protecting children from neglect and abuse is even more significant. This state interest may justify violating the dignity of those who we fear are at risk for neglecting and abusing their children. Thus, when poor parents are conceptualized as at high risk for maltreating their children, it facilitates the construction of a jurisprudence that authorizes the constant violation of these parents' dignity.

Expanding Our Understanding of "Intervention"

It bears repeating that the jurisprudence has established that individuals' family privacy rights may be infringed legitimately by the state in order to protect children from abuse and neglect. Scholars have tended to conceptualize these interventions narrowly, as only those efforts that child protective agencies make after they have received information suggesting that a particular child has been victimized. There are several interventions that a state may make:

1. It can investigate a family, ascertaining whether there is sufficient evidence of child maltreatment to take further action.[4]

2. If there is insufficient evidence of child maltreatment and the state has no authority to take further action, it can offer voluntary in-home or community-based services to a family, attempting to reduce the likelihood that a child will be abused or neglected in the future.

3. If there is sufficient evidence of child maltreatment, the state can re-move the child from the parent's home and place him in foster care or in the care of a relative, mandating that the child remain outside of the parent's care until the parent has satisfied all of the conditions for reuni-fication outlined in a permanency plan.

4. The state can terminate a parent's legal rights to her child if it deter-mines that the termination is in the child's best interest, freeing the child to find a permanent home with an adoptive family (McGrath 2012).

Most scholars conceptualize this list as the universe of interventions that the state makes in its efforts to protect children from abuse and neglect. How-ever, in this chapter I propose that the list should be expanded to include the screenings that all recipients of Medicaid-subsidized prenatal care must endure in some form upon initiating healthcare. As detailed in the Introduc-tion, poor pregnant women in California must have an assessment of their "psychosocial functioning" and must answer questions about their "social support system, personal adjustment to pregnancy, history of previous preg-nancies, . . . goals for herself in this pregnancy, general emotional status and history, wanted or unwanted pregnancy, acceptance of the pregnancy, sub-stance use and abuse, housing/household, education/employment, and financial/material resources" (22 California Code of Regulations 3 § 51348). Poor pregnant women in New York must endure similar questions, under-going a screening that asks about

> the unplanned-ness and/or unwantedness of the current pregnancy, the wom-an's intention to give up the infant for adoption or to surrender the infant to foster care, an HIV-positive status, a history of substance abuse, a lack of familial or environmental support, marital or family problems, a history of domestic violence, sexual abuse, or depression, mental disability, a lack of social welfare benefits, a history of contact with the Administration for Children's Services (the child protective agency in New York State), a history of psychiatric treatment or emotional disturbance, and a history of homelessness. (Bridges 2011a, 129)

Poor pregnant women in other states have to submit themselves to similar in-terrogations (Gilman 2008).

This chapter argues that these interrogations should be understood as in-terventions for two reasons. First, they, like all the interventions that child pro-tective agencies make, endeavor to protect children from abuse and neglect.

The screenings are designed to determine which mothers possess characteristics that make them more likely to maltreat their children once they are born.

Second, and more importantly, this chapter understands these interrogations as interventions because the women who have to endure them experience them as interventions. A poor woman, who has been asked the battery of questions that the state requires, knows that the state is trying to determine whether or not she will be a bad mother. The description that family law scholar Doriane Coleman (2005) offers of the harms visited upon those who are subject to child welfare investigations is instructive:

> A knock at the door by an official who suggests that someone . . . has given the state reason to believe that a child in the family is being abused or neglected by the very people who are intended to cherish her is the ultimate challenge to the strength and existence of this central premise in a family, and thus is also the ultimate vehicle for shame for its members. (498)

Medicaid interrogations are that knock on the door by an official. They are that sign that the state has been given reason to believe that a child may be abused or neglected by the very people who are intended to cherish her. Poor women are shamed by the necessity of disavowing that they will fail their children so tragically.

That these screenings are reasonably experienced as interventions and ought to be conceptualized as such is made evident if one simply imagines how a woman with private health insurance, a private doctor, and class privilege would experience them. Imagine this woman being shuttled into the office of a government employee whom she has never seen before. Imagine this woman being asked by a stranger how she is adjusting to pregnancy. What is her general emotional status? Does she have a history of substance abuse? What about a history of domestic violence, sexual abuse, or depression? Is she having marital or relationship problems? Where is she working? How much is she earning? How much is her partner earning? Is he going to make enough money to support her child when he or she is born? Is her family supportive of this pregnancy? It is not at all unreasonable to imagine that this woman would be offended. Some versions of this woman would be outraged. And most of these women would feel like their privacy has been invaded.

Nothing suggests that women without class privilege are not similarly offended and outraged. Indeed, there is very little reason to believe that poor women do not similarly feel that their privacy has been invaded. And to the extent that a poor woman does not feel this way, it may be due to her poverty having disciplined her to expect such privacy invasions. That is, a wealthier woman's sense of offense and outrage may derive from the unanticipated nature of these governmental intrusions; they are quite unusual. However, for poor women, governmental intrusions of this sort are *de rigueur*.

We might compare these interrogations to the stops and examinations that the police conduct on black and brown people. These are interrogations that we have come to understand as harmful. They are injurious because they are a symptom of racial inequality: They demonstrate that criminality is thought to attach to black and brown bodies—criminality that does not attach in similar ways to white bodies. And we understand these interrogations to be dangerous because of their effects: They reveal that black and brown persons are less valuable members of the body politic—that they are second-class citizens. Moreover, black and brown persons learn through these encounters just where they stand in the nation's cultural imagination.

Interrogations of poor pregnant women are similarly harmful. As a symptom of class inequality, they demonstrate that pathology is thought to attach to poor bodies in a way that it does not attach to wealthier bodies. And they are dangerous because of their effects: They reveal that poor women are less valuable members of the body politic. Again, poor women learn through these encounters with the state that they do not have equal standing in the nation's cultural imagination.

Consider legal theorist Dorothy Roberts's (2003) description of the effect that the child protective state has on poor individuals and poor communities: "Everyone in the neighborhood has either experienced state intrusion in their family or knows someone who has. Parents are either being monitored by caseworkers or live with the fear that they may soon be investigated" (180). This description is edifying for two reasons. First, it shows the appropriateness of analogizing interrogations conducted by a state interested in protecting children with interrogations conducted by the police. Like the indigent mothers that Roberts describes who must live with the pervasiveness of the child protective state, everyone in poor neighborhoods has had contact with the police or knows someone who has. They all live with the fear that their next encounter with the penal state will soon come.

Second, the description is instructive because it illuminates the harm of forcing particular people and communities to live with omnipresent and unconstrained state power. Roberts describes communities that are distrustful and suspicious of the state. These are people who feel themselves to be in an antagonistic relationship with the government—people who are aware that they have no means of keeping the state out of their lives. These are disenfranchised people.

The jurisprudence tells us that the "family is not beyond regulation" (Moore v. City of East Cleveland, 431 U.S. 494, 499 (1977)) and that parental liberty is not absolute. Accordingly, family privacy rights are never meant to be a *complete* shield against government intervention. The jurisprudence instructs us that the state legitimately infringes an individual's right to family privacy and intervenes into her family when it has a suspicion that child maltreatment might be occurring.

But, what if poverty gives the state a legitimate reason to suspect child maltreatment? This means that the state *always* has the authority to infringe the poor's right to family privacy, and it means that they do not even enjoy a *partial* shield against government intervention. Those who subscribe to this book's moderate claim would take this fact as evidence of the frailty of poor mothers' existing privacy rights. However, those who subscribe to this book's strong claim would reach a different conclusion: The fact that poor mothers' ostensible family privacy rights are always already infringed is evidence that there are other processes at work—that alongside the articulated rules stating that all persons bear family privacy rights are unarticulated rules about who may be included within the class of rightsbearers. They would conclude that these unarticulated rules affirm that poor mothers are not competent privacy rightsbearers and, as such, that poor mothers have been informally disenfranchised of their rights to family privacy.

The Overrepresentation of the Poor in the Child Welfare System

Poor families are overrepresented in the child protective system. A national incidence study once compared the prevalence of child maltreatment in families with annual incomes above $15,000 to those with annual incomes below $15,000. It found that

> maltreatment was over five times higher in low-income families than high-income families (29.3 versus 5.5 per 1,000 children). Two thirds of all cases of maltreatment identified by the study involved families with incomes below $15,000. (Besharov 2000, 183)

In a similar vein, Roberts (2003) has described a map that the Illinois Department of Children and Family Services prepared showing the distribution of child abuse and neglect cases across the city of Chicago:

> Neighborhoods with the highest concentration of cases form an L-shaped pattern colored in red. There is another map of Chicago with the same color coding that shows level of poverty across the city. The poorest neighborhoods in the city form an identical L-shaped pattern. (2003, 176)

This fact, and many others, leads Roberts to a conclusion that others have reached as well: "Poverty is key to explaining why almost any child gets in the system" (174).

The families that child welfare authorities investigate tend to be poor. The families about which child welfare authorities can substantiate allegations of child maltreatment tend to be poor. The families from which children are removed and placed in foster care or in the care of relatives tend to be poor. The families that are dissolved after a court terminates the legal rights of the parents tend to be poor. This is the reality.

It forces us to ask why. Why is it that poor families are more frequently accused of abusing and/or neglecting their children? And why is it that poor families are more frequently found to have maltreated their children? Scholars have offered several possible explanations.

The Confusion of Poverty with Neglect

One theory is that state authorities tend to confuse poverty with neglect. This theory posits that what child protective authorities interpret as evidence of neglect is often just the trappings of poverty. Writing in this vein, family law scholar Kay Kindred (1996) states that one of the primary reasons for the overrepresentation of the poor in the child welfare system "may be that definitions of neglect encompass many behaviors and circumstances that are direct results of poverty" (532–33). Similarly, social worker Leroy Pelton (1999) has noted that "[M]aterial hardship is not merely related to what we call child neglect; it is so intertwined with 'neglect' as to often be indistinguishable from it" (1484).[5]

Indeed, if one examines the definitions of neglect that child welfare authorities have formulated, one can easily see how *a poor parent, due to her indigence, might find it impossible to avoid neglecting her child*. One manual for social workers in child protective service (CPS) schematizes child neglect as follows (adapted from DePanfilis 2006, 12–14):

- Physical neglect
    - Nutritional neglect: when a child is undernourished or is repeatedly hungry for long periods of time
    - Clothing neglect: when a child lacks appropriate clothing, such as not having appropriately warm clothes or shoes in the winter
    - Other physical neglect: includes inadequate hygiene
- Medical neglect
    - Denial of healthcare: the failure to provide or to allow needed care as recommended by a competent healthcare professional for a physical injury, illness, medical condition, or impairment
    - Delay in healthcare: the failure to seek timely and appropriate medical care for a serious health problem that any reasonable person would have recognized as needing professional medical attention. Examples . . . include not getting appropriate preventative medical or dental care for a child, not obtaining care for a sick child, or not following medical recommendations
- Inadequate supervision
    - Exposure to hazards
    - Smoking: second-hand smoke, especially for children with asthma or other lung problems
- Environmental neglect . . . characterized by a lack of environmental or neighborhood safety, opportunities, or resources
- Educational neglect
    - Failure to address truancy
    - Failure to enroll a child in school

One could understand this schematization as nothing more than a description of various types of child neglect. However, one could just as easily view this schema as a description of what it means to be poor. When one is poor, one will be hungry repeatedly, sometimes for long periods of time. When one is poor, one will not have appropriate clothing for the weather. One will not be able to visit the doctor when one is ill. One will live in unsafe neighborhoods that lack resources. One will find it difficult to make a hungry, sick, poorly clothed child attend school.

Thus, we arrive at a disturbing explanation for the fact of child protective authorities' overwhelming presence in the lives of poor families: The conditions of poverty are the conditions of neglect. Poverty and neglect are simultaneous. Essentially, one neglects one's child by being poor. Note that if this is true, then it makes sense to effectively or actually deprive poor mothers of their family privacy rights, as the family privacy rights function to make it difficult for the state to protect poor children who, *by definition*, are being neglected.

This justification for depriving poor mothers, and poor parents generally, of their family privacy rights does not depend on the moral construction of poverty; it does not depend on the presumption that poor mothers are behaviorally or ethically deficient. The state can recognize the need, and the obligation, to protect children from poverty without also subscribing to the notion that these children's parents are to blame for their dire circumstances. But, the moral construction of poverty certainly makes it easier for the state to have little ambivalence as it goes about the brutal task of intervening in, breaking up, and, in some cases, disbanding families. If, parents have *chosen* to be poor, then they have also *chosen* to be neglectful to their children. The state and state actors need not lament having to make inventions that hurt parents when the parents are responsible for the circumstances that lead to the state's need to make the intervention. In those cases, the parents *deserve* to be hurt.

Additionally, the moral construction of poverty makes removing children from their impoverished parents—as opposed to providing parents with goods and services that reduce the effects of poverty—the most logical and efficient solution. If poverty is a manifestation of a moral failing, the state merely puts a bandage on a potentially mortal wound when it protects children by reducing the effects of their parents' poverty. While reducing the effects of poverty would protect children from poverty-qua-neglect, it would not protect children from parents who have demonstrated, through the fact of their poverty, that they are more fundamentally flawed. I expand on this notion below.

Poverty Makes It Difficult to Avoid the Harmful Consequences of Imprudent Behavior

Another explanation for why poor families are disproportionately subjects of CPS interventions is that negligent behavior is more likely to result in actual injuries to a child when a poor parent engages in that behavior. Roberts (2003) has made this observation, noting that "[c]hildren are often removed from poor parents when parental carelessness increases the likelihood that . . .

hazards will result in actual harm. Indigent parents do not have the resources to avoid the harmful effects of their negligence" (175).

When honest, most parents will admit that they have made mistakes while performing the difficult, sometimes overwhelming task of raising a child. When wealthy parents make these mistakes, the harm that those mistakes could potentially cause are less likely to come to pass. When poor parents make these mistakes, however, their poverty means that the harm that those mistakes could potentially cause are more likely to be realized.

As an example, consider the fact that exposing an asthmatic child to secondhand cigarette smoke is regarded as the stuff of neglect. When a poor mother improvidently exposes her child to cigarette smoke, poverty means that the child is more likely to be asthmatic. (Poor children, for a variety of reasons—which include unhealthy environmental conditions in poor neighborhoods, the high amount of allergens in the housing in which poor people live, and a lack of preventative medical care—are much more likely to suffer from asthma (U.S. Environmental Protection Agency 2008)). Because healthcare is much more difficult to access for the poor, the poor asthmatic child is less likely to have medications that can prevent a severe asthma attack. Further, if a poor child has an asthma attack that must be treated in a hospital, the child is more likely to be cared for in a public hospital by providers who will alert child welfare authorities. Meanwhile, when a wealthier mother, equally improvidently, exposes her child to cigarette smoke, her relative wealth may mean that the child is less likely to be asthmatic. Her relative wealth may mean that, if her child is asthmatic, she will have access to the medications necessary to stave off a serious asthma attack. And even if an asthma attack is serious enough to warrant hospitalization, she is more likely to be cared for in a private hospital by a private doctor, who may be less likely to report the parent to the state.

It might be useful to follow this example a bit further. Asthma is a significant cause of school absenteeism among children (U.S. Environmental Protection Agency 2008). Note that child welfare authorities define a parent's failure to address truancy as a species of neglect. Poverty may mean that a poor child is more likely to miss school because she is asthmatic and to lack access to the healthcare that could make the condition one that does not interfere with school attendance. Simultaneously, the wealthier asthmatic child is more likely to have access to the healthcare that will render her asthma a controllable health condition that does not interfere with her ability to attend school without interruptions.

In sum, poverty increases the probability that risky behavior will become harmful behavior. This may explain the overrepresentation of poor families in the child welfare system.

Actual Higher Rates of Abuse

Yet another theory about why it is that poor families are more frequently investigated for child abuse and neglect, and are more frequently found to have maltreated their children, is that poor families more frequently abuse and/or neglect their children. This disturbing theory posits that the reason there are more poor families than wealthier families in the child welfare system is because poor families simply harm their children more often than their wealthier counterparts.

The reasons that commentators have offered for why poor parents disproportionately harm their children have centered on stress. That is, it is stressful to be poor. Being poor means that a person will be worried about her finances. It means that she will have to worry about finding a job and keeping the job; it frequently means that she will have to worry about making ends meet despite her having a job. Being poor means that she will have to worry about whether she has a safe, secure place to live. It often means that she will have to worry about being sick and lacking the means to discover just what ails her and how to be cured of it. Being poor means that she will have to worry about transportation—how she will simply get from point A to point B. It often means that she will have to worry about her physical safety. Being poor means that she will have to worry about signing up for welfare benefits and dealing with the privacy intrusions that are part and parcel of receiving state assistance. Further, given the known fact that child protective agencies intervene in poor families at disturbingly high rates, being poor means that she will have to worry about having her kids taken away from her. People coping with such stresses "may not have the time or emotional capacity to provide for the basic needs of their children" (DePanfilis 2006, 35).

It may be helpful to elaborate further: Living in a poor neighborhood without resources—a neighborhood that may also have higher rates of crime and violence—is stressful. Moreover, poor communities "are also associated with less social contact or support, which is another risk factor for neglect" (DePanfilis 2006, 31).

Being a single parent is stressful: "There is less time to accomplish the tasks of the household, including monitoring and spending time with children and earning sufficient money, when there is only one parent or caregiver. Single parents often have to work outside the home, which might mean they are not always available to supervise their children" (DePanfilis 2006, 34). Thus, single parenthood is a risk factor for neglect.

The stresses associated with poverty may lead some to self-medicate with drugs and alcohol. As one would expect, substance abuse makes it difficult for a parent to care for her child properly and to attend to her child's needs. This is not to argue that the poor—poor mothers, specifically—are more likely to abuse drugs or alcohol. Several studies purport to show that wealthier mothers are just as likely to abuse substances as are poor mothers. In one frequently cited study, conducted by Ira Chasnoff (1985) during the racialized and sensationalized "crack baby" epidemic of the 1980s, researchers tested 715 pregnant women for drug use. They found no significant difference in the usage rates of illicit drugs between the poor women who sought care from a public clinic (16.3 percent) and wealthier women who sought care from private doctors (13.1 percent).[6] Thus, substance use and abuse may be as prevalent among wealthier classes as poorer classes. However, substance abuse, when combined with poverty, may put a parent at risk for neglecting her child. That is, when a person is addicted to drugs or alcohol, it is more likely that her addiction will render her unable to be an effective parent when she is poor. Thus, substance abuse, when it intersects with poverty, is a risk factor for neglect.

In sum, being poor is associated with a "set of characteristics that have been repeatedly found to be accurate predictors for child maltreatment" (Bartholet 2009, 900). These characteristics—"unemployment, single-parent status, substance abuse, and living in a significantly disadvantaged neighborhood" (900)—produce stress. And coping with stress, which is part and parcel of being poor, makes a person more at risk for child maltreatment. This may mean, quite devastatingly, that poor parents harm their children more frequently than do wealthier parents.

If it is true that poor parents actually abuse and neglect their children more frequently than do their wealthier counterparts, then it makes sense to deprive them of privacy rights in order to protect children. It makes sense to conduct the dignity-harming interventions that Medicaid requires in order for state actors to attempt to ascertain whether a particular poor mother stands at an increased risk—above the baseline risk that being indigent represents—for maltreating her child once born. It makes sense to ask all poor pregnant women to confess their propensities for abuse and neglect—to ask about their employment status, their immigration status,[7] their housing situation, their history with drug and alcohol use and abuse, their history with sexual abuse and intimate violence, their eligibility for welfare benefits. It makes sense to conduct the dignity-harming interventions that Medicaid requires even if these coerced confessions *insult* poor pregnant women—even if the result is that poor pregnant women are constructed as, and feel like, second-class citizens.

If poverty puts parents at risk for abusing and neglecting their children, and if protecting these children requires stripping parents of effective family privacy rights that shield their families from state interventions, then poverty justifies depriving (either in the moderate or strong sense) a class of people of a particular set of rights. Economic inequality serves as a justification for legal inequality.

Depriving poor mothers of privacy rights because poverty is a predictor of child maltreatment does not necessarily depend on the assumption that poor people are behaviorally or ethically flawed. One can believe that a poor parent may neglect her child because of reasons that have nothing to do her character—because she is coping with severe strains and anxieties and does not have the emotional bandwidth to attend to her child's needs. However, the moral construction of poverty makes it easier to feel comfortable with depriving the poor of rights. If they are to blame for their poverty, then they *deserve* to be inserted into a dignity-denying regime of surveillance and intervention.

Further, when we live in a system that effectively or actually denies poor individuals family privacy rights because poverty makes them more likely to maltreat their children, it creates the perception that the poor are, in fact, deficient. Family law scholar Ana Novoa (1999) captures this idea, writing that it is "disheartening" that the poor are disproportionately represented in the child welfare system:

> What is even more disheartening are the common beliefs about the poor and child protection. First, that the poor overpopulate the system because they are substance abusers and criminals. Second, that they overpopulate the system because they are intellectually and/or physically impaired. And third, using the same false reasoning, that the poor are therefore more likely than the general public to abuse or neglect their children. (17)

Thus, our legal system reinforces the truth of the moral construction of poverty for those inclined to believe in it.

The Visibility of the Poor

A final theory of the overrepresentation of poor families in the child protective system looks to the visibility of these families. This explanation assumes that poor parents engage in the same problematic (and unproblematic) behaviors as do their wealthier counterparts. However, the difference between wealthier and poor parents is that, as a direct consequence of their poverty, the lives of the poor are subject to more observation by third parties—parties who may have a legal duty to report possible child maltreatment to authorities. Because of dependence on public aid and public resources—on public transportation, public hospitals, public building inspectors, and so forth—poor families are more likely to come to the attention of child welfare agencies (Appell 1997, 584). Essentially, this theory suggests that poor families are simply more visible to the state than are wealthier families and, due to this visibility, the state has more opportunities for regulating them.

Yet, what this explanation overlooks is that the wealthy are quite visible to the state, as well. Consider historian Nancy Cott's (2002) ruminations on the present-day disestablishment of marriage, by which the state is less invested in defining and policing romantic and domestic unions:

> The formality and conformity of marriage-like arrangements matter far less in the law now than in the past, because support can be traced through cohabitation and biological parenthood. And no state needs to work through household heads to locate or govern family members: *the interweaving or intrusion of government presence in the lives of individuals through their employment, schooling, immigration, taxation, and social welfare, travel, and so on, has advanced so far that all are already in the state's grasp.* (213, emphasis added)

Cott's sense that we "all are already in the state's grasp" is critical. All of us, wealthy and poor alike, are visible to the state. If the state chooses to involve itself in the lives of the poor while refusing to do the same in the lives of those who are wealthier, we have to understand it as a *choice*—not a product of the fact that the wealthy live more private lives.

Consider as well legal theorist Martha Fineman's (1995) work unmasking the inevitability of dependency. She has shown, in compelling ways, how the state helps wealthier families manage dependency by offering them tangible support. She notes that

> [p]rivate families receive many hidden direct and indirect subsidies through tax, inheritance, marriage and other laws. Employer contributions to health and

life insurance policies are not counted as income. . . . Middle class deductions, such as that for interest paid on mortgage debt or certain child care expenses, are considered appropriate even through they remove income from the taxable pool. (2205–206)

While Fineman makes these observations to demonstrate just how society supports wealthier families—and to observe that society generally views the subsidization of wealthier families as unproblematic while it loathes any subsidization that the government offers poor families—we might note that these discrete moments where the state offers tangible support to wealthier families are also *opportunities* for the state to observe and problematize these families. Because the state does not take these moments as opportunities to regulate families, we largely fail to recognize them as opportunities for regulation. Instead, we solely understand those contacts that the poor have with state actors—in public clinic emergency rooms, with public building inspectors, in public transportation, with public benefits providers—as the stuff of visibility. Because the wealthy do not have these same encounters with these same state actors, we think that the wealthy are not visible. But, we are wrong.

The issue of testing pregnant women and new mothers for substance abuse advances the case. A number of child welfare experts agree that one form of child maltreatment that ought to bring a mother within the jurisdiction of a child protective agency is exposing a newborn to drugs (Chavkin 1992). Thus, a pregnant woman who gives birth to an infant who tests positive for controlled substances will be subject to the full gamut of child welfare services interventions (227–28).

Many studies dispute the proposition that poor mothers use drugs at higher rates than wealthier mothers. (e.g., Chasnoff 1985). Nevertheless, poor mothers are screened more frequently into child welfare agencies because of documented drug use. Scholars explain this disproportion in terms of visibility: Poor mothers are simply more visible than wealthier mothers, thereby making their drug use more visible. The argument is that, because of their poverty, poor mothers are more likely to deliver their babies in public hospitals. Public hospitals, unlike their private complements, are more likely to test infants at birth for the presence of drugs (Roberts 1991). Consequently, child protective authorities are much more likely to be alerted to poor mothers' drug use than they are to that of wealthier mothers. In sum, the argument is that, by virtue of their use of public resources (in this case, the public hospital), poor mothers are more visible and therefore more susceptible to public intervention.

But, although poor mothers' use of public hospitals might demonstrate their visibility, wealthier mothers' use of private hospitals and birthing centers *does not* demonstrate their invisibility. The only thing that would demonstrate the invisibility of wealthier mothers is if they delivered in spaces with no third-party involvement at all. They do not. In other words, when wealthier mothers give birth, they are quite visible —to their private doctors, their midwives, their doulas, and other hospital and birthing center personnel. Moreover, as healthcare workers, most states require private doctors, midwives, doulas, and hospital and birthing center personnel to report child maltreatment to government authorities (Roberts 1991).

By virtue of delivering their children with the assistance of third parties, wealthier mothers are visible to the state. Their infants could be screened for drugs just as easily as are the infants of poor mothers. Like their public counterparts, private hospitals and birthing centers could implement policies requiring the testing of all infants at birth for exposure to controlled substances. Indeed, the reasons that motivate public hospitals to test infants for their exposure to controlled substances could just as easily motivate private hospitals and birthing centers to do the same. It is good medical practice to know whether all infants—not just the poor ones—have drug metabolites in their system, as such knowledge may be therapeutically relevant. It is not in the interests of any infant—rich or poor—to release her into the unsupervised custody of a woman who may be struggling with drug or alcohol addiction. Essentially, wealthier mothers' giving birth in hospitals and birthing centers is an opportunity for the state to observe them and, if the evidence supports it, to intervene in their families. The only reason we do not recognize it as an opportunity, as the stuff of visibility, is because the state has decided not to use it as such.

The wealthy are as seen and as seeable as the poor. The crucial distinction between the two, however, is that the latter's poverty subjects them to a presumption that they are behaviorally or ethically deficient. This conclusion is buttressed by the fact that, even when wealthier families are seen in the same contexts and exhibit some of the same indicia of dysfunction as their poor counterparts, they have entirely different encounters with the state.

Roberts (2003) discusses a report on suspected cases of child abuse referred to authorities from Boston hospitals. The report found that "families who were Medicaid-eligible . . . were more likely to have their children removed. . . . Severity of condition was not significantly associated with outcome" (175). And legal scholars Daan Braveman and Sarah Ramsey (1997) discuss a study of child abuse and neglect reporting by hospitals[8] that

> found that reports were less likely when families were white or were middle- or upper-income, either because doctors do not suspect abuse or feel that they can be more effective in working directly with the parents. Families with annual incomes of $25,000 or more had better than a two-to-one chance of having their recognized child maltreatment go unreported. (462)

Consider as well a report authored by the Casey-CSSP Alliance for Racial Equity in the Child Welfare System (the Alliance) that documents and theorizes the disproportionate numbers of black children that currently are within the jurisdiction of child protective agencies (Hill 2006). The Alliance theorizes that the disproportionate representation of *black* children in the child welfare system is partially a result of the disproportionate representation of *poor* children in the child welfare system. Moreover, they theorize how poor children come to be disproportionate subjects of child welfare investigations:

> Research studies have found child maltreatment to be reported more often for low-income than middle- and upper-income families with similar presenting circumstances. For example, research has revealed that doctors are more likely to diagnose physical injuries among poor families as "abuse" and to diagnose them as "accidents" among affluent families. (18)

What these studies demonstrate is that, essentially, doctors view families through lenses that color what they see. The lenses, informed and constituted by cultural discourses, presuppose the dysfunction of poor mothers and poor parents while making no similar presupposition about their wealthier counterparts. In this way, we can understand why a doctor will see "abuse" in a poor child's arm fracture while seeing "accident" in the arm fracture of his wealthier equivalent. We can understand why a healthcare provider would feel that when bad things happen to a poor child, it is a direct consequence of parental failure while simultaneously feeling that when bad things happen to a wealthier child, it is the result of life's unpredictability. We can make sense of why a provider would feel that when a poor child is injured, it is necessary to call state authorities who can envelope the family within an apparatus that can manage the deficiencies of the family's head; yet, when a wealthier child is injured, it is unnecessary to make a similar call, as no state apparatus is needed at all—as no deficiency is at issue. That which is at issue for wealthier parents is bad luck, bad timing, or bad circumstances. That which is at issue for poor parents is bad character.

That child protective agencies assume character and behavioral deficiencies of poor mothers may explain why some scholars have noticed that the interventions that these agencies make into poor families are often not focused on removing the risks to which children may have been exposed, but rather are focused on fixing perceived flaws in mothers. Appell (1997), for one, notes that children may be removed from their parents because their families are facing homelessness and they have been forced to reside in unsafe housing. However, instead of addressing this risk by helping the parents secure safe housing, child welfare authorities attempt to reform the parents—by forcing them to attend parenting classes, secure employment, receive counseling, and live up to middle-class norms. Roberts (2002) has made a similar observation, writing that after child welfare authorities remove children from their homes, "[t]he issue is no longer whether the child may be safely returned home, but whether the mother has attended every parenting class, made every urine drop, participated in every therapy session, shown up for every scheduled visitation, arrived at every appointment on time, and always maintained a contrite and cooperative disposition" (80).

Essentially, the state is not interested in preventing specific risks from materializing. Instead, it is interested in correcting the context in which those risks exist. The idea is that if the context is improved, then it decreases the possibility that the risks will ever materialize. The context, of course, is the parents—the mothers. Improving these contexts, these women, better ensures that whatever immediate harm children were in when they came to the attention of the state will not bear out or be repeated. Thus, when a state is in the business of correcting women, child welfare authorities understandably "expand the scope of state intervention beyond child protection into every realm of mothers' lives in the name of making them good mothers" (Appell 1997, 580).

Certainly, if one proceeds from the assumption that a poor mother has done something pathological to end up as a *poor* mother, then it makes sense for child protective agencies to approach the prospect of child endangerment holistically and to focus on reforming the parent—who can either place a child in danger or save her from it. Consider the case of *In re N.M.W.* (461 N.W.2d 478 (Iowa Ct. App. 1990)), which involved the removal of a 6-year-old girl from her mother's home because of the home's unhygienic condition:

> Inside the apartment, the worker discovered the entire front room to be strewn with a collection of garbage, clothing, and other general clutter. Ashtrays were

found filled to overflowing with some knocked over. Windows and screens were missing and garbage materials were embedded in the carpet. A side closet was packed with a mixture of clutter and refuse. A bedroom was filthy with garbage. Additionally, two litters of cats were living under the bed. Apparently a total of eleven to twelve cats lived in the apartment. The same squalid conditions existed in the kitchen. The floor was filthy and the garbage container was left uncovered. The refrigerator had smeared food on parts of it and was empty of food except for milk, eggs, and ketchup. Dishes were stacked in the sink, on the counter, and on the table. Also, a cat box filled with cat excrement was found in the kitchen. In the bathroom, the cats had defecated along the bathtub and some of N.M.W.'s clothing was stuck to the feline fecal material. (479–80)

Disagreeing with the majority's approval of the child's removal, the dissent noted, "If this mother came from a higher economic level, she could do as many parents do who have neither the desire or ability to clean their houses. She could hire a cleaning service" (483). The dissent noted the economic inefficiency entailed by removing the child from the home: "A few hours of cleaning service would have cost the state less than the judicial time and court appointed attorney fees spent to litigate the adequacy of this woman's housekeeping skills through the state's appellate courts" (483).

But, if one views this case, and this mother's home, through an ideology that posits the flawed character of the poor, then one can see how providing a cleaning service to this mother would not have really eliminated the risks to which the child had been exposed. Essentially, the state of the home is not the problem. Rather, the state of the home is simply a symptom of a larger pathology—a pathology that touches on the moral character on the woman who would allow her home to arrive at such a state. One can see an argument that something has to be *wrong* with a person—morally and, perhaps, psychologically—for her to be willing to live in conditions like the ones that described N.M.W.'s mother's home. If this is the case, then hiring a cleaning service for N.M.W.'s mother and returning the child to the home is simply insufficient. While the individual risks attendant to living in an unsanitary home would have been removed, N.M.W. would still be at the mercy of a woman whose character is so compromised that she is willing to live in squalor. Only an irresponsible state could allow a child to live so precariously. Or so the argument goes.

Appell (1997) observes that children are often removed from their parents' homes because a child protective agency has found that the parents have been unable to provide adequate childcare. She writes that poor mothers "depend on informal kinship and community networks for babysitting. If a mother leaves her child with a neighbor or an aunt, rather than with a nanny or a licensed day-care center, she is considered to have neglected her child" (585–86). She theorizes that poor mothers' departures from middle-class behaviors—as when they rely on informal and uncompensated networks of family and friends for childcare—are interpreted as failures that expose their children to risk and, in turn, justify state intervention for the purpose of protecting those at-risk children. She asks the reader to contrast the image of a lone babysitter tending to a middle-class child in a quiet, neatly kept home with the "description of parenthood in a black, working-class neighborhood: 'Children are almost never alone and very rarely in the company of one other person. A crying baby is fed, tended, held, and fondled by anyone nearby. Each child seems to be the concern of each adult" (586). She theorizes that this scene would look like child neglect "to someone used to exclusive, isolated, maternal parenting" (586).

However, if one views this scene through an ideology that posits the behavioral or ethical deficiency of the poor, one can see an argument for how the mother's inability to afford childcare that mimics the care provided to wealthier children is not really the problem. One can see an argument for how simply providing the poor mother with the means to pay a babysitter who could care for the child in the mother's home will not address the real issue. One can see how the scene that Appell describes might be understood as merely a sign of a larger disorder—a disorder that implicates the moral character of the woman who would leave her child in such conditions. One can see an argument that there has to be something wrong with a person who would think it acceptable to allow her small child to be in the care of a motley group of outsiders—with no one person being able to provide an account of the child's safety and well-being at all times. Accordingly, by providing the poor mother with the means to hire a babysitter, one could eliminate the discrete risks attendant to childcare in the form that Appell describes. However, leaving the child in the custody of the poor mother would leave the child at the mercy of a woman whose judgment is so compromised that she is willing to expose her child to *chaos*. Only an irresponsible state could allow a child to live so precariously. Or so the argument goes.

Note that the moral construction of poverty justifies disruptive state interventions in poor families, as opposed to benevolent state support of poor families, under all of the theories outlined in this chapter concerning the over-representation of poor families in the child welfare system:

1. If definitions of child neglect merely describe what it means to be poor, then the state might protect children by lifting their parents out of poverty or by improving the conditions in which poverty forces them to live. However, if a poor parent's defective character has led to her poverty, then lifting parents out of poverty or improving their conditions will still leave children in the care of a person with a defective character.

2. If poverty increases the likelihood that careless behavior will result in harm, the state might protect children by, again, lifting their parents out of poverty or otherwise changing the conditions that make risk materialization more likely. However, if a poor parent's compromised character has led to her poverty, then making interventions that are less disruptive to the family will still leave children in the care of a person with a compromised character.

3. If poverty causes stress, which, in turn, interferes with a poor parent's ability to adequately care for her child, then the state might protect children by financially supporting their parents such that they can be relieved of some of the stresses that are concomitant with poverty. However, if a poor parent's dysfunctional values and ethics have led to her poverty, then relieving a parent of stress will still leave children in the care of a person with dysfunctional values and ethics.

This means that the state intervenes in poor families in the way that it does—dramatically, harshly, completely—because the moral construction of poverty counsels that rupturing families while trying to fix bad parents is the proper course of action. It is the only effective way to protect children from maltreatment.

There Has Been No Exchange of Rights for Benefits

As discussed in the previous chapter, those who are committed to traditional rights discourse resist the idea that our legal landscape could be one in which an entire class of people have been deprived of a right that our Constitution purports to endow to all persons. When confronted with the strong claim—that poor mothers have been informally disenfranchised of the family privacy rights that could prevent the privacy invasions that the state makes through Medicaid prenatal care and other public benefits programs—many traditionalists would respond with the assertion that poor mothers have exchanged their privacy rights for state assistance. The claim is that although poor mothers have privacy rights to begin with, they trade these rights for benefits.

However, it is misguided to believe that if a poor pregnant woman declined to receive welfare benefits, she would enjoy privacy and would be able to keep the state out of her family's affairs. That is, it is wrong to believe that poor mothers' and poor families' lack of privacy is contingent on their receipt of Medicaid or other state assistance. This is because the *lack of a receipt of benefits* justifies the state intervening into families in order to protect children.

What would happen if a poor, pregnant woman refused Medicaid benefits? As a *poor* woman in the United States, this would mean that she would be not be able to afford to pay out-of-pocket for medical care. Therefore, she would not be able to receive prenatal care. Interestingly, pregnant women's failure to receive prenatal care has justified state intervention in their lives. Consider *State v. McKnight* (576 S.E.2d 168 (S.C. 2003)), in which the Supreme Court of South Carolina affirmed the conviction of a cocaine-addicted woman, Regina McKnight, for homicide by child abuse after her baby died shortly after birth. The hospital had taken a urine sample from McKnight after the baby's stillbirth in order to screen it for drugs—a screening to which McKnight had consented. The reason the hospital conducted the drug test on McKnight was that the hospital's protocol required a drug screening if a patient could not establish that she had received prenatal care.

A similar protocol was at issue in *Ferguson v. City of Charleston* (532 U.S. 67 (2001)) in which the Supreme Court held that screening pregnant women's urine for drugs is a search under the Fourth Amendment when it is conducted for law enforcement purposes. In *Ferguson*, the public hospital at the center of the case had a policy establishing that any given patient's urine would be screened for cocaine if one or more of nine criteria were met. Those criteria included "[n]o prenatal care," "[l]ate prenatal care after 24 weeks gestation," and "[i]ncomplete prenatal care" (71). It is important to keep in mind that while the Court took issue with the hospital's use of the protocol for law enforcement purposes, the Court did not disapprove of the hospital's use of the protocol for other purposes—for example, to identify women who are struggling with drug addiction or poverty, such that services or public benefits may be offered to them.

What *McKnight* and *Ferguson* reveal is that a lack of prenatal care raises the suspicions of the state. While those cases involved distrust activating the criminal law arm of the state, this worry may also activate the child protective arm of the state. In other words, the state often uses a woman's inability to document that she has received prenatal care as a justification for involving her and her family in its child welfare system.

The failure to receive prenatal care is a form of "neglect," and that justifies the state's intervention into the family to "protect" the child. Indeed, as I discussed in *Reproducing Race*, Alpha Hospital, a large public hospital in New York City, had some version of this policy (Bridges 2011b). A social worker described the protocol in the following terms:

> If somebody comes . . . to deliver and it seems like they haven't been getting prenatal care here or elsewhere, what happens is that [the hospital] will hold the baby until they can get a nurse to go to the home and see if everything is taken care of there. And once they get clearance, then the lady can take the baby home. (Bridges 2011b, 48–49)

In this way, if a poor woman receives Medicaid, she is subject to privacy invasions; if she does not receive Medicaid and, therefore, prenatal care, she is still subject to privacy invasions.

Moreover, even if a poor mother manages to keep the state from intervening in her family around the time of the baby's birth, her refusal to receive Medicaid or other state-subsidized health insurance will make it difficult or even impossible for her to ensure that her child receives the ongoing medical care that he needs. Note that when a parent does not get "appropriate preventative medical or dental care for a child," does not "obtain[] care for a sick child," or does "not follow[] medical recommendations," this has been identified as a form of "medical neglect" that can justify coercive interventions by CPS (De-Panfilis 2006, 12–13). Again, if a poor mother receives Medicaid, she will be vulnerable to privacy invasions; if she does not receive Medicaid, she still will be vulnerable to privacy invasions.

What is true with respect to refusing Medicaid is also true with respect to other forms of welfare benefits. If a woman decides that she does not want to trade her ostensible family privacy rights for Supplemental Nutrition Assistance Program benefits (SNAP, which used to be called food stamps) or Special Supplemental Nutrition Program for Women, Infants, and Children benefits (WIC, which provides food for poor postpartum women, infants, and children up to age 5 who are found to be at nutritional risk), she will find it difficult to adequately feed her children. When a child is "undernourished or is repeatedly hungry for long periods of time," it is "nutritional neglect," according to child welfare experts (DePanfilis 2006, 12). As a form of physical neglect, it justifies coercive state interventions into the family by CPS.

If a woman decides that she does not want to trade her ostensible family privacy rights for cash assistance from the Temporary Aid for Needy Families program, she will find it difficult to provide basic necessities for her children. "When a child lacks appropriate clothing, such as not having appropriately warm clothes or shoes in the winter," it is "clothing neglect," according to child welfare experts (DePanfilis 2006, 12). As a form of physical neglect, it justifies coercive state interventions into the family by CPS.

If a woman decides that she does not want to trade her ostensible family privacy rights for public housing benefits, she will find it difficult to adequately shelter her children. The failure to provide shelter has been understood as a form of neglect that can justify coercive interventions into the family by CPS (Cahn 1999; Wallace and Pruitt 2012). Associated with the inability to provide shelter for a child is the inability to provide the means with which a child can bathe and brush her teeth daily. "Inadequate hygiene" is a form of physical neglect that can justify coercive interventions into the family by CPS.

If a woman decides that she does not want to trade her ostensible family privacy rights for state benefits of any kind and instead tries to make ends meet with a job, she will likely find the task to be impossible (Edin and Lein 1997; Wacquant 2009). Moreover, her effort will likely take her out of the house and away from her children, requiring her to leave them in the care of others. Parents in this situation, on occasion, have had to resort to desperate measures: "[T]wo Illinois parents were successfully prosecuted for a child abuse felony for leaving their children, aged two and nine, alone in a parked car outside their place of employment in twenty-one degree weather for about three hours" (Braveman and Ramsey 1997, 457–58). Even if such desperate measures are not prosecuted as crimes, indigent working parents may nevertheless be found to have provided "inadequate supervision"—a form of neglect that can justify coercive interventions in the family by CPS.

Essentially, poor parents will find that the families that they create are supervised, regulated, interfered with, and managed without regard to whether they receive a welfare benefit. Their lack of privacy is not a function of their dependence on state aid; it is a function of their poverty. Their poverty justifies depriving them of the means for preventing the state from interfering in their families. As long as children are there, the child protective state feels the need to be there as well.

4　Informational Privacy

When scholars invoke the term "informational privacy," they could be talking about any number of things.[1] They could be using the term to refer to the ability (or inability) to keep confidential, disaggregated, and non-commoditized the data that are generated from one's travels in both cyberspace and physical space. The following section discusses this type of informational privacy.

Or, scholars could be using the term to refer to individuals' ability to constrain the government from disclosing information that it has gathered from them. This type of informational privacy, which the Court has intimated might enjoy constitutional protection, is also explored below.

The term might also refer to an individual's interest in preventing the government from subjecting her to interrogations that demean her, degrade her, and remind her that she exists at the bottom of the social hierarchy. This was the interest that Rocio Sanchez sought to vindicate when she challenged the city of San Diego's practice of requiring persons who had applied for welfare benefits to submit to intrusive questioning—questioning that ostensibly was designed to confirm the applicant's eligibility for assistance.[2] After Sanchez submitted an application to receive benefits from CalWORKS, California's Temporary Assistance for Needy Families (TANF) program, an investigator met her at her home and questioned her about her husband and where he could be found, the date of her last encounter and communication with him, and why the couple had decided to separate (Gilman 2012). This particular interrogation ended after the investigator had searched her home, presumably for signs of her husband, and left so that he could seek more information about Sanchez from her neighbors. Sanchez encountered the investigator again several days later when she returned to clean the apartment from which she had recently moved. When she arrived, her interrogator was already there, checking the residence for evidence of her husband. He questioned her further about her husband, asking why she never had filed a domestic violence complaint and why she still spoke to his sister if the relationship had ended (Gilman 2012).

Sanchez challenged San Diego's policy on Fourth Amendment grounds—a challenge that made sense in light of the fact that CalWORKS investigators search the physical homes of beneficiaries without first securing a warrant. However, it also seems clear that the investigations that San Diego requires would be terribly debasing *even if investigators never crossed the threshold of beneficiaries' homes.*

In this chapter I explore informational privacy in its various manifestations. Here I argue that poor mothers have been deprived, either in the moderate or the strong sense, of the informational privacy right that the Court has described in its cases. I contend that this deprivation is due to the sense that, when poor mothers bear these rights, the rights will not yield the value that justifies their provision in the first instance.

Further, in this chapter I describe a type of informational privacy right that has not yet been articulated adequately in the case law and in scholarship. This right, absent compelling circumstances, would prevent the state from asking questions that serve to demonstrate that the person being interrogated is an undesired and undesirable member of the body politic. This right would prevent the state from coercing those who are the most marginalized and the most vulnerable to make confessions that might be taken to justify their marginalization and vulnerability.

Before getting to that exploration, however, we will first examine privacy invasions made possible by the digital age and investigate the possibility that poverty might allow the poor to enjoy more privacy than their wealthier counterparts. We will then consider a provocative argument that some scholars have made: Individuals who are members of subordinated populations, like poor mothers, would do better if they had *less* informational privacy.

Privacy in the Digital Age

As many law students learn in their first-year torts class, Samuel Warren and Louis Brandeis famously authored their eloquent articulation of the need for courts to recognize a common-law right to privacy after new technology—the portable camera and the penny press—threatened the individual's "inviolate personality" in ways that had not been possible before (Gray and Citron 2013b, 385–86). Just as technological advances endangered privacy at the turn of the nineteenth century, when Warren and Brandeis were moved to pen their influential *Harvard Law Review* article, technological advances endanger privacy in the present day.

Most commentators agree that the era of the "Internet of Things" has arrived (Brill 2015). This is an era characterized by the presence of interconnected networked devices—like wearable health and fitness sensors; high-tech baby monitors that can be affixed to infants to track their sleeping habits, breathing patterns, and heart rates; and "smart" appliances in homes that can detect residents' daily patterns—that are always on, are always with us and, together, ensure the total surveillance of everyday movements, habits, and intellectual endeavors (Peppet 2014).

Coexisting with the Internet of Things is the proliferation of closed-circuit television (CCTV) systems in urban areas. As a result of this phenomenon, we should expect to be recorded around 300 times a day as we undertake the banalities of our daily life (Nissenbaum 2010). Further, many localities have installed cameras on or around traffic lights to catch drivers who run red lights. The upshot is that these new technologies, together with old technologies—like phone records, swipe-card entry points, and credit cards (which, whenever whipped out to make a purchase, document the buyer's location and the time of use)—create comprehensive records of our movements through physical space, as well as our interests, likes, desires, needs, and physiological states.

In recent years, we have learned that the government has been very intentional in its efforts to create comprehensive records about its subjects. Government contractor Edward Snowden revealed that the state has been engaging in massive surveillance programs in the United States and abroad (Hu 2015). Due to his disclosures, we now know about PRISM, an antiterrorism program that may have required the most popular Internet companies—including Google, Yahoo, and Facebook—to release to the National Security Agency (NSA) private communications that their users sent (Gellman and Poitras 2013). And we now know that the NSA sought, and was granted, an order that required Verizon (and other major telephone providers) to produce "on an ongoing daily basis" call records for all telephone communications "between the United

States and abroad or wholly within the United States, including local calls" (Greenwald 2013).

As privacy scholars David Gray and Danielle Citron (2013a) report, the domestic surveillance programs that the government has implemented "seek to provide government agents with contemporary and perpetual access to details about everywhere we go and everything we do, say, or write, particularly when using or in the company of networked technologies" (64). In other words, new technologies have enabled the state to more perfectly monitor us (Balkin 2008). Although the USA Freedom Act of 2015 now imposes some limits on the collection of telecommunication metadata, it is likely that the national surveillance state will continue for the foreseeable future.

New technologies have also made it easy to bring together dispersed pieces of data. Fusion centers are what information aggregation looks like when the government tries its hand at it. It is at these sites that multiple private- and public-sector databases of information—everything from "traffic tickets, property records, motor-vehicle registrations, immigration records, tax information, public-health data, car rentals, credit reports, postal services, utility bills, insurance claims, suspicious-activity reports, and data brokers' digital dossiers" (Citron and Henry 2010, 1116)—are amassed with the hope that analysts can identify potential criminal activity and, perhaps, prevent it.

On the private sector side, information aggregation is big business. Consider Choicepoint and Acxiom, companies that collect and combine information from various databases and sell the amassed information to both private and public sector customers (Gray and Citron 2013a). These businesses make it plain that in the digital age, information is a commodity that can be bought and sold for handsome profits.

The power, and danger, of aggregated information is not simply that comprehensive dossiers can be produced about any given individual. Rather, the promise and peril of information aggregation is that it allows third parties to know individuals in a way that would be impossible if the information remained dispersed. Big Data—a term that refers to a "technology and process [that] comprise a technique for converting data flows into a particular, highly data-intensive type of knowledge (Cohen 2013, 1920–21)—is valuable in the private sector because it helps marketers and companies identify the consumers who will most desire the goods and services that purveyors are trying to sell (Strahilevitz 2013). As the consumer browses and shops online, his tastes and preferences are recorded by monitoring his clickstream. Analysts can employ "increasingly sophisticated mathematical and statistical techniques [that make] it possible to extract descriptive and predictive meaning" from the consumer's clickstream and past behavior (Nissenbaum 2010, 42). The result is that, while online, the likely consumer will be inundated with advertisements for products and services that algorithms suggest he will find desirable. If the algorithms are sufficiently predictive, he will, indeed, click on the links that have been tailored to match his preferences, and he will, indeed, purchase the goods found there.

An important part of the danger of Big Data and data mining in the private sector may be that it is so appealing. It is not the surveillance that poor mothers endure—the battery of questions about sexual history that they must answer in order to receive prenatal care or the police scrutiny that they experience when they simply walk around in their neighborhoods. Instead, the surveillance that Big Data makes possible "beckon with seductive appeal. Individual consumers willingly and actively participate in processes of modulation, seeking the benefits that increased personalization can bring" (Cohen 2013, 1916).

However, the peril that data mining poses goes beyond the surveillance of subjects. Big Data may also produce a distinct type of subject—a "predictable citizen-consumer whose preferred modes of self-determination play out along predictable and profit-generating trajectories" (Cohen 2013, 1917). This is bad for democracy, privacy scholar Julie Cohen argues. As statistical techniques get more refined, consumers will find themselves exposed *only* to information online that they find agreeable. They will navigate a cyberspace that conforms "to their political and ideological commitments" (2013, 1917). Over time, they may lose knowledge of how to engage with ideas that challenge their own, and they may lose the desire to even have this knowledge. In essence, persistent collection of data about our intellectual pursuits changes the sort of citizens that we become (Richards 2015). The society that unregulated Big Data produces is not one that is conducive to the generation of anything new—in the realm of politics, art, culture, and ideas (Cohen 2013).

The threat that Big Data poses on the public side, when the government uses data mining for its purposes, is quite different from the threat posed on the private side. When the government uses Big Data to its advantage, the result is a more perfect domination. Legal scholar Jack Balkin (2008) has made this argument, putting data mining into conversation with philosopher Michel Foucault's theory of the Panopticon. Whereas states deploying panoptic power control its subjects by "watching or threatening to watch," the state deploying the power of Big Data controls its subjects by "analyzing and drawing connections between data" (12). He elaborates:

> The problem today is not that fear of surveillance will lead people to docile conformity, but rather that even the most innocent and seemingly unimportant behaviors can increase knowledge about both ourselves and others. Normal behavior does not merely acquiesce to the state's power; it may actually amplify it, adding information to databases that makes inferences more powerful and effective. (Balkin 2008, 13)

Essentially, Big Data allows the state to produce an exquisite knowledge about subjects. This is a knowledge not just about what they *do*, but a knowledge about who they *are*. And one need not be a disciple of Foucault to understand that knowledge is power (Foucault 1990). The result is that when the state's knowledge about its subjects approximates perfection, state power approximates perfection. Governance approximates perfection. Dominance approximates perfection.

While the courts responded to Warren's and Brandeis's call to arms by recognizing a common-law right to privacy, the U.S. government has not responded in a satisfactory way to the dangers posed by life in the digital age. Consider that the European Union passed the European Data Protection Directive in 1995, updating it in 2012 with the General Data Protection Regulation (Cohen 2000). These efforts enable individuals to limit and control how their personal information is collected, managed, distributed, and used. However, the United States has not done anything that approximates the European effort to protect individual privacy. To date, the federal government has not passed a comprehensive statute that regulates what, when, where, why, and how information is collected, used, and distributed to others. Instead, at the federal level, the United States has taken a sectoral approach, regulating a particular area of activity or type of information. Individual privacy protections are passed in a piecemeal fashion whenever the political will to do so arises. For example, in 1988, Congress passed the Video Privacy Protection Act—prohibiting video rental stores from disclosing customers' rental histories—after a video rental store disclosed the rental history of Judge Robert Bork, who had been nominated to the Supreme Court, without Bork's knowledge or consent (Schwartz 1999).

There are many problems with the U.S. approach to informational privacy regulations. First, it can produce nonsensical results. For example, as informational privacy scholar Paul Schwartz notes, while businesses that rent videos are prohibited from disclosing information about a customer's rental history under the Video Privacy Protection Act, "the law contains no safeguards regarding disclosure of video content chosen from a Web site" (1999, 1633). Second, the fact that we protect individuals' informational privacy only as a *reaction* to new events or technologies means that we enjoy less privacy than we would enjoy if the state took a more *proactive* approach. Informational privacy scholar Lior Strahilevitz (2013) explains the phenomenon clearly:

> When a new technology or practice emerges to challenge existing assumptions about privacy in the United States, months or years go by before it will be restricted in any way, since the new behavior falls within a gap in our sectoral statutory framework. . . . Moreover, as disclosure becomes increasingly common, privacy norms are altered, and what may have been considered intrusive eighteen months ago is no longer deemed troubling today. (2036)

The relative lack of informational privacy protection in the United States, and the fact that cyberspace resembles a wild, wild West where laws regulating activity are few and far between, should not be interpreted to mean that these areas of modern life ought not, or do not need, to be regulated. On the contrary there *is* a general sense that we need some sort of regulation. This sense has become stronger in light of our growing realization that the failure to regulate will make it devastatingly difficult for individuals to remain inaccessible to third parties and that such inaccessibility is necessary if we are to have a competent citizenry.

Thus, the information age has robbed us of informational privacy. Importantly, some observers have argued that this is an area of life where poor people enjoy more privacy than their wealthier counterparts. They claim that this is due to the "digital divide," the fact of the poor having less access to robust networked technologies (Allard 2002). They argue that, as a consequence of this divide, the poor are less likely to be tracked and less likely to have their information gathered, aggregated, and/or commoditized.

In light of this, some have concluded that the poor and the wealthy are similarly situated. They argue that the poor are subjected to surveillance due to their living in high-crime communities with substantial police presences, their reliance on government benefits and services that collect detailed and intimate information about them, and, if they are racial minorities, their being "heavily supervised at work, watched in stores to deter shoplifting, scrutinized, and profiled when they drive their cars or walk outside their neighborhoods" (Allen

2013, 245); they argue that, on the other hand, the wealthy are equally subjected to surveillance due to their living important parts of their lives online. However, concluding that everyone—poor and wealthy alike—lack privacy, and equally so, is inaccurate and inappropriate.

We can begin by noting that, to the extent that wealthier people *lack* networked privacy, it is because, in some important sense, they have unwittingly traded their privacy for the use of networked technologies. To the extent that poorer people *possess* networked privacy, it is because their indigence precludes them from even getting to the bartering table and making the trade. It is difficult to describe networked privacy as something that the poor "enjoy" when it results from their inability to access goods that are available to the general population. A better description is that networked privacy is something that has been forced upon the poor. As such, networked privacy is hardly a privileged position. Instead, it is a state of being that reveals one's marginalization.

But, more importantly, the supposition that the poor enjoy more networked privacy than the wealthy is not correct. This is simply because the digital divide has been significantly closed. A recent study conducted by the Pew Research Center revealed that access to the Internet is practically universal. While a study conducted in 2011 showed that poorer individuals were more likely to report that their primary means for accessing the Internet was their cell phone, this had changed by 2012, when these people largely reported that they were able to access the Internet with a desktop or laptop computer (Zickuhr and Smith 2012).

Now, that which distinguishes the wealthy and the poor may no longer simply be sheer access to the Internet; rather, the distinguishing characteristic may be the *quality* of access to the Internet. Only 41 percent of those living in households with annual incomes of less than $30,000 had access to broadband, high-speed Internet at home, as compared to 89 percent of those living in households with annual incomes of more than $75,000 (Adler 2014).[3] If the time that the poor spend on the Internet is less enjoyable than the time spent by the wealthier—because it is riddled with delays, slowly loading websites, and the inability to view certain content and engage in certain activities, like downloading large files and streaming video—then it seems plain that the poor would spend less of their time in cyberspace.

Moreover, the fact of poverty changes the types of activities that one does online. While wealthier individuals go online to shop and manage bank accounts, for the poor, these types of activities are frequently financially infeasible or simply irrelevant. The only online activity in which the wealthy and poor engage in equal amounts appears to be social networking (Zickuhr and Smith 2012).

Thus, if it still makes sense to speak about a digital divide, then the term does not reference a gap in the ability to access the Internet; instead, it references a gap in the quality and the amount of the time that the poor and the wealthy spend engaging in networked activities, as well as differences in the types of activities in which the two groups engage.[4]

However, it is paramount to recognize that the poor, like their wealthier counterparts, are online. Further, the poor, like their wealthier counterparts, are being tracked while online. Yet, the poor's poverty results in their having qualitatively different online experiences than their wealthier counterparts.

We must keep in mind the reason why it is currently profitable to amass personal information in the digital age: Aggregations of information can be sold to individuals or corporations who can, in turn, use the information to market products or services to potential consumers. Modern businesses aspire to "one to one marketing,"—a "'mass customization' of products and customer relations through the gathering and manipulation of finely grained personal data" (Schwartz 1999, 1641). The object of the information trade is "the creation of individualized economies of attention, in which we are known by our preference and habits and captured by our loyalties" (Cohen 2010, 885).

But, what happens when the individuals who are tracked online are revealed not to have disposable income that they can spend on consumption? Communications scholar Joseph Turow (2012) has exposed how marketers of products identify these persons as "waste." Their wealthier counterparts, on the other hand, are identified as "targets":

> Those considered waste are ignored or shunted to other products the marketers deem more relevant to their tastes or income. Those considered targets are further evaluated in the light of the information that companies store and trade about their demographic profiles, beliefs, and lifestyles. The targets receive different messages and possibly discounts depending on those profiles. (Turow 2012, 88)

This point deserves underscoring: While both the wealthy and the poor are subjected to privacy invasions, those invasions result in the wealthy getting better deals on more coveted products; meanwhile, the poor are left to pay more for less desirable products.

In essence, the wealthy and the poor both lack networked privacy. However, that lack entrenches the poor's marginalization while it reinforces the privilege of the wealthy.[5] Moreover, if one has one eyes trained on the private sector, one will miss that the government is very much involved in the information trade as well. Indeed, "Government is an important secondary beneficiary of informational capitalism, routinely accessing and using flows of behavioral and communications data for its own purposes" (Cohen 2013, 1916). Several federal agencies—including the Federal Bureau of Investigation, the Drug Enforcement Agency, and the Department of Homeland Security—have multimillion-dollar contracts with information brokers (Cohen 2010; Nissenbaum 2010).

Further, the constitutional limits imposed on the government's ability to acquire information about individuals do not constrain the government when it gets the information from an intermediary, such as a data broker (Gray and Citron 2013b). Such is the "third party doctrine," which provides that if an individual shares information with a third party, the Fourth Amendment does not restrict the government from acquiring the information from that party; this is in contrast to the amendment's restrictions on the government if it attempted to extract the information from the individual directly (Smith v. Maryland, 442 U.S. 735 (1979)). Thus, if private actors are able to track our movements through the GPS applications installed on our cell phones, then the government, via these private actors, may be able to track our movements in this manner; and if private actors are able to divine our tastes, affinities, needs, and desires through the things that we post on social media or the websites that we visit in cyberspace more generally, then the government, via these private actors, may be able to know these things about us as well (Gray and Citron 2013b).

The significance of the government's involvement in the information trade is that its interest is *not* pecuniary—the interest that makes persons the target of the "will to know" in the private sector. Instead, the government's participation in information economies springs from its ostensible effort to ensure the safety of American people and the security of American interests. If it is true, as this book contends, that the poor figure within the country's imagination as a problematic population that desperately needs to be monitored and controlled, then we can reasonably conclude that the government's involvement in the information trade—motivated as it by an interest in managing dangerous persons and populations—imposes greater burdens on the poor relative to their wealthier counterparts.

While the wealthy may be made vulnerable by companies' desires to know their desires, the poor are made vulnerable by the government's desires to control those who have been marked as deviant. The vulnerabilities are different in kind. They may also be different in degree. Moreover, we might wonder about which vulnerability is more insidious: the one that results in an individual being surrounded by stimuli that have been filtered to match her known preferences or the one that results in an individual's exposure to state power and violence. When we compare the harm that a wealthier person experiences when she is inundated with ads for products she covets with the harm that a poor person experiences when her local fusion center identifies her as prone to "radicalization" and, consequently, the appropriate subject of enduring surveillance, we can reasonably conclude that the latter harm is much more significant (Citron and Pasquale 2011; U.S. Senate 2012).

Privacy scholar Helen Nissenbaum (2010) has made an argument that speaks to this point. She notes that some have claimed that the issue is not that information is being collected, accumulated, and shared, but that it is not being done evenly. These advocates of the "transparent society" have argued that we ought not to fight for restrictions on our being watched, but rather should fight to ensure that all are watched equally. In response, Nissenbaum writes, "Despite the liberating ring of this argument, it is misguided . . . [as we live in] a world in which power, as well as information, are unevenly distributed" (211). Nissenbaum might be read to counsel that even if we produce a society in which we all are watched equally, equal observation will not result in equal exposure. Power differentials will leave us differently exposed. Accordingly, if what this chapter suggested earlier is true—that, the digital age has allowed state power to approximate perfection, governance to approximate perfection, and dominance to approximate perfection—perfected state power, governance, and dominance will only be sought with respect to some populations. These are the problematic ones, the deviant ones, the dangerous ones. The poor, exponentially more than the wealthy, figure within political and popular discourse as the group that needs to be the object of the state's pursuit of perfect governance and dominance.

In conclusion, poverty is not a shield against informational privacy invasions in the digital age. Rather, poverty functions to produce different sources and types of informational privacy invasions. Poverty has never been a position of privilege in this country. This remains true in the digital age.

Less Privacy May Be Better

For many years, the general feeling among privacy scholars has been that our present lack of informational privacy—that is, our inability to keep sensitive information as well as personally identifiable information from third parties—was an unfortunate circumstance and one that law and society ought to take steps to avoid. Representative of this sentiment is *The Panoptic Sort*, privacy scholar Oscar H. Gandy's (1993) early critique of technologies that allow for persons and institutions to discriminate against individuals based on personal information that suggests that those individuals may not be consumers from whom sizable profits might be generated. Sociologist and legal theorist David Lyon (2003) extended Gandy's critique by observing that the discrimination that the lack of informational privacy makes possible does not simply prevent persons from becoming the objects of attention for those selling inessential goods and services. Instead, the exclusions that the lack of informational privacy and the existence of sorting technologies enabled were much more profound: "[S]urveillance today sorts people into categories, assigning worth or risk, in ways that have real effects on their life-chances. Deep discrimination occurs, thus making surveillance not merely a matter of personal privacy but of social justice" (2003, 1).

However, some have challenged the conclusion that the absence of informational privacy is injurious. Indeed, some have made the opposite case, arguing that informational privacy itself may be injurious. They assert that a state of affairs within which individuals' personal information is freely accessible to all may be preferable to one in which privacy protections exist. Strahilevitz (2013) has offered such a counternarrative about informational privacy. His first insight is that protecting privacy produces winners and losers. Some will benefit when privacy is protected, and others will benefit when privacy is not protected. The policy question then is, *Who* should benefit? Which entities should win? And will their having won produce net social welfare gains or losses? The received wisdom is that powerful actors—data brokers, corporations, the government—are the sole beneficiaries of the failure to protect privacy.

But, Strahilevitz's second insight is a challenge to that wisdom, suggesting that disadvantaged persons and groups might benefit from the absence of informational privacy. He observes that without good information about an individual, decision-makers may engage in *statistical discrimination*, which occurs when persons discriminate against an individual because he belongs to a group that is statistically more (or less) likely to engage in a behavior or possess a characteristic that the decision-maker finds problematic (or desirable) (Fang and Moro 2011). He gives the example of an employer who is averse to hiring ex-felons in a context in which black males are disproportionately represented among the population of persons who have been convicted of a felony (Strahilevitz 2008a). In an attempt to avoid hiring ex-felons, an employer may engage in statistical discrimination against black males; that is, he may not hire any individual black male candidate because the candidate belongs to a group that is statistically more likely to possess a characteristic (i.e., the status of being an ex-felon) that the employer finds problematic.

Strahilevitz proposes that the way out of the problem of statistical discrimination is not informational privacy—that is, making inaccessible information about whether or not a person is, in fact, an ex-felon. Instead, he proposes that

[i]n the information age, we should consider approaching the statistical discrimination problem from the opposite direction: using the government to help provide decisionmakers with something that approximates complete information about each applicant, so that readily discernable facts like race or gender will not be overemphasized and more obscure but relevant facts, like past job performance and social capital, will loom larger. (2008a, 371–72)

Further, he argues that access to complete information will not solely benefit those who are disadvantaged along the axis of race and/or gender, but will also benefit those who are disadvantaged along the axis of class. With full information about consumers, producers will be able to engage in price discrimination, selling their products at prices that differ according to the buyer's ability to pay. Poor persons will be able to purchase products that they otherwise may not be able to afford if their willingness to pay is greater than the cost of producing the product, but less than what the product would cost if the price were the same for everyone (Strahilevitz 2013).

The terrain that Strahilevitz imagines the poor and other subordinated groups inhabiting in the absence of informational privacy is a fairly attractive one; but, this is only true if profit and consumption are the ultimate values. However, if other values are privileged—like dignity and equality—then one can see some of the ugliness of a landscape in which complete information is freely available. Admittedly, it may seem a bit incongruous to privilege any value above profit and consumption where markets are concerned. As informational privacy scholar Cohen (2012b) rhetorically asks, "[I]sn't it exactly the point of markets to separate people from their disposable surplus in exactly the proportion that they have it?" (246–47). If that is the point of markets, then arguments in favor of informational privacy seem irrational. But, if markets are necessarily situated within social contexts that are riven with inequality, and if we are concerned about how those markets may function to exacerbate (or diminish) inequality in the larger social context, then we would not privilege profit and consumption over all else. Instead, we would allow our other concerns—about economic and social justice, for example—to determine what we think is permissible in the market and, therefore, whether and how we regulate the market.

If we are concerned about justice, we may be worried about the price discrimination that Strahilevitz uncritically lauds. Just as price discrimination may allow poor persons to access goods that would be inaccessible to them if everyone were charged the same price, the logic of price discrimination also permits charging higher prices to consumers because they are poor (Nissenbaum 2010). This is the logic that governs the provision of credit. Wealthier individuals, because they are wealthy, are charged less for credit (i.e., they are offered lower interest rates); meanwhile poorer individuals, because they are poor, are charged more for credit (i.e., they are offered higher interest rates). What this looks like on the ground is that the poor mothers who are the focus of this book pay more than their wealthier counterparts for the same good— credit. We should also keep in mind that, due to their poverty, poor mothers are more likely to use whatever credit that they can obtain to purchase essentials, like food, childcare, healthcare, housing, the gasoline that will get them to and from their low-wage jobs, and so on. The result is that *these essentials end up costing more for poor mothers.* Price discrimination facilitates this scenario, which will strike many as being inconsistent with our notions of economic and social justice.

In a similar vein, price discrimination also enables providers of goods to charge more based on the urgency of need (Nissenbaum 2010). This is the phenomenon of umbrella purveyors doubling or tripling the price of their wares during a rainstorm and locksmiths charging more for "emergency services"— services that are usually sought when people have locked themselves out of their cars and houses. "Payday loans" might be another example of the phenomenon, whereby lenders lend money to persons at high interest rates in advance of their next paycheck (Johnson 2002). Check-cashing services may be yet another example, where consumers pay large (some may say exorbitant) fees for the ability to get cash from a check almost instantly. If one understands that the product that these particular financial services sell is the conversion of a financial instrument into cash, then one can understand payday loans and check-cashing services as instances of price discrimination—that is, circumstances where prices are responsive to the urgency of the consumers' needs. For consumers whose needs are not as dire, lower prices are charged for the product. For these fortunate consumers, the price of the product—which is, again, the conversion of a financial instrument into cash—is simply the fees associated with a checking account. However, for consumers whose needs are more urgent—because they desperately need cash in advance of their next payday or because they cannot wait three to five days for a check to clear—the price of converting a financial instrument into cash is quite high. The point here is that price discrimination is not as beneficial to the poor as Strahilevitz suggests.[6]

Upon closer examination, Strahilevitz's general argument—that it is possible that a regime of completely accessible information will be better for disadvantaged groups than one in which there are informational privacy protections—rests upon some problematic assumptions about the how race and class operate in the contemporary United States. Correcting those assumptions makes one less sanguine about how subordinated groups will fare without informational privacy protections.

We can begin with Strahilevitz's claim that statistical discrimination may lead employers to refuse to hire black males due to a reluctance to hire someone with a criminal history. He writes, "Assuming the decisionmaker lacks reliable access to information about applicants' criminal records, he may choose to hire a Caucasian female over an equally qualified African American male, based on the relatively high percentage of African American males and the relatively low percentage of Caucasian females who are involved in the criminal justice system" (Strahilevitz 2008b, 1683). However, what Strahilevitz fails to acknowledge is that perhaps the reason the employer does not want to employ someone with a criminal background is *because* black males are disproportionately represented in that group. In other words, Strahilevitz assumes that the category—persons with a criminal background—can be disarticulated from race, gender, and class. But, this is untrue. Instead, the category likely has become salient for the employer, and it is likely that the category has become a *disfavored* one to the employer, because of the race, gender, and class of the persons who comprise it. To elaborate, white persons are statistically more likely to be addicted to opioids (Ford and Rigg 2014). They are also statistically more likely to use powder cocaine (Fellner 2009). However, the groups of opioid addicts and powder cocaine users are likely not ones that the employer even *contemplates* as ones from which he wants to avoid hiring when making employment decisions. And this is because of the race, gender, and class characteristics of those who comprise the group.

Moreover, we should be interested in the fact that Strahilevitz (2008b) identifies the relevant category to the employer as those with a "criminal background" (1683). Why is that the salient category for the employer? Why not a more granular category of persons with a criminal background? For instance, why not use "serial killers" as the category—a category disproportionately populated by white males (Reynolds 2007). Why does the employer wish to avoid hiring someone who may have been convicted of possessing a gram of marijuana over someone who may have committed multiple homicides? Race, class, and gender likely have something to do with it.

Additionally, Strahilevitz does not confront the fact that information, in and of itself, does nothing to diminish the power of the stories that we tell about race. If *racist* racial discourses retain their truth value, then complete information will not help racial minorities. Let's elaborate on this point: Strahilevitz (2008b) observes that white persons are more likely than black persons to be prescribed opioids, even when they have the same access to health insurance, present with the same symptoms, and report the same level of pain. He concludes that the reason for this phenomenon is doctors' belief that black patients "are abusing prescription medication, diverting medication to the black-market, overstating symptoms, or failing to comply with protocols for taking medications or recuperating" (2008b, 1697). He prescribes fully accessible information as the cure: If doctors documented whether or not patients were actually engaging in these problematic practices in their medical records, and "[if] the contents of these medical records were easily transferred from one physician to other physicians likely to encounter a particular patient, then doctors would not need to engage in statistical discrimination on the basis of race and other problematic proxies" (2008b, 1697).

However, a comprehensive medical record with a detailed account of a black patient's benign history with opioids—a record that shows that he has never abused prescription medications, has never diverted medications to the black market, and so forth—does not challenge narratives that declare that black people are simply the *type of people* who abuse prescription medications and divert medications to the black market, and so forth. This is a narrative about propensity, inclination, and culture. If this racist narrative is not challenged, then black patients will remain the *type of people* who abuse prescription medications. And if black patients are these types of people, then a doctor acts reasonably when she refuses to prescribe opioids to them—even when their medical records reveal that they have never engaged in the problematic behavior. Racist discourses about black patients counsel that patients with an unblemished medical record simply not have engaged in the problematic behavior *yet.*

The panoptic regime in which poor mothers live—a regime that is devoid of informational (and other) privacy protections—is precisely the regime that Strahilevitz describes as desirable. What he misses is that the regime is demeaning. The pursuit of information about poor mothers is based on the supposition that they, because of the fact of their poverty, are presumptively incompetent mothers. Like providing information demonstrating that a black patient has not abused opioids *yet,* more information about an individual poor mother does not change the baseline supposition that poor mothers, as a group, are presumptively incompetent.

It bears underscoring that the pursuit of full information about an individual poor mother would not even be attempted without the baseline supposition about the group to which she belongs. This is why wealthier mothers are not subjected to the panoptic regime; they belong to a group whose competence is assumed. As such, Strahilevitz misses that a world without informational privacy protections would be one in which persons belonging to disadvantaged groups—racial minorities, the poor—would have to give as much information about themselves as possible in order to show that the problematic, unchallenged assumptions about the groups to which they belong do not describe them as individuals. They would have to divulge information to establish that they are exceptions to the rules. Meanwhile, persons belonging to advantaged groups would have the privilege of divulging no information about themselves, allowing others to assume that the unproblematic, unchallenged assumptions about the groups to which they belong also describe them as individuals. This is a world where the subordinated would have to endure complete exposure, while the privileged would have the luxury of remaining shielded. This is hardly a just world.

The Value of Informational Privacy

If poor mothers do not enjoy informational privacy, then we ought to ask why. This book contends that the answer to this question can be found in the moral construction of poverty. In other words, scholars have long argued that informational privacy generates value. This value justifies protecting informational privacy—whether that protection is in the vehicle of a constitutional right or otherwise. This section explores various values that informational privacy is thought to generate and argues that poor mothers are not given informational privacy because their enjoyment of it is thought to produce no value.

Informational Privacy Facilitates Decisional Autonomy

There is a close relationship between informational privacy and an individual's ability to make personal decisions without intervention from third parties. As such, when an individual enjoys informational privacy, she can enjoy decisional autonomy. Conversely, when an individual's informational privacy is nonexistent or jeopardized, her ability to make autonomous decisions is similarly diminished.

The Court recognized the simultaneity of informational privacy and decisional autonomy in *Whalen v. Roe* (429 U.S. 589 (1977)), the first occasion for the Court to consider whether a right to informational privacy is buried somewhere in the Due Process Clause. The case concerned a law that allowed the New York State Department of Health to keep a centralized computer file that contained all of the names and addresses of persons who had been prescribed certain drugs. These drugs, which the regulatory framework at issue called "Schedule II drugs," were those for which there were both lawful and unlawful markets. The purpose of the law was to help the state monitor the distribution of the drugs so as to prevent them from being diverted into illegal channels.

A group of patients who regularly received prescriptions for Schedule II drugs challenged the law. They argued that the statute illegitimately burdened their "individual interest in avoiding disclosure of personal matters"—a nascent right to informational privacy (599). They claimed that this right was burdened by the possibility that a state employee with access to the centralized computer file or with the responsibility for maintaining the security of the file may intentionally or negligently cause the names contained therein to become public. The Court disagreed, noting that the information was kept in a non-networked database in a secured case and that, consequently, there was no meaningful risk of public disclosure. However, the Court did state that if there was a real risk of public disclosure, the law might raise constitutional questions.

Interestingly, the plaintiffs also argued that because the statute burdened their claimed informational privacy right, it also functioned to burden their right to privacy-qua-decisional autonomy. The Court described this argument:

> The mere existence in readily available form of the information about patients' use of Schedule II drugs creates a genuine concern that the information will become publicly known and that it will adversely affect their reputations. This concern makes some patients reluctant to use, and some doctors reluctant to prescribe, such drugs even when their use is medically indicated. It follows . . . that *the making of decisions about matters vital to the care of their health is inevitably affected by the statute.* (Whalen v. Roe, 429 U.S. 589, 600 (1977); emphasis added)

The Court ultimately upheld the statute—but not because it denied the connection between informational privacy and decisional autonomy. Instead, it found that because the collected information was protected from unwarranted disclosure, the plaintiffs' decisional autonomy also was sufficiently protected.

Scholars have observed that a connection exists between informational privacy and decisional autonomy about matters concerning reproduction, what people working in the field call *reproductive privacy*. For example, Jerry Kang (1998) has observed that

> information privacy—e.g., keeping the fact of pregnancy to oneself—can create the breathing space away from familial or societal censure necessary for decisional privacy—e.g., to choose whether to have an abortion. Or, in reverse, consider how decisional privacy shields an individual from disclosing to the state her justifications for exercising some choice, thereby fortifying her information privacy. (1203–204)

The Court once struck down a statute that burdened the informational privacy interests of women who had undergone abortions because it functioned to burden women's ability to make autonomous decisions about having an abortion. *Thornburgh v. American College of Obstetricians and Gynecologists* (476 U.S. 747 (1986)) involved a challenge to the Pennsylvania Abortion Control Act, which imposed significant reporting requirements on facilities that provided abortion services. Abortion providers had to supply a report to the state that included extensive information about women who had undergone abortions, including their name, age, race, marital status, number of prior pregnancies, and method of payment. In striking down the statute, the Court determined that it was insignificant that the collected information was not to be part of the public record. Instead, it emphasized that

> Pennsylvania's reporting requirements raise the specter of public exposure and harassment of women who choose to exercise their personal, intensely private, right, with their physician, to end a pregnancy. Thus, they pose an unacceptable danger of deterring the exercise of that right, and must be invalidated. (767–68)

The Court reasoned that the burden on an individual's decisional autonomy that results from the collection of her personal information justified prohibiting the collection of that information—even when the information is protected from unwarranted disclosure. A commentator observed that the Court refused to accept this very same analysis in *Whalen*: "In reaching the decision, the [*Thornburgh*] Court seemed to rely on the reasoning rejected in *Whalen*, stating that the threat of public disclosure and the resultant 'chilling' effect on a patient's behavior were enough to reject the statute" (Bodger 2006, 598).

So, how does this help us to understand why poor mothers are denied informational privacy? Well, poor mothers are also denied reproductive privacy, as Chapter 5 of this book explores. Thus, if informational privacy facilitates reproductive privacy, then denying poor mothers informational privacy helps the state and society accomplish the end of ensuring that poor mothers cannot be sovereigns over their reproductive bodies and lives. If the value of informational privacy is that it allows individuals to control their reproductive destiny, then allowing poor mothers to realize that value is ultimately counterproductive insofar as society does not *want* poor mothers to control their reproductive destiny. Denying poor mothers informational privacy helps to wrest control over reproductive decision making away from poor mothers and helps to give that control to a state that endeavors to supervise and manage their fertility.

Informational Privacy Prevents Social Control

Neil Richards and other scholars have argued that informational privacy creates the conditions for individuals to participate in activities that they might want to shield from third-party observation (Kang 1998; Richards 2015). Without privacy, individuals may not engage in these activities. Indeed, this is the reason why society is largely comfortable with denying privacy in all of its myriad forms (including informational privacy) to incarcerated persons and, to a lesser extent, formerly incarcerated persons who have been released on parole. Society feels that it has good reason to believe that, if given privacy, these categories of persons will do things that they ought not to do—things that are crimes or that otherwise threaten the health and safety of others (Kang 1998). Accordingly, we deny them privacy for the express purpose of preventing them from participating in these activities. We deny them privacy in order to control them.

Therein lies the second justification for respecting individuals' privacy: for those categories of persons from whom we do not presume criminality—those whom we assume will contribute positively to the body politic—we believe there is a value in allowing them to engage in activities that they would prefer to shield from third-party observation. We believe it is valuable to create the conditions of possibility for their participation in behaviors that are unpopular or countercultural. Thus, we protect informational privacy because we *want* people to experiment with alternative pursuits and thoughts. We believe that this experimentation is a social good. As Cohen (2000) describes it, pervasive monitoring will

> incline choices toward the bland and the mainstream. The result will be a subtle yet fundamental shift in the content of our character, a blunting and blurring of rough edges and sharp lines. But rough edges and sharp lines have intrinsic, archetypal value within our culture. . . . The condition of no-privacy threatens . . . to chill the expression of eccentric individuality. (1425–26)

Philosopher Ruth Gavison (1992) has written that a "society without privacy . . . likely will not . . . have robust individuals who are willing to experiment, dare, and challenge their governments and the positive morality of their societies" (456). Moreover, this is the hallmark of totalitarian governments: These are governments that deny their citizens privacy *because* they do not want them to experiment, dare, and challenge their governments and the positive morality of their society. Thus, denying privacy is a mechanism for social control. Making otherwise private behaviors known to third parties enhances "the power of social norms, which work more effectively when people are being observed by others in the community" (Solove 2006, 493).

And so it should become clearer why informational privacy is denied to poor mothers. We, as a society, want to control them. We want to prevent them from experimenting with behaviors that are unpopular or countercultural, as we do not trust that anything valuable will result from their experimentation. Indeed, powerful discourses in society claim that the reason why they are *poor* mothers and poor *mothers* is because they have rejected social norms and the majority's morality. Thus, if denying privacy is a technique for increasing the power of those social norms—if denying privacy is a technique for forcing individuals to conform to the dictates of the majority's morality—then denying poor mothers privacy is a mechanism for bringing a problematized segment of society into conformity.

In essence, scholars have theorized that the value of privacy is that it allows those who otherwise obey social mores to experiment with the margins of thought and behavior. Insofar as we deny privacy to poor mothers, it is because society believes that there is no value in allowing those who *disobey* social mores to experiment with these margins. To many, it not only is valuable, but imperative, to bring those disobedient sectors of society away from the margins of thought and behavior and toward the mainstream.

Interestingly, privacy scholar Daniel Solove (2002) theorizes that because denying privacy has the effect of discouraging and potentially eradicating thoughts and behaviors, it is fair to describe our society as one that gives privacy to practices that we value. He writes, "When we state that we are protecting 'privacy,' we are claiming to guard against disruptions to certain practices. Privacy invasions disrupt and sometimes completely annihilate certain practices" (1129). Thus, identifying those practices that we surround with a shield of privacy is an exercise in cartography to the extent that it allows us simultaneously to map those practices that we deem to be socially valuable. What, then, is revealed by the fact that we do not surround poor mothers' lives with a shield of privacy? It reveals that we do not believe their lives to be socially valuable. We do not believe that their lives contribute to the greater social good.

Informational Privacy Protects Human Dignity

Lastly, some scholars have theorized that the value of privacy, including privacy in its informational dimensions, is that it protects human dignity. We might be reminded that the grandfathers and architects of modern privacy torts, Warren and Brandeis (1890), argued that the right to privacy derived from "inviolate personality" (205). Commentators subsequently have claimed that what Warren and Brandeis meant by "inviolate personality" was, simply, dignity. Writes philosopher Ferdinand Schoeman,

> "Inviolate personality" is taken to include . . . notions such as individual dignity and integrity, personal uniqueness, and personal autonomy. . . . Respect for these aspects of human dignity is the basis for according to individuals the right to determine to whom their thoughts, emotions, sentiments, and tangible products are communicated. (1984,18)

Consider here Cohen's (2012b) ruminations on the purchase of informational privacy. She defines privacy as imperfect knowledge, a "condition in which there remain important and durable gaps in the information about oneself that is accessible to others" (244). She calls this "semantic discontinuity," defined as the "opposite of seamlessness" and present where there are "inconsistencies within systems of meaning" (Cohen 2012a, 239). She observes that Big Data, data mining, and other technologies facilitate the closing of gaps in the information that we have about persons and make semantic discontinuity elusive. She is right. But, it is also true that cruder methods for extracting information——that is, the consultations with social workers to which poor mothers must submit when they receive state benefits, the relationships with child protective services (CPS) caseworkers that poor mothers must have when they are low-wage laborers and can only earn enough to provide for their children in ways that amount to "child neglect"—also make semantic discontinuity elusive. In other words, cruder methods for extracting information also make it difficult to create gaps in the knowledge about oneself that is available to others.

Moreover, while cruder methods of extracting and amassing information are quite effective in completing the knowledge that third parties have about the poor mother, she must also endure the government's use of high-tech methods of acquiring information. Consider the tracking of poor persons' food purchases through Electronic Benefits Transfer (EBT) cards distributed as part of the Supplemental Nutrition Assistance Program. Consider close-circuit television, the monitoring of persons through physical space, and the *greater* attention one can expect to be paid to monitoring *poor* persons through physical space. Cohen writes that

> [w]hile it might seem tempting, for example, to calibrate disability benefits based on the precise level of need, or to engage in real-time monitoring of Medicaid recipients' food purchases to supervise nutritional choices, a liberal democratic society cannot simply deploy surveillance technologies to close the gap unfilled and unfillable by perfect technologies of justice. (2013, 1931)

She writes that to deploy these surveillance technologies is not "dignifying" (1931).

The previous chapter argued that class frequently operates to make the dignity of those who are poor easy to discount. This is not to argue that classism makes it *impossible* to recognize the dignity interests of those without

class privilege. Rather, this is to argue that classism makes it easy to priori-
tize other interests—like the interest in protecting children from impoverished
(but not necessarily neglectful) parents and the interest in protecting the public fisc—over poor people's interest in maintaining their dignity *despite* their
poverty. This is especially true when our particular brand of classism in the
United States is informed by, and is a product of, narratives that blame the
impoverished for their impoverishment. These narratives go a long way toward
explaining why our present is one where poor mothers' private lives have been
constructed as matters that are in the public interest.

The Constitutional(?) Right to Informational Privacy

The Court has thrice wrestled with the question of whether the Constitution
protects a right to informational privacy, and it has answered with a resounding "maybe." The first occasion for the Court to consider whether this right
is buried somewhere in the Due Process Clause was *Whalen v. Roe* (429 U.S.
589, 600 (1977)). As discussed above, the case concerned a law that allowed the
New York State Department of Health to keep a centralized computer file that
contained all of the names and addresses of persons who had been prescribed
certain drugs. Importantly, the Court in *Whalen* never explicitly held that the
Fourteenth Amendment actually contained a right to informational privacy. It
simply held that, even if an individual's interest in avoiding disclosure of personal information rose to constitutional significance, the New York law at issue
in *Whalen* did not violate that hypothetical right.

Nevertheless, the Court was open to the possibility that the Constitution
protected an individual's interest in keeping her personal information from
becoming known to third parties, and it was well aware that this interest was
threatened by the "accumulation of vast amounts of personal information in
computerized data banks or other massive government files" (605). However,
the Court noted that statutes or regulations prohibiting disclosure of personal
information usually protected that interest. Thus, it would not have occasion to
definitively decide whether the Constitution actually protected a right to informational privacy until it was presented with a law that required collecting personal information without also shielding that information from unwarranted
disclosure. Until that case presented itself, the right to informational privacy
would remain hypothetical.

The Court's second occasion to wrestle with whether there is a constitutional basis for an informational privacy right came just months after the de-

cision in *Whalen*.[7] In *Nixon v. Administrator of General Services* (433 U.S. 425 (1977)), former President Nixon challenged a law that ordered the seizure of 42 million pages of documents and 880 tape recordings that had been generated during his time in office. Archivists were to screen the materials with the expectation that items that were purely personal would be returned to Nixon while items that had some historical value would be preserved. Nixon argued that the screening process amounted to a violation of his right to informational privacy—a right that the Court in *Whalen* had just recently implied existed. The *Nixon* Court disagreed.

In the course of disagreeing, however, the Court never stated clearly whether this implied right to informational privacy did, in fact, exist. Taking a page from the *Whalen* playbook, the Court argued that even if the Constitution did protect this hypothetical right, the challenged law would not violate it, as there were ample precautions in place designed to prevent the unwarranted disclosure of Nixon's private information.[8] If the law did not contain these safeguards, only then would the Court have the opportunity to decide whether the Constitution required them—that is, whether there existed a right to information privacy that demanded that private information that the government collects either be protected from undue dissemination or go uncollected altogether. The law at issue in *Nixon* did not allow the Court to answer that question.

The third and last time the Court addressed the question of whether the Constitution contains a right to informational privacy was in *National Aeronautics and Space Administration v. Nelson* (562 U.S. 134 (2011)). In this case, a group of people who worked as contract employees for NASA challenged as an invasion of their (still only hypothetical) informational privacy right intrusive background checks that they were forced to undergo as a condition of their employment. The checks sought information about whether the employees had ever been in treatment or counseling for drug addiction and asked "employers, schools, landlords, and references" whether they knew of any "'adverse information' concerning the employee's 'violations of the law,' 'financial integrity,' 'abuse of alcohol and/or drugs,' 'mental or emotional stability,' 'general behavior or conduct,' or 'other matters'" (141–42). The Court upheld the background checks without deciding, once and for all, whether the Constitution actually contained a right to informational privacy. Rather, it merely "assume[d], without deciding, that the Constitution protects a privacy right of the sort mentioned in *Whalen* and *Nixon*" (138).

As *Whalen* and *Nixon* emphasized that the laws at issue in those cases contained protections that guarded against the unwarranted disclosure of the collected information, the Court in *Nelson* thought it quite significant that the Privacy Act of 1974 regulated the information collected pursuant to the NASA background checks.[9] The Court believed that the act, which requires that the government obtain written consent before disclosing any information to third parties and which imposes criminal penalties for unauthorized dissemination, "provided adequate privacy protection" and thereby negated the necessity of the Court reaching the million dollar question: Does the Constitution constrain the government from collecting private information if it does not also make efforts to prevent third parties from accessing that information without meaningful consent?

Although the Supreme Court has never announced definitively that a right to informational privacy exists, the circuits have trudged ahead and recognized the right. Because the Court has not offered much help in delineating the contours of the right, the right that the circuits have recognized has assumed a variety of different forms. In some circuits, burdens on the right to informational privacy are reviewed with an intermediate scrutiny, while in others they are reviewed with a strict scrutiny ("Leading Cases" 2011). Some circuits vary the level of scrutiny with the nature of the information involved. Thus, laws that implicate extremely sensitive information are reviewed with a more rigorous scrutiny than laws implicating information that is less intimate. Moreover, there are splits in the circuits on the question of what type of information triggers constitutional protection. Some circuits only protect the privacy of information that implicates fundamental rights; meanwhile, other circuits protect any information about which the individual has a reasonable expectation of privacy.

Keep in mind that all of these tests involve a balancing of interests: The individual's interest in the nondisclosure of her information must be weighed against the government's interest in collecting the information. And it is imperative to recognize that when courts are engaged in comparing the relative weight of interests, they are operating within a culture. That culture informs courts' appreciation of the weight of the competing interests. Consequently, we should not be surprised if we see courts—embedded in a society featuring many narratives blaming poor mothers for their indigence and problematizing their insistence upon bearing children—failing to give much weight to the interests of poor mothers in keeping their private information private. When societal discourses preclude the possibility that courts will give any significant value to poor mothers' interests, a test requiring judges to weigh poor mothers' interests against governmental ones is an overdetermined one. In other words, a right that leads to the invariable sanctioning of government power is hardly a right.

Williams v. Berry (977 F.Supp.2d 621 (S.D. Miss. 2013)), a recent district court case from Mississippi, is instructive. The case concerned the Mississippi Child Care Payment Program, a federally funded program that subsidizes indigent parents' childcare costs. Prior to 2013, parents could simply sign their names on a sheet at childcare facilities when they dropped off and picked up their children; the sheets provided documentation of parents' use of childcare services. However, in 2013, the Mississippi Department of Human Services began to require instead that beneficiaries of the program submit to a finger scan whenever they dropped off and picked up their children.

A beneficiary of the program, Elizabeth Williams, challenged the requirement that she submit to twice-daily finger scanning as an infringement on her right to informational privacy. She argued that because only beneficiaries of the Mississippi Child Care Payment Program were required to use the finger-scanning technology, her status as a program beneficiary was disclosed to all those around her whenever she used the technology upon dropping off and picking up her child. The court, unsurprisingly, failed to appreciate the significance of her interest in keeping private her status as a welfare recipient. It upheld the constitutionality of the finger scans, holding that they were not searches under the Fourth Amendment. And in response to the plaintiff's claim that the finger scans violated her Fourteenth Amendment right to informational privacy, the court observed that the Fourteenth Amendment prevented *governmental* disclosure of sensitive data. "The fact that others may observe Williams . . . being fingerscanned and deduce therefrom that she is a recipient of government assistance does not constitute *government* disclosure of personal information" (637).

But, the interest that Williams asserted ought not to be dismissed. No narrative exists in our culture that commends, or even defends, poor mothers who need to rely upon public benefits for their survival. Instead, society swirls with narratives about their irresponsibility, their blameworthiness, and their desire to exploit the government programs that are designed to sustain them. Williams sought to avoid being identified with that disparaged group. She sought the luxury of having others assume her moral equivalence to them and not assume her bad character, laziness, and greed. Although she had been damned within cultural and political discourses, she wanted to avoid the broadcasting of her damnation to those in her immediate vicinity. The court failed to appreciate the significance of that interest.

One should also bear in mind that while the court did not, and likely could not, understand the magnitude of a poor mother's interest in keeping private her status as a welfare recipient, the court had no issue at all in understanding the magnitude of the *government's* interest in deterring fraud. Denying the claim that the finger scan was a Fourth Amendment search, the court wrote with conviction about the weight of the government's interest in protecting its fisc from exploitation. It noted that the finger-scanning requirement was a means of ensuring that when the government issued a payment for childcare services provided, the child was actually in attendance at the facility that day. And it noted that the government's interest in "ensuring that public funds are used for their intended purpose" (Williams v. Berry, 977 F.Supp.2d 621, 634 (S.D. Miss. 2013)) has long been recognized as a legitimate one. It looked to the Court's opinion in *Wyman v. James*, in which it upheld the requirement that all AFDC beneficiaries in New York submit to searches of their homes, for the proposition that state agencies that administer welfare programs like the one at issue in *Williams v. Berry* (2013) fulfill "a public trust." It quoted *Wyman* at length:

> The State, working through its qualified welfare agency, has appropriate and paramount interest and concern in seeing and assuring that the intended and proper objects of that tax-produced assistance are the ones who benefit from the aid it dispenses. Surely it is not unreasonable, in the Fourth Amendment sense or in any other sense of that term, that the State have at its command a gentle means, of limited extent and of practical and considerate application, of achieving that assurance. One who dispenses private charity naturally has an interest in and expects to know how his charitable funds are utilized and put to work. The public, when it is the provider, rightly expects the same. It might well expect more, because of the trust aspect of public funds, and the recipient, as well as the caseworker, has not only an interest but an obligation. (Williams v. Berry (citing Wyman), 977 F.Supp.2d 621, 634–35 (S.D. Miss. 2013))

The court's ode to the state's interest in guarding its funds from exploitation is quite noteworthy. It is a bit perverse, and telling, that the court is able to appreciate the significance of interests possessed by the "state"—a nonhuman, albeit anthropomorphized entity—while failing to appreciate the significance of interests possessed by living, breathing women. The court is able to empathize with an entity that actually does not have feelings, but unable to empathize with actual, feeling people. This speaks volumes about the denigrated, indeed dehumanized, status of poor mothers within society.

Finally, as explained above, if a state entity that has collected information has protections in place that are designed to prevent the information's unwarranted disclosure, then any right to informational privacy that may or may not exist likely is not infringed. The Federal Privacy Act of 1974 referenced in *Nelson*, which generally proscribes the disclosure of information that is collected by the federal government, served in that case to constitute the protection from unwarranted disclosure that helped the information-collection scheme at issue to survive constitutional scrutiny. In fact, the Privacy Act will also be the protection from disclosure implicated in any challenge to the information-collection schemes that Medicaid and TANF implement (Gilman 2008).

Crucially, the Privacy Act contains exceptions that allow for the nonconsensual disclosure of collected information. Intriguingly, one of those exceptions "allows disclosure to other jurisdictions for law enforcement" (5 U.S.C. § 552a). The result of this exception is that when a population is imagined to be inclined toward criminality, then that population exists in a state of exception under the Privacy Act. Undeniably, welfare beneficiaries are one of those populations thought to be comprised of criminal elements (Gustafson 2011). The irony should be apparent: The act that provides protection from the disclosure of information, and thereby saves the constitutionality of information-collecting regimes, itself provides for disclosure.

Of course, the Privacy Act and the statutory right to informational privacy that it creates have substance for those who are not thought to be relevant to law enforcement—those who are not imagined to engage in criminality in the absence of vigilance. But, for poor mothers receiving welfare benefits, the right to informational privacy, as enfeebled by the Privacy Act's law enforcement exception, offers no protection.

The inherent weakness of poor mothers' ostensible informational privacy right is demonstrated from time to time. Legal scholar Wendy Bach (2014) writes of "several instances in which welfare agencies have collaborated with law enforcement to apprehend individuals for reasons utterly unrelated to their public benefits" (333–34). She writes about a program called Operation Talon, in which

> Food Stamps offices collaborate with law enforcement to apprehend individuals with outstanding warrants. After a computerized match is run between the

> relevant database, individuals receive a pretextual letter asking them to come
> in to discuss an issue concerning their benefits. When they arrive, they are met
> by law enforcement and arrested. Between 1996 and September 20, 2009, 14,645
> individuals were arrested under this program. (334)

Indeed, a right against the disclosure of information that cannot protect against
the disclosure of information is hardly a right.

The Interest in Preventing
the Collection of Private Information

The Court as yet has refused to rule definitively on whether the Constitution
protects an individual's interest in preventing the government from collecting
private information when the government cannot guarantee that the information will not end up in unauthorized hands. That is how the Court framed the
issue in *Whalen* and then again in *Nelson*. And that is how the circuits have
formulated their various rights to information privacy. But, this framing of
the issue may miss the concerns that actually motivate people to seek to prevent the government from collecting their private information. That is, many
times, individuals who have challenged laws that require them to divulge certain information—whether that information is sensitive or not—are not simply concerned about that information landing in the wrong hands; rather, they
have been offended by the fact that the government poses the question in the
first place. In other words, they want to prevent the government from collecting certain information because, even if no unauthorized person ever gains
access to the information, it is degrading when the government asks the question and collects the information in the first instance. Further, what makes a
pursuit of information degrading does not turn on whether the information
being pursued can be linked back to a specific individual or whether it is sensitive; rather, the degrading character of the pursuit turns on the assumptions
made about the person that are motivating the interrogation.

Relevant to this claim are the plaintiffs in *Nelson*, who, you may recall, ob-
jected to a background check that involved the government asking whether
they had ever been in treatment or counseling for drug addiction and asking
"employers, schools, landlords, and references" whether they knew of any "'adverse information' concerning the employee's 'violations of the law,' 'financial
integrity,' 'abuse of alcohol and/or drugs,' 'mental or emotional stability,' 'general behavior or conduct,' or 'other matters'" (National Space and Aeronautics
Administration v. Nelson 2011, 141–42).

As discussed above, the Court in *Nelson* noted *Whalen*'s emphasis on regulations that imposed duties on the government to safeguard against the unwarranted disclosure of the information collected and, finding that the Privacy Act adequately provided those safeguards, rejected the plaintiffs' challenge. But, the Court's focus on the fact that existing safety measures protected against the undue disclosure of the employees' private information might have missed the point entirely. The point may have been the umbrage that persons justifiably take when they are asked certain questions. Indeed, in his concurrence, Justice Scalia actually got the point. He understood that the *Nelson* plaintiffs were not concerned about the possible unwarranted disclosure of their private information once collected. Instead, they were concerned about the collection of that information in the first place.[10]

Consider a story told to me by "Sia," a pregnant black patient who was receiving prenatal care from the obstetrics clinic of a large public hospital in New York City when I met her.[11] I had asked her about her experiences receiving Medicaid-subsidized healthcare prior to her pregnancy. She told me that, despite the fact that she had always had Medicaid and, therefore, had always been able to visit the doctor regularly, she only had gone to the doctor when she felt very ill. I asked her why she had she forgone the opportunity to receive consistent healthcare when it was available to her. She responded with the following story:

> One time, I was not feeling well. I had been coughing, and the cough was not going away. And whenever I laid down to sleep or whatever, I felt like it was hard to breathe. So, I decided to go to the doctor to get checked out—to make sure that nothing really serious was going on. So, I make the first appointment that was available, and it is with this doctor who I had never been to before. The nurse takes me to the room and tells me to take off my clothes and put on a hospital gown. Fine. So, I'm sitting there on the examining table—cold, because it's always cold in doctors' officers. And the doctor walks in—white lady. And she takes one look at me. . . . You know, I have a lot of tattoos. I have them everywhere. They're beautiful. They're art, you know. And I paid a lot of money for them. [laughs] Anyway, the doctor walks in, takes one look at me, sees the ink on my arms and asks me, "Did the person who did your tattoos use clean needles?" And I'm like, "What the fuck?" [laughs] Why in the world would you ask me something like that? [laughs] What about me makes you think that I would get tattooed with dirty needles? In some back alley. . . . Is it because I'm black? Because I'm on Medicaid? I look like I've been in a jail? If she had actually paid attention to what she was looking at, she would have seen that [the

tattoos] are very high quality. They're not the type of thing that you would get if you went to somebody who's not using sterilized needles.

Sia was not concerned about the possibility that third parties would access the information that her doctor collected about her tattoos. Instead, she was offended by the fact that her doctor had even asked the question. The question revealed her doctor's perception of her. It revealed that her doctor perceived Sia as someone who *might* have gone to an unlicensed, back alley tattoo artist. It revealed that her doctor perceived Sia as someone completely different from how Sia perceived herself—a woman adorned with beautiful, expensive art.

With this in mind, one can see a different interest asserted in *Nelson* than the one the Court identified. One can see how the plaintiffs might have experienced as *insults* questions about drug addiction, financial well-being, mental health, and criminal pasts. The questions might have revealed their employers' perceptions of them as people who *might* have used drugs, been financially unstable, struggled with a stigmatized mental illness, and engaged in criminal or other problematic activity.

That the plaintiffs might have been insulted by these perceptions is strengthened by the fact that they were *not* poor people. The Court notes that among the employees who challenged the background checks were "the lead trouble-shooter for . . . th[e] $568 [million] Kepler space observatory, the leader of the program that tests . . . all new technology that NASA will use in space, and one of the lead trajectory designers for . . . the Galileo Project and the Apollo Moon landings" (National Space and Aeronautics Administration v. Nelson 2011, 151). By all accounts, the plaintiffs in *Nelson* were successful, highly trained people with great jobs. It likely was insulting to them that the government would insinuate that these highly trained scientists *might* be drug-abusing criminals with mental health issues. The right to informational privacy that they asked the government to recognize would have protected them from those insults.

Still, even if one properly recognizes the interest that the employees sought to protect, it is possible that one will arrive at the conclusion at which the Court arrived and believe that the background checks are constitutional. As the Court notes, the government has an interest in "ensuring the security of its facilities and in employing a competent, reliable workforce" (150). The government's interest in hiring "reliable, law-abiding persons who will 'efficiently and effectively' discharge their duties" (152) may outweigh the individuals' interest in avoiding having degrading questions posed to them. Nevertheless, it is important to recognize the latter interest as one that individuals have—and one that, in some cases, ought to override the government's interest in asking demeaning questions.

Significantly, the interest in preventing governmental collection of certain information, independent of any worry that others may access the collected information, is one that is more valuable to those who are most subordinated in society. This is an argument that poverty law scholar Michele Gilman (2012) has made quite convincingly in her scholarship. She writes that the web of informational privacy protections that U.S. law provides—constitutional, statutory, and common law—defends the interests of those with class privilege, as the middle and upper classes are more likely to be affected negatively by the misuse of data. However, while the poor might also be concerned about the misuse of their private data, they might be more concerned with "the humiliating procedure[s] by which personal information is gathered" (1418). She notes that no area of our law, including constitutional law, "protect[s] anyone from the embarrassment that occurs when the government or private entities gather information in an intrusive or demeaning manner in the first place. This mistreatment tends to happen disproportionately to the poor and other marginalized groups" (1423).

Thus, the existing law is concerned with protecting individuals from the vulnerability that is concomitant to the disclosure of personal and potentially embarrassing information—like their "credit histories, student records, debts, bank records, tax returns, television viewing habits, health information, and . . . video rentals" (1423). However, when it comes to protecting individuals from the dignity-harming aspects of information collection, "the courts are silent" (1418). Thus, when the D.C. Circuit denied a challenge to an intrusive background check in a case where "information [was] collected by the government but not disseminated publicly," it was entirely correct when it noted that the plaintiffs "could cite no case in which a court has found a violation of the constitutional right to privacy where the government has collected, but not disseminated, the information" (American Federation of Government Employees, AFL-CIO v. Department of Housing & Urban Development, 118 F.3d 786, 793 (D.C. Cir. 1997)). The latter interest, which is one that might be of vital importance to the most marginalized members of society, is one that has gone unrecognized in the law.

Consider a woman who is poor enough to qualify for public benefits. This is a woman who is never celebrated within cultural and political discourses. Quite the contrary, most of society's narratives describing her are ones that construct her fertility as a social problem, claim that she exercises her problematized fertility to exploit the government's benevolence, and predict that the child that she raises will be, like her mother, a drain on society's resources. Her reproduction is viewed as the abject version of the reproduction in which those with class privilege engage: It is *not* the product of some aching biological urge, nor is it an attempt to wipe the slate clean and give a child the opportunity to live a life that is filled with more love and less sorrow than the life that the parent has come to live. Instead, it is irresponsible. It is conniving. It is dangerous. It is a public health concern.

Now, imagine that woman being forced to answer the questions that public benefits programs demand of her. Imagine her having to recount the status of her relationship with the father of her unborn child. Imagine her having to relate that she has been addicted to drugs, convicted of possessing contraband, expelled from her high school, sexually adventurous, the recipient of multiple abortions, or unemployed. Imagine her having to affirm that the father of the baby with whom she is currently pregnant is not the father of her older children. Imagine her having to confess that she is an undocumented laborer and that she gets paid "under the table" as a housekeeper or a waitress. Imagine her having to share that a relative sexually abused her when she was a child or that she abused alcohol as a young adult. Imagine her having to relate that her diet consists mostly of fast food and that the only exercise she gets is walking to and from the closest subway station.

Imagine this particular woman having to answer the battery of questions that Medicaid requires her to answer—questions that are neither immediately relevant to a doctor's ability to assess her health or relevant to her ability to successfully parent her child. (Indeed, because these questions are not posed as a matter of course to wealthier people, we should be skeptical that they can help assess whether a person will be able to successfully parent a child. If they accurately predicted a parent's likelihood of abusing or neglecting her child, we would presume that *all* mothers and fathers would have to answer similar questions.) The poor mother forced to reveal such information understandably may be embarrassed, ashamed, demeaned.

Collecting private information that further damns poor mothers within cultural and political discourses may be experienced as an insult to dignity. Importantly, no court has recognized the interest that individuals—but especially marginalized individuals—have in avoiding these harms to dignity. If the courts did recognize this interest, and if our courts were concerned about protecting the dignity of *all* individuals in the polity, then the Constitution might be interpreted to require that the state only collect information that is necessary to determine the level of benefits a person should receive and that facilitates her connection to other social services *only if she desires that connection.*

It is important to recognize that collecting private information from a poor mother can be experienced as a real harm even when the woman does not have anything particularly embarrassing to reveal. She possesses an interest in keeping her private information to herself even when her life conforms to the social norms that those with social and political power celebrate—that is, she is a citizen, permanent resident, or documented immigrant; she has had only one or very few sexual partners; she has never been subjected to punishment by the criminal justice system; she has never experimented with drugs (let alone been addicted to them); she has never been a victim of intimate or sexual violence; and so forth. There are two reasons why this interest in preventing the government from collecting certain information persists even when the information that would be collected is acceptable when judged by the majority's norms.

First, the knowledge that the government ultimately amasses about the poor pregnant woman and the poor mother is total. After the indigent woman has answered the entire battery of questions that she must answer in order to receive public benefits, the government has created a dossier on her that is quite exhaustive. Indeed, the profile the government is able to generate from the questions that it poses is comprehensive—ranging from the woman's physiological characteristics (her heart rate, her blood pressure, her weight) to sociological characteristics (her socioeconomic status, her citizenship status, the highest level of education that she has achieved, her diet and frequency with which she exercises) and psychological characteristics (she is excited or anxious about her pregnancy and the prospect of beginning or expanding her family, she is happy to be a mother).

It recalls the case of *Nader v. General Motors* (255 N.E.2d 765 (1970)), which concerned General Motors's surveillance of Ralph Nader—a campaign that it launched to gather information that could discredit the activist and the book that he was about to publish. (Nader's book claimed that General Motors was largely unconcerned with ensuring the safety of the vehicles that it produced (Smith 2011). Among other things, General Motors followed Nader; asked his friends, enemies, family, and neighbors about details of his life; tapped his phone and eavesdropped on his conversations; watched him take out money from the bank; and sought information about his tax filings. None of the information about Nader that General Motors acquired revealed that Nader lived a life that was inconsistent with social norms. In a narrow holding, the court found that Nader nevertheless had suffered an invasion of privacy, likely because it recognized that the information that General Motors acquired and sought to acquire would have allowed it a total knowledge about Nader. Solove's (2002) description of the case is instructive:

> General Motors' campaign of harassment, surveillance, and investigation created a form of systemic oppressiveness, an exercise of power that is profoundly suffocating and threatening to a person's private life. This type of power has a significant potential to render people vulnerable and helpless . . . (1150)

Upon acquiring a total knowledge about a recipient of public benefits, the government exercises a power that is suffocating and threatening to the beneficiary. It simultaneously renders her vulnerable and helpless while revealing her already existing vulnerability and helplessness—vulnerability and helplessness that are products of her sociopolitical location. A poor mother may experience the interrogation as doubly painful both because it facilitates social control while at the same time revealing her as the type of person that society wants to control.

Second, even if a poor mother has nothing particularly embarrassing or deviant (in the sense that her past and present do not deviate too significantly from social norms) to confess during the informational canvassing to which she must submit as a condition of her receipt of public benefits, she still presents herself to her interrogator as a failure. She has failed as a purveyor of her labor—a cardinal demand of capitalism. And she has failed in the sense that she has been unable to attach herself to a person, traditionally a man, who has succeeded as a purveyor of his labor. Indeed, the state's interrogation tends to make obvious that it believes the woman to be a failure. While the woman may hold herself in high esteem prior to her encounter with the state—she has intimate knowledge of how truly *difficult* it is to simply survive at the intersections of unprivilege, yet she has survived!—the true harm is that she may walk away from the interrogation convinced that the state's view of her is persuasive. Relevant here is Allen's (2011) claim that those who intrude upon our privacy "can form humiliating, despicable pictures of their victims that interfere with their victims' self-concepts and self-esteem, *making them doubt they are the people they have worked to be*" (15, emphasis added).

Moreover, because the moral construction of poverty suggests that it is reasonable to presume that a person is poor due to bad values and bad behavior, then the information given by the indigent mother whose life has otherwise conformed to social norms can be understood as an effort to rebut that presumption. It is a performance of respectability that middle-class women simply do not have to do. If the individual interest in preventing the government from collecting certain private information were recognized and protected, then it would have structural effects: It would produce an equality of treatment between poor and non-poor mothers, even when the narratives that are told about the two sets of mothers are far from equal.

On Confessions and the Value of Limiting the Government's Ability to Interrogate

Solove (2006) recognizes interrogation—that is, posing intensely intimate or intrusive questions to another—as a privacy invasion. He writes, "Privacy law's theory of interrogation is not only incoherent, it is nearly nonexistent. Despite recognizing the harms and problems of interrogation—compulsion, divulgence of private information, and forced betrayal—the law only addresses them in limited situations" (505). Interrogation is the practice that poor mothers must endure when they turn to the state for financial assistance or when, after refusing to turn to the state for financial assistance, they find themselves within the net of a CPS investigation. And interrogation is the event that threatens poor mothers' decisional autonomy, facilitates social control over them, and injures their dignity.

While Solove is correct that privacy law has yet to develop a satisfactory theory about interrogation, scholars working in the area of criminal procedure have spilled a lot of ink thinking about it. The Fifth Amendment protects an individual from being "compelled in any criminal case to be a witness against himself" (U.S. Constitution, Fifth Amendment). The Court has interpreted this clause as erecting limitations on police interrogation practices. Criminal procedure scholars have done insightful analyses of the justifications for the limitations that the Court has imposed. It is possible that this body of scholarship might shed some additional light on this chapter's inquiry into an individual's interest in preventing the government from interrogating her and collecting certain information about her. And it might help us understand why society has not been moved to erect limitations on governmental interrogations when the state distributes public benefits to indigent mothers.

It is instructive to identify what the state requires poor mothers to do as a "confession." This label accurately describes the nature of the exercise. Women are induced to detail all of the transgressions against social norms that they have committed. Indeed, the record that is produced after a woman has answered all of the questions that public benefits programs pose to her is a record of her past crimes, sins, indiscretions, shames, and failures. "Confession" is the best word to describe this record. Further, identifying the information communicated by a mother attempting to receive state benefits or attempting to release herself from the jurisdiction of CPS as a confession allows us to look to scholarship about confessions to understand what precisely is so discomfiting about this particular practice. Comparative literature scholar Peter Brooks's (2001) work is a productive site from which to draw.

Brooks identifies two types of confessions: the religious confession and the criminal confession. The intent behind, and the goal of, the religious confession is expiation. The penitent confesses her sins in order to achieve, or at least begin the process of achieving, forgiveness. The act of confessing soothes the penitent because her shame is no longer hidden. She takes ownership of her past misdeeds. She also takes ownership of the penalties authorities think appropriate to mete upon her. As such, the act of confession gives the penitent permission to move beyond her past transgressions—to leave them behind her.

However, the criminal confession is quite different. While the consequence of a religious confession is moral consolation and rehabilitation, the consequence of a criminal confession is punishment. When an accused person confesses his crime to a police interrogator, he establishes his guilt, and he paves the path to his conviction.

Therein lies the potential for conflict: If one confesses one's sins to an agent of the church, one hopes for relief and succor. However, if one confesses one's sins to an agent of the penal state, one can only hope for discipline and punishment.

The problem is that, in practice, it may be difficult to disentangle the religious confession from the legal confession. As Brooks asks, "If confessing to a priest is good for you, are we to say that confessing to a police interrogator is not?" (2001, 3). Moreover, law enforcement agents may leverage the religious aspects of confessions in order to extract an admission of wrongdoing. They may promise absolution with conviction on their minds. When law enforcement agents suggest that the meanings that attach to religious confessions also attach to legal confessions, they encourage accused persons to assume the posture that they assume when confessing their sins to religious authorities. And that may be an injustice. Writes Brooks, "The institutionalization of confession as a means of legal conviction nonetheless must always make us uncomfort-able, since the state in search of confession plays on the consolatory aspect of confession as a means to entrap for disciplinary purposes" (112).

What Brooks observes about the vexed nature of confessions in the criminal context is also true in the context of the poor mother seeking public benefits from the state or seeking a way out of the CPS bureaucracy. The woman is en-couraged to recall all of her past failures and to share them with a social worker who is employed by the state. Indeed, a woman might be more inclined to treat her Medicaid, TANF, or CPS confession as a religious confession because the specter of punishment is not readily apparent; it is certainly less apparent than it is in the criminal context.

Moreover, society encourages us to think of social workers as charged with the duty to *help* their clients. We imagine that they intervene in order to improve the quality of the lives of their clients and to ensure their overall well-being. Thus, it is not unreasonable for an indigent mother to think of her requisite conversation with social workers as healing and corrective. (In fact, Brooks (2001, 166–67) notes that the nature of the "situation of interlocution is in the manner therapeutic.") It is not unreasonable for the confessant indigent mother to trust her confessor social worker and to engage in the self-exploratory work in which she would engage if she was confessing to a religious authority. It is not unreasonable for the confessant to be open and honest, hiding nothing be-cause she sees only the value of revealing the entirety of her past sins and none of the value in dissimulation. It is not unreasonable for the confessant to expect that absolution, support, and relief will flow from her confession.

However, unlike the priest, the social worker does not have an uncom-plicated relationship to his confessant. His loyalties are divided. He is a *state agent*. He has a duty *to the state* to extract a confession from the woman and to share it with state agencies. He has a duty to make sure that other state agents remain involved in the woman's life if the information that he obtains justifies it. He is obliged to ensure that the woman remains encased in bureaucracies that will supervise her, regulate her, and discipline her. He is obligated to iden-tify her as a subject who ought not to enjoy privacy in any real sense of the word and is obligated to facilitate an unadulterated and unlimited state power in her life.

If we are disquieted by the fact that criminal confessions mimic religious confessions and thereby incite the criminally accused to act against their inter-ests, then we ought to be disquieted by the fact that something eerily similar is operating in the civil context. As there is an injustice when law enforcement evokes expiation when the consequence is actually conviction, there is an injustice when public assistance and CPS invoke healing and help when the consequence is actually state management of a woman and her family. The Fifth Amendment attempts to erect strictures around the government's ability to collect information from those accused of crime. A right to informational privacy that the Court has not yet recognized—a substantive due process right that would limit the government's ability to extract confessions in noncriminal settings—is a much needed analogue to the Fifth Amendment.

The origins of the Fifth Amendment's protection against self-incrimination are in the oath ex officio, which the Star Chamber and the High Commission courts used in England (Stuntz 1995). Persons were made to take the oath, by which they were required to answer truthfully all questions that were posed to them. To describe the oath ex officio as hated is an understatement. By the mid-seventeenth century, John Lilburne, who was prosecuted for political agitation in England, would famously argue that the oath ex officio violated a person's "fundamental right . . . [as] no man's conscience ought to be racked by oaths imposed, to answer to questions concerning himself in matters criminal, or pretended to be so" (Miranda v. Arizona, 384 U.S. 436, 459 (1966)). Historians largely agree that the Fifth Amendment was an effort to prevent the importation to the United States of practices like the loathed oath ex officio (Stuntz 1995).

The most famous articulation of what the Fifth Amendment requires came with the Court's decision in *Miranda v. Arizona*, which is now familiar in popular culture. In *Miranda* the Court held that statements made by those who have been arrested while in police custody will be presumed to be coerced and therefore inadmissible in subsequent court proceedings, unless the arrestee has been explicitly apprised of her right not to speak as well as the consequence of the waiver of that right. The *Miranda* Court waxed philosophically about the privilege against self-incrimination:

> [T]he constitutional foundation underlying the privilege is the respect a government—state or federal—must accord to the dignity and integrity of its citizens. To maintain a "fair state-individual balance," to require the government "to shoulder the entire load," to respect the inviolability of the human personality, our accusatory system of criminal justice demands that the government seeking to punish an individual produce the evidence against him by its own independent labors, rather than by the cruel, simple expedient of compelling it from his own mouth. (460)

Thus, the Court identifies two justifications for the privilege: a structural interest in maintaining a fair balance of power between the government and the individual ensnared in its criminal justice system and an interest in guarding the dignity of the individual. On this latter justification, the Court theorizes that a person who has been compelled to share information that is not in his self-interest to share has suffered an injury to his dignity. Moreover, even when a person chooses not to make harmful statements about herself, there is the sense that merely placing her in that fraught situation is injurious. As Justice Goldberg in *Murphy v. Waterfront Commission of New York Harbor* (378 U.S. 52 (1964)) stated, the absence of a Fifth Amendment right to remain silent would expose a person to the "cruel trilemma of self-accusation, perjury or contempt" (55).

There is little reason to believe that the justifications for the privilege against self-incrimination in the criminal context do not translate into noncriminal contexts. That is, although the Fifth Amendment was intended to constrain the government when it seeks to bring the force and violence of the criminal justice system to bear against an individual, the value of imposing that constraint does not simply vanish if criminal punishment is not implicated. The freedom to avoid being compelled to say harmful things about oneself, which is the essence of the privilege against self-incrimination, is valuable outside of the criminal justice system.

We can begin with dignity. As it harms an individual's dignity to be forced to make statements that are wildly against his interests in the criminal context, it also harms an individual's dignity to be forced to make statements that are against his interests in noncriminal contexts. Brooks (2001) writes that confessions—those circumstances in which one has to give voice to one's transgressions against the legal, religious, or moral order—invariably entail "a penitential state that may involve disgrace, even abjection" (9). Given this reality, he asks "[D]oesn't it often appear a violation of human dignity?" Consider political scientist Robert Gerstein's (1984) defense of the right against self-incrimination. He writes that persons who have transgressed the norms embodied in our criminal codes still feel themselves to be members of the moral polity. As such, it is quite brutal—indeed, it inflicts a painful indignity—to force the transgressor to confess that he has disobeyed the norms of his own community. Gerstein writes,

> What I am thinking about is violations in the core area of criminal law, violations which involve serious injury to the interests of others and therefore serious immorality, committed by one of the vast majority of people for whom the

criminal law is designed: people who to one degree or another feel themselves to be part of the same moral community with those whose interests they have injured, and who therefore see the violation as a moral issue. (1984, 250)

The analogy to the circumstance of a poor mother turning to the state to ask for benefits or attempting to extricate herself from a CPS "open case" should be apparent. The information that these programs require poor women to divulge is information that may describe the confessor's disobedience to the norms of the polity of which she considers herself a member. She may have to reveal that she has struggled with substance abuse and addiction. She may have to reveal that she has been the victim of intimate violence—a victimhood that large portions of society still fail to recognize as a status deserving of sympathy and support, but instead envisions as an affliction that the abused have brought upon themselves by failing to leave their abusers (Ellerin 2000). She may have to reveal that she has broken moral norms dictating that sexual intercourse should only occur in monogamous relationships, should only occur with one partner at a time, or should never be exchanged for money or gifts. She may have to reveal that she has broken the norms embodied in the criminal law or the norms embodied in immigration laws.

Moreover, even when a poor mother does not have anything particularly salacious to confess, she invariably will have to reveal that she has broken community norms that assert that it is *immoral* to allow one's motherhood to intersect with one's poverty. When a woman is seeking public benefits, she invariably will have to reveal that she has broken community norms that proclaim that it is *immoral* to depend on the state for one's economic survival. The necessity of confessing these departures from the mores of the body politic in which the poor mother is a member may injure the dignity of the woman making the confession in a way that is analogous to the injuries to dignity against which the Fifth Amendment protects in the criminal context. Writes Gerstein (1979),

> The designation of conduct as criminal means the attachment of a significant stigma to it. To compel a public admission of what is understood to be guilt by community standards thus degrades the individual from his status in the community as a free moral agent; he would have good reason to regard this accusation as a serious affront to his personal dignity. (353)

The same is true of that which Medicaid, TANF, and CPS require women to divulge. They require indigent mothers to admit to a social position to which significant stigma is detached. Compelling the admission of it—even in the absence of a formal, criminal accusation of wrongdoing—is a serious affront to the personal dignity of the woman so compelled.

It is instructive to examine an argument that criminal procedure scholar David Dolinko (1985) makes in his insightful critique of the privilege against self-incrimination in the criminal context. He considers the claim that the privilege is justified because it is cruel to punish people for doing something anyone similarly situated would do. The claim is that everyone compelled to tell the truth about their criminal involvement would lie when the truth that is to be told would expose them to criminal punishment. The claim is that the Fifth Amendment prohibition against compelling a person to be a witness against himself prevents the "hypocritical cruelty" that would result if we punished persons for doing what we ourselves would do. However, Dolinko observes that, in a lot of other contexts, we punish people for doing things that we would do if we were in their situation:

> Consider, however, the legal treatment of narcotics addicts. An addict is subject to criminal punishment for violating the laws against possession of narcotics, even though most of us would break those laws were we in the addict's place (i.e., were we addicted). Courts have rejected constitutional and common-law attacks on the propriety of this punishment. [This example illustrates] that there are situations in which the criminal law does punish people for behaving as most of us would behave in their place. . . . If we ask how one might defend punishing an addict for conduct that is almost inevitable for a person in his position, a likely answer would be that the addict should never have gotten into that "position"—that is, he can justly be blamed for having embarked on, and persisted in, the course of conduct that led to his addiction. Even though almost all of us would possess narcotics if we were in the addict's position, we can punish him without hypocrisy, because he is culpable for placing himself in that position . . . [T]here is no such impropriety if X can fairly be blamed for getting himself into the predicament in the first place. (1985, 1097–99)

Dolinko's argument sheds light on why the Court has refused to interpret the Constitution to contain a right that would prevent the government from collecting private information in noncriminal contexts. In a very important sense, we feel that people who are subject to the prying questions that the government asks have gotten themselves into the predicament in the first place. Those who have been prescribed the highly addictive drugs that were the subject of the controversy in *Whalen* consented to taking the stigmatized drugs that their doctors thought best for their various conditions; as such, they are largely responsible for being in a situation where they take a drug for which there is an illegal market. Nixon voluntarily assumed the office of president of the United States, a position that comes with a slew of duties, obligations, and burdens; as such, he is largely responsible for being in a situation where another public official would be called upon to examine his private effects. The NASA contractors in *Nelson* voluntarily accepted employment with the agency; as such, they are responsible for being in a situation where the government would attempt to ascertain whether they would be trustworthy employees. Poor mothers either have turned to the state for assistance or have possibly neglected their children; as such, they are responsible for being in a situation where the government would pose innumerable intimate questions to them.

Yet, still, poor mothers requesting welfare benefits or in the throes of a CPS investigation present a qualitatively different situation from those of the patients receiving healthcare from qualified medical doctors in *Whalen*, the former president in *Nixon*, and the highly compensated scientist contractors in *Nelson*.

Whereas the patients, the president, and the contractors may be thought to have responsibility for getting themselves in the predicament of being subjects of the government's inquisitiveness, poor mothers are not simply *responsible* for their predicament. According to the moral construction of poverty, they are to be *blamed* for their predicament. They have a culpability that the *Whalen* patients, the president, and the NASA employees lack. The moral construction of poverty counsels that these women have chosen to be indigent. And they have chosen to become pregnant—a condition that magnifies and exacerbates the culpability inherent in the status of simply being poor. They are more akin to the addicts who Dolinko believes are properly punished for possessing drugs and who suffer no indignity when compelled to give information that facilitates their criminal punishment. A vast conceptual distance separates poor mothers from the plaintiffs in *Whalen*, *Nixon*, and *Nelson*.

We return finally to the other justification for the privilege against criminal self-incrimination that the Court identified in *Miranda*: the structural interest in preventing gross imbalances of power between the state and the individual. Solove (2006) has articulated his sense that the act of interrogation always creates an imbalance of power—even when the state is not the entity posing the question and even when the questions have nothing to do with a criminal investigation:

> [I]nterrogation can create harm. Part of this harm arises from the degree of co-erciveness involved. . . . People take offense when others ask an unduly probing question—even if there is no compulsion to answer. One explanation may be that people still feel some degree of compulsion because not answering might create the impression that they have something to hide. (2006, 501)

In essence, the mere posing of questions shifts power to the entity posing the questions, even when the interrogator poses the question illegitimately and even when the person being interrogated may legitimately refuse to answer.

The effect that the act of interrogating has of shifting power toward the interrogator and away from the person being interrogated is amplified when the state is the interrogator and the questions being posed are actually legiti-mate. As such, some understand the Fifth Amendment privilege against self-incrimination as a tool for managing this power shift.

A state that necessarily wields more power than the individual that is its subject poses a question about autonomy. To the extent that the Fifth Amend-ment privilege against self-incrimination is an effort to prevent the state from taking advantage of its superior power vis-à-vis the individual—a power that the state enjoys by virtue of its existence—then the privilege is an effort to en-sure that individuals remain autonomous, even when they have been accused of committing a crime.

What is true in the criminal context is also true in noncriminal contexts. That is, the state's power vis-à-vis the individual does not significantly decrease simply because it proceeds along paths that do not implicate its law enforce-ment agents, criminal courts, and penal institutions. It remains powerful still when it provides the necessities of life—housing, money that will allow a par-ent to feed and clothe her child, healthcare that will enable a healthier preg-nancy. Indeed, the lesson of Foucault and his theory of the biopolitical state is that the government wields incredible power when it endeavors to sustain its citizens' lives and protect their health; this power matches, if not exceeds, the power that the state wields when it endeavors to punish wrongdoers and deny them life and liberty (Foucault 1995). When a modern state with this kind of biopolitical power asks a question, even an inappropriate and illegitimate one, the individual in need of assistance reasonably feels compelled to answer it. Thus, if we are concerned about ensuring that individuals remain autonomous, then we would want to provide them with a tool that manages the inherent power imbalance between individual and state. We would want to recognize a right that limits the government's power to demand confessions and collect intensely personal information in noncriminal contexts as well.

However, even if the Court recognized that individual autonomy is valuable outside of prosecutions and that its protection in noncriminal contexts redounds to the benefit of society generally, poor mothers are differently situated. Popular and political narratives about their moral shortcomings and character deficiencies counsel that their autonomy is not quite as important as those who are succeeding within market capitalism. Indeed, the moral construction of poverty contends that their self-government has resulted in their indigence and their production of children whom society will eventually have to support. Far from being valuable, their autonomy runs counter to the good of society. Hence, while law and society might come to be concerned about the differential in power between the state and the individual in noncriminal contexts, it likely will remain unconcerned when the individual affected is poor and pregnant or parenting.

We currently exist within a legal landscape in which the state enjoys enormous power in relation to its indigent subjects. The rights that are designed to limit the power of the state have been perverted by the stories that we tell about poverty. In context after context, doctrines function to limit state power when it implicates the wealthier and to allow state power to reign unrestricted when it implicates those who are poor. Simply stated, we are largely unconcerned about imbalances of power between the state and individual when the individual is poor. In many cases, we actively encourage it. It may be the height of optimism to expect that we would begin to be concerned about this power differential in noncriminal contexts should the Court decide to recognize a right that is designed to manage it.

5 Reproductive Privacy

We might define *procreative liberty* as the ability to decide whether to have a child without being subject to the government's power to compel the individual to act in alignment with the government's desires. It may be an understatement to describe the choice to become a parent or to eschew parenthood as a difficult one for many men and women. (This is not to deny that this decision may be the easiest decision in the world for some.) Moreover, the decision is invariably more complex for women. We live in a society wherein motherhood has been constructed as the apotheosis of womanhood; yet, society remains arranged in a way that disadvantages women by their very motherhood (Roberts 1993a).

Because the choice to become a mother is a choice both about the minutiae of one's life as well as its general arc, we have come to believe that, as a general matter, the government should abstain from involving itself in that choice. And we have developed a legal tool, reproductive privacy rights, to enforce government abstention and to enable individuals to enjoy procreative liberty. Yet, if we examine the experience of poor women, we see that they do not enjoy procreative liberty at all. This chapter conducts that examination, arguing that poor mothers do not enjoy procreative liberty because they have been deprived of reproductive privacy rights, either in the moderate or strong sense.

Three brief notes are helpful before beginning the exploration. First, there are many possible definitions of procreative liberty. For example, legal scholar and bioethicist John Robertson (2003) defines procreative liberty as "a liberty or claim-right to decide whether or not to reproduce. As such, it has two independent justified aspects: the liberty to avoid having offspring and the liberty to have offspring. . . . [E]ach [aspect] may be conceived as a different right, connected by their common concern with reproduction" (447). Absent from Robertson's definition is a concern about the government's potential impact on the individual's decision about whether or not to reproduce. Yet, attention to the government's role in influencing this decision is paramount—if only because the government is a potent force in modern life and, as a result, has the ability to influence individual decision making significantly.

In other words, individuals are not decontextualized, free-floating entities. On the contrary, they are embedded within contexts, and they are very much affected by power. As a result, the decisions that they make are very much affected by power. It is for this reason that a person does not freely make the choice to become a mother or to avoid motherhood when the government has used its power to produce a particular choice. Consequently, the definition of procreative liberty that this chapter offers is one that builds government power into its understanding of liberty. A person is not "at liberty" to do any one thing when the state has worked to ensure that she does that very thing.

The second issue to note is that the government-qua-law is not the only force that impacts reproductive decision making. Surely, a woman's religious and moral convictions, the strength of her relationship with her intimate partner (if any), her family, her community, non-legal sociocultural discourses (including racial ones), and, of course, her class also influence her reproductive decisions. And, surely, this is not an exhaustive list. Consequently, one might argue that if one claims, as this chapter does, that a woman is not at liberty to decide whether or not to become a mother when the law radically influences her decision, then a woman similarly is not at liberty to decide whether or not to become a mother when any of these non-legal forces radically influence her decision.

Because of the impossibility of escaping these forces, one might then conclude that procreative liberty is an impossibility. *No one* enjoys procreative liberty. However, in this chapter I distinguish legal influences on reproductive decision making from non-legal influences, and this is simply because this book is concerned with the law. I am concerned with how the *law* has produced stratified experiences of pregnancy and motherhood and with interpreting the law to reveal the assumptions about poverty (and gender and race) that are reflected in it. Thus, this chapter inserts legal influences into the definition of procreative liberty while not similarly inserting non-legal influences. Accordingly, when a woman's religion, family, and community influence her decisions around motherhood, she still enjoys procreative liberty. However, when the *government-qua-law* leads her into or away from motherhood, she does not enjoy that liberty.

The third point is that we might not use the language of "liberty" at all to define what is at stake with reproductive privacy rights. We might instead say that reproductive privacy rights are concerned with guaranteeing procreative "autonomy." Indeed, the widely influential legal scholar and philosopher Ronald Dworkin (1996) understands the Court's case law around reproduction as being concerned with procreative autonomy, not procreative liberty. However, Dworkin's definition of procreative autonomy—which he describes as "the right of women to decide for themselves not only whether to conceive but whether to bear the child"—is indistinguishable from most definitions of procreative liberty (104). Accordingly, the choice to use the language of liberty versus autonomy does not change the analysis. That said, in this chapter I prefer to use the language of procreative liberty (and not procreative autonomy) for linguistic simplicity.

Here is my reasoning for this choice. In this chapter I argue that the value of being able to decide whether or not to bear a child is that it allows individuals to be autonomous; it affords them control over the direction that their lives will take, and it allows them to constitute themselves as the people they would like to be. Accordingly, if I used the language of procreative autonomy in this chapter, then I would have to argue that *procreative* autonomy enables *general* autonomy. To avoid having to refer to two types of autonomy, I use the language of procreative liberty instead. Thus, in the chapter I can assert, simply, that procreative liberty enables autonomy. And when poor women are denied procreative liberty, they are denied the ability to be fully autonomous, self-creating directors of their lives.

Medicaid Abortion Funding Restrictions

We begin our analysis of the constraints that function to deny poor women procreative liberty by looking first to the Supreme Court's decision in *Maher v. Roe* (432 U.S. 464 (1977)). The litigation began when two Medicaid beneficiaries—one a 16-year-old junior in high school and the other a single mother of three children—challenged a Connecticut regulation that limited the state's Medicaid coverage to therapeutic, or "medically necessary," abortions. The state refused to fund its Medicaid program to cover the non-therapeutic, or elective, abortions that the plaintiffs sought. Had the plaintiffs' pregnancies threatened to leave them wounded, mentally ill, or dead, they could have used Medicaid to cover the costs of terminating their pregnancies. However, because the plaintiffs' pregnancies did not threaten their physical or mental health—"only" functioning to force a young girl into early motherhood and to force a woman to have a fourth child when she already found it impossible to economically support her three children—Connecticut refused to subsidize their abortions costs.

The plaintiffs argued that the state's policy of funding only therapeutic abortions violated the Fourteenth Amendment's Equal Protection and Due Process clauses. The Court disagreed. It rejected the equal protection challenge summarily, finding that "an indigent woman desiring an abortion does not come within the limited category of disadvantaged classes so recognized by our cases" (470–71). Because indigent women saddled with unwanted pregnancies are not a suspect class, the Court held that it was appropriate to review laws that burdened them with rational basis review. Unsurprisingly, under this deferential standard of review, the Court found Connecticut's Medicaid funding policy consistent with the Fourteenth Amendment's command of equal protection.

Although it was relatively easy for the Court to dispatch the equal protection challenge to Connecticut's Medicaid program, it had to engage in a bit of sophistry to deny the plaintiffs' due process challenge. The plaintiffs had argued that Connecticut's decision to deny poor women Medicaid funding for nontherapeutic abortions violated their substantive due process right to privacy. Just four years earlier, the Court had held in *Roe v. Wade* that the Due Process Clause forbids states from denying individuals the ability to terminate an unwanted pregnancy prior to fetal viability. In *Maher v. Roe*, the plaintiffs argued that the prohibition on Medicaid funding for nontherapeutic abortions did just that: It denied poor women the ability to terminate unwanted pregnancies prior to fetal viability. As such, the plaintiffs argued that the Connecticut law—like the Texas law criminalizing abortion that the Court in *Roe v. Wade* found to be inconsistent with the Due Process Clause—violated their substantive due process right to reproductive privacy.

If one accepts the plaintiffs' framing of the issue, then it is hard to see how the Court could uphold the Connecticut regulation without simultaneously overturning *Roe v. Wade*. That is, if one conceptualizes the Connecticut law as that which impeded indigent women's access to abortion, then it would be indistinguishable from the unconstitutional Texas law that made the performance of an abortion a crime and, in so doing, impeded women's access to abortion. While Texas used its criminal law to obstruct women's access to abortions, Connecticut simply used its Medicaid law to accomplish the same. Thus, in order to leave its holding in *Roe v. Wade* undisturbed, the Court in *Maher v. Roe* had to deny that it was the Connecticut law that impeded indigent women's abortion access.

The Court did just that. Instead of identifying Connecticut's decision to deny coverage of nontherapeutic abortions as the cause of poor women's inability to access abortion in the state, it identified their poverty as the cause. It argued that the "indigency that may make it difficult—and in some cases, perhaps, impossible—for some women to have abortions is neither created nor in any way affected by the Connecticut regulation" (Maher v. Roe 1977, 474). The Court noted that *Roe v. Wade* had interpreted the Constitution to prohibit *laws* that made it difficult or impossible for women to terminate unwanted pregnancies. It had not at all interpreted the Constitution to prohibit things that were outside of the law, like poverty, that made abortion unattainable for women.[1] As such, Connecticut was under no obligation to remove that obstacle—poverty—from women's path to abortion.[2]

Harris v. McRae, decided three years later, picked up where *Maher v. Roe* left off. In *Harris*, the Court was called upon to determine the constitutionality of the Hyde Amendment, a federal regulation prohibiting the use of federal Medicaid funds for even medically necessary, therapeutic abortions. While the Hyde Amendment currently allows for indigent women to use Medicaid funds to terminate pregnancies that endanger their lives or that are products of rape or incest, it denies funds to terminate pregnancies that endanger women's health (Soohoo 2012). Thus, the Hyde Amendment leaves poor women to be maimed by their pregnancies. *Harris* compelled the Court to determine whether the brutality that the regulation inflicts on indigent women was consistent with the commands of the Constitution.

Using the logic of *Maher*, the *Harris* Court held that the Constitution was not at all disturbed by the prohibition on federal funding for even medically necessary abortions.[3] As in *Maher*, the Court reasoned that indigent women requiring therapeutic abortions were not a suspect class and, accordingly, that a law that burdened them raised no equal protection problems. And as in *Maher*, the Court reasoned that the law, the Hyde Amendment, was not the obstacle that impeded poor women's access to medically indicated abortions. The Court reasoned that their poverty was the obstacle. Finally, as in *Maher*, the Court argued that the government was under no obligation to "remove" poverty, an impediment that no state or federal law had created.

Maher v. Roe and *Harris v. McRae* did not in any way *prohibit* individual states from using their own monies to fund nontherapeutic and therapeutic abortions. The Court made it quite clear that states retained the option to cover poor women's abortion costs with state funds. Unfortunately, most states have declined to exercise that option. Currently, thirty-two states fund their Medicaid programs in line with the federal standard, allowing indigent women to use Medicaid funds to terminate pregnancies only when those pregnancies endanger their lives or are the consequence of rape or incest (Guttmacher Institute 2016). Remarkably, South Dakota's Medicaid program does not even cover the costs of abortions for women who are survivors of rape or incest; Medicaid beneficiaries in South Dakota can only use their Medicaid insurance to terminate pregnancies that may kill them.

Seventeen states exceed the federal standard and structure their Medicaid programs to cover therapeutic, medically necessary abortions. However, although seventeen states have committed themselves to protecting poor women's health, few states have made a commitment to protecting poor women's procreative liberty, robustly formulated. That is, only seven states—California, Hawaii, Maryland, Massachusetts, Minnesota, New Jersey, and New Mexico—implement Medicaid programs that cover the costs of nontherapeutic, elective abortions.[4] Again, only eight states facilitate poor women's enjoyment of the freedom that wealthier women enjoy. This is the freedom to avoid having a child because the woman has decided that, although carrying a pregnancy to term may not threaten her physical life, it would nevertheless threaten her social, emotional, relational, familial, aspirational, *thick* life and ought to be avoided for that very reason.

While much ink could be spilled exploring the government's rationale for denying poor women the means to terminate an unwanted pregnancy, some space will be devoted here to acknowledging the individualist explanations of poverty that undergird the government's funding decision and the Court's approval of it. In *Maher* and *Harris*, the Court wondered about what would happen to a poor woman who wanted an abortion but who could receive no financial assistance from the state to help her toward that end. Fascinatingly, it concluded that, in most cases, she would simply acquire the abortion that she desires by turning to the "private sources" that presumably exist all around her and are always at her disposal (Harris v. McRae 1980, 314; Maher v. Roe 1977, 474).[5]

Legal scholar Susan Appleton (1996) explains that "the cases emphasized the absence of any cognizable effect on the challengers. Indigent women seeking abortions were no worse off than if the government got out of the Medicaid business altogether" (63). The Court acknowledges that states' refusal to provide coverage for abortion services in their Medicaid programs may prevent *some* women from acquiring the abortions that they desire. But, women who are forced to bear pregnancies that they would terminate if given public funds appear to be exceptions to the rule. They are rarities, with the Court writing that poverty "may make it difficult—and in some cases, perhaps, impossible—for some women to have abortions" (Maher v. Roe 1977, 474). That is, only "in some cases" would the Medicaid funding structure prevent "some" women from terminating unwanted pregnancies. And even in those cases, only "*perhaps*" would women find it impossible to obtain an abortion.

The Court is extremely skeptical that Medicaid funding policies will affect the trajectory of poor women's pregnancies. Thus, the Court assumes that, with or without state assistance, poor women are in control of their reproductive present and future. Indeed, the Court likely assumes that they control whether or not they get pregnant in the first place. Senator Orrin Hatch argued in favor of the Hyde Amendment by noting that poor women could avoid the constraints imposed by the regulation by simply "exercising increased self-restraint"—practicing abstinence (124 Cong. Rec. 31, 900 (1978)). He also proposed that if a poor woman fails at abstinence and finds herself bearing an unwanted pregnancy, all she has to do is "sacrific[e] on some item or other for a month or two," thus enabling her to "afford [her] own abortion" (900).

For the Court, Hatch, and others, poor women are powerful agents exercising dominion over their lives. If they find themselves pregnant, it is because they chose to indulge their sexual desires. If after choosing to indulge their sexual desires, they find themselves carrying to term an unwanted pregnancy and giving birth to a child, it is because they chose not to pull together the private resources to pay for an abortion. These assumptions are consistent with the moral construction of poverty, discourses that similarly assume that individuals are in control. If an individual finds herself impoverished, it is because she has failed to control her laziness, her gambling, her addiction, her vice, her libido, her inherent criminality, and so forth. Thus, individualist explanations of poverty and its attribution of an unqualified agency to those who are poor are what underlie the Medicaid abortion funding restrictions and the Court's legitimation of them.

There are two additional points that deserve mention. First, we should acknowledge just how Medicaid abortion funding restrictions serve as a compromise in the battle over abortion rights in this nation. Those who oppose abortion conceptualize the practice as the slaughter of innocents and insist that it be criminalized and never again performed in the country, if not the world. Those who support abortion rights conceptualize abortion as a medical procedure that all women should be able to access because abortion access is, for scores of women, essential to their ability to command their destiny. In light of the reality that neither side of the conflict likely will realize their preferred state of affairs, Medicaid abortion funding restrictions are a happy medium: They please abortion rights supporters because wealthier women's access to abortion remains unconstrained, and they please abortion opponents because, in preventing taxpayer monies from going toward abortion care, they place abortion outside the reach of many women. As legal scholars Janet Dolgin and Katherine Dieterich (2012) formulate it, Medicaid funding restrictions allow "members of Congress to satisfy a powerful, vocal pro-life constituency while protecting access to abortion for middle- and upper-class women" (392).

One could use the language of rights to describe the compromise that Medicaid abortion funding restrictions represent. One could say that by weakening poor women's abortion rights, wealthier women's rights are strengthened (or are allowed to go undisturbed). This formulation of the compromise is consistent with the moderate claim.

However, the strong claim would formulate the compromise differently. The strong claim contends that when a poor woman cannot exercise her abortion right because laws that the Court has found to be consistent with the Constitution make exercise of that right impossible, then we misspeak when we describe this woman as bearing a right to an abortion. The strong claim would contend that the more accurate description is that poor women lack abortion rights; they have been informally disenfranchised of them. And if this is true, we see that weakening poor women's abortion rights does not protect wealthier women's rights; rather, *depriving* poor women of abortion rights allows wealthier women to remain enfranchised. That is, poor women's lack of rights subsidizes wealthier women's rights. The injustice of this fact is striking.

Finally, we must be reminded that poor women's lack of abortion rights is not a function of their having exchanged those rights for assistance from the state. This is not a case of poor women signing up for Medicaid and, at that point, being unable to acquire the abortions that they were able to acquire prior to their receipt of the benefit.[6] Rather, this is a case of poor women being unable to access abortion with or without Medicaid. They have exchanged no rights for state assistance. The meaninglessness of their rights (consistent with the moderate claim) or their rightlessness (consistent with the strong claim) exists whether or not they receive a welfare benefit. Their deprivation is a function of their poverty.

TANF Family Caps

The Medicaid funding restrictions are a pronatalist policy inasmuch as they encourage, and frequently compel, women to give birth to children by denying them the means to terminate unwanted pregnancies.[7] But, the government's pronatalism toward poor women is met by an antinatalism that takes the form of "family cap" or "child exclusion" policies in state Temporary Assistance for Needy Families (TANF) programs.

In states that do not adopt a family cap policy, the number of individuals in a family determines the size of the family's TANF grant. Accordingly, if the number of individuals in a family increases—because of the birth of a child or the addition of another dependent person into the household—the size of the grant increases. A family cap policy freezes the amount of a family's grant, making it unresponsive to increases in the family's size.[8] Under the Aid for Families with Dependent Children program, TANF's predecessor, states had to obtain a waiver from the federal government in order to implement a family cap policy (Smith 2006). Under the TANF program, states need not obtain a waiver; the program explicitly gives states the discretion to implement such policies. Currently, family cap policies are in place in seventeen states (Center on Reproductive Rights and Justice 2016).[9]

Family cap policies are antinatalist because, in their refusal to provide financial support for growing families, they discourage TANF beneficiaries from bearing additional children. There are many rationales for these policies. Most of them are consistent with the moral construction of poverty. In *Dandridge v. Williams* (397 U.S. 471 (1970)), Maryland defended its family cap policy with the argument that it provided an incentive to the heads of indigent families to seek "gainful employment" (483). In *C.K. v. Shalala* (883 F.Supp. 991 (D.N.J. 1995)),

New Jersey presented a similar defense of its family cap policy, contending that placing a "ceiling on benefits provides an incentive for parents to leave the welfare rolls for the workforce" (1014). This rationale assumes that there are jobs out there that welfare beneficiaries could get if they just tried.

The family cap policy, then, is just a kick in the pants—a spur designed to get indigent people off of the couch, out of the door, and back into the workforce. This rationale assumes that people are unemployed because they choose to be—because they are lazy, unmotivated, and irresponsible. Of course, structuralist explanations of poverty reject the contention that people are unemployed, and poor, because they just lack the initiative—the get-up-and-go—to find themselves a job that could support themselves and their families. Segments of the economy have contracted or disappeared, felons have been disenfranchised and subjected to collateral consequences, the system of public education is in shambles, jobs do not pay a livable wage, affordable and reliable childcare is chimerical, persons are physically and/or mentally disabled, and so on. The causes of unemployment are myriad. It is a political choice to believe—like New Jersey, Maryland, and the Court that accepted Maryland's argument—that we can solve the problem of unemployment by simply incentivizing the unemployed to seek "gainful employment."

Consider as well that family cap policies are also defended with the claim that they encourage those who are receiving welfare benefits to use contraception. Maryland took this tack in *Dandridge v. Williams* (1970), arguing that the policy provided "incentives for family planning" (484). And in *C.K. v. Shalala* (1995), the court accepted the proposition that the family cap policy "sends a message that recipients should consider the static level of welfare benefits before having another child, a message that may reasonably have an ameliorative effect on the rate of out-of-wedlock births that can only foster the familial instability and crushing cycle of poverty currently plaguing the welfare class" (1014).

The *C.K.* court makes it clear that it believes that poor people's insistence upon having children outside of marriage is that which is responsible for poverty. The court appears not to realize, or care, that the family cap policy that it upholds similarly discourages *marital* births. That is, the policy does not make distinctions based on the marital status of the beneficiary. Thus, the policy does not problematize and condemn the fertility of *unmarried* poor people; it problematizes and condemns the fertility of *poor* people. The policy does not proclaim that if one is unmarried and poor, one ought not to have a baby;

the policy proclaims that if one is simply poor, one ought not to have a baby. Nevertheless, the court in *C.K. v. Shalala* proclaims that if poor people would just stop having children outside of marriage, then poverty itself—or, at least poverty in its cyclical form, the "crushing cycle of poverty"—would be closer to being overcome.

The court here ignores that there is nothing inherent about nonmarital births that make poverty an inevitable result. Rather, nonmarital births tend to induce poverty because we, as a society, have decided not to support them. Certainly, there are steps that we could take that could make single parenthood a financially tenable pursuit. We could raise the minimum wage; we could provide universal healthcare in every state; we could make safe and reliable childcare affordable and accessible; we could compensate parents for the labor involved in raising a child. But we have largely decided not to take these steps. Instead, we have left single parents, specifically single mothers, to find ways to purchase the goods, like childcare and healthcare, that will support their families. And, occasionally, we pass laws that are designed to make it even more difficult for single parents to support their children—family cap policies exemplifying these.

It deserves mention that if family cap policies are supposed to reduce the number of children born to welfare beneficiaries, they simply do not work. Indeed, Congress was presented with testimony maintaining that "there is no solid evidence for concluding that eliminating benefits will significantly reduce nonmarital births" (McClain 1996, 383). Linda McClain observes,

> Nor has evidence of actual demographic patterns—that is, that the families of women [receiving cash assistance] are no bigger than those of the rest of the population and, indeed, tend to be smaller—exerted any countervailing effect on the imagery of the welfare recipient/rational actor procreating in response to incentives. Moreover, the initial evaluation of New Jersey's family cap measure reveals no statistically significant difference between birth rates of women subject to the cap and those who are not. (1996, 383)

So, again, if family cap policies are supposed to reduce the number of children born to welfare beneficiaries, they do not work. However, if family cap policies are supposed to make it difficult for indigent parents to support the children that they do have, then they are wildly successful. And if these policies are calculated to *punish* poor women—for allowing their poverty to intersect with their parenthood, for failing to produce families that fit into the middle-class model, and, if they are unmarried, for disobeying the majority's morality by engaging in extramarital sex and having children outside of wedlock—then they perform just as they are intended.

If we return to the definition of procreative liberty proffered at the beginning of the chapter—if procreative liberty is the ability to decide whether to have a child without being subject to the government's power to compel the individual to act in alignment with the government's desires—we see that family cap policies deny indigent women that very thing. Moreover, they are *designed* to do just that. Legislators and political pundits have been very clear that their support of family cap policies is due to their hope and belief that the laws will decrease the birth rate among beneficiaries of cash assistance welfare programs. Appleton (1996) notes that the intent to deny indigent mothers procreative liberty has "been touted by the decision makers for all the world to see. The most often expressed purpose of welfare reform, to stop welfare mothers or unmarried teenagers from reproducing, is reflected in every measure or proposal" (64).

Let's now return to the fact that reproductive privacy rights are supposed to protect procreative liberty. Yet, the purpose of family cap policies is to deny poor mothers the ability to make unconstrained decisions about whether or not to bear a child; that is, their purpose is to deny poor mothers procreative liberty. Thus, the *intent* of family cap polices is to violate poor mothers' ostensible reproductive privacy rights. Let's return as well to the fact that the Court has sanctioned these policies, finding that they pose no constitutional issues at all (Dandridge v. Williams, 397 U.S. 471 (1970)). We are not dealing with a law that, in its pursuit of other legitimate aims, indirectly burdens a constitutional right. Instead, we are dealing with a law whose direct aim is to burden, and violate, a constitutional right. Indeed, the law fails if it does not violate poor individuals' ostensible reproductive privacy rights. As Appleton (1996) observes, the success of family cap policies is measured by whether or not there is a reduction in the "illegitimacy ratio" (64).

Yet, the Court has held that these laws, whose purpose is to violate poor mothers' rights, actually do not violate those rights. The moderate claim invites us to believe that poor mothers have rights that are violated by laws that not only intend and function to violate these rights, but also have the blessing of that institution that determines the boundaries and content of the right. This is an odd invitation. It may be less odd to conclude, as the strong claim would, that poor mothers do not have these rights at all.

The Current Landscape

If procreative liberty is the ability of a woman to decide whether or not to become a mother without the government using its enormous power to force her to make the decision that the government wants her to make, then a poor woman only enjoys procreative liberty when the government does not attempt to influence her reproductive decisions. There are two circumstances wherein a poor woman enjoys procreative liberty:

1. If she lives in a state that does not have a family cap policy in its TANF program and that structures its Medicaid program to fund both non-therapeutic and therapeutic abortions as well as the costs attendant to childbirth

2. If she lives in a state that both does not have a TANF program at all *and* refuses to fund nontherapeutic abortions, therapeutic abortions, and the costs attendant to childbirth

In the first circumstance, the state does not influence a woman's decision about whether to become a mother because it provides financial support for both paths. Because the government is not using its economic power to direct a woman to curb her fertility or to carry a pregnancy to term, the woman is left free to decide whether having a child is the right course for her. Expectedly, external forces—like pressure exerted by her family or intimate partner, her religious or moral beliefs, cultural discourses asserting the impropriety of abortion and/or mothering while poor, her personal desires concerning the life that she wants to live and the life that she wants to provide for any children that she has—will bear on her decision. But, procreative liberty means that the *government* is not one of those external forces. And the government is not one of those external forces bearing on a woman's reproductive decision making when it financially supports both motherhood and the avoidance of motherhood.

Similarly, the government is not an external force bearing on a woman's reproductive decision making when it financially supports neither motherhood nor the avoidance of motherhood. This circumstance abandons indigent women to the wilderness of the market. It leaves them in the situation in which wealthier women find themselves—bearing the onus of purchasing the healthcare that will facilitate the births of healthy children, the goods and services that will facilitate the rearing of healthy children, and the medical procedure that will avoid the necessity of the first categories of items. Yet, this circumstance is cruel. It is cruel because it leaves poor women in the situation in which wealthier women find themselves, but without the means that wealthier women enjoy. Nevertheless, I am willing to argue that a government that fashions this legal landscape allows its indigent subjects procreative liberty—albeit a tragic and emaciated liberty—because it does not use its economic power to determine the trajectory of a woman's pregnancy.

Luckily, this second circumstance—wherein women enjoy a brutal, withered liberty—does not exist in the United States. Every state has chosen to implement a Medicaid program with federal monies (Perkins 2002). Because the federal government requires that states receiving federal Medicaid monies must cover prenatal care and childbirth expenses for eligible pregnant women, every state covers those costs (Perkins 2002). Further, every state has implemented a TANF program, providing (temporary) financial support to families (Center on Budget and Policy Priorities 2015). Thus, no state abandons indigent women to the market.

However, while we might be appreciative that every state supports a poor woman's decision to become a mother (at least initially, before family cap provisions are triggered or before the five-year limitation on TANF grants comes into effect), our appreciation ought to be cabined by the acknowledgment that this support does not mean that poor women enjoy procreative liberty. Poor women only enjoy procreative liberty when a state matches its economic support of motherhood with economic support of therapeutic *and* nontherapeutic abortion. Interestingly, only five states—Hawaii, Maryland, Minnesota, New Mexico, and California—allow women procreative liberty, funding therapeutic and nontherapeutic abortions as well as declining to implement a family cap policy in its TANF program (Falk 2016; Guttmacher Institute 2016).

While it is commendable that poor women enjoy procreative liberty in these five states, we must keep in mind that their enjoyment of this liberty is not in any way commanded by the Constitution. This liberty is not the consequence of a reproductive privacy right demanding that the government support both paths that a pregnancy could take. That poor women enjoy procreative liberty in five states is a consequence of the generosity of those states, not the requirements of poor women's "rights." Indeed, the Court has interpreted their "rights" to require nothing from the state.

It is worthwhile to note that the denial of procreative liberty to poor women has taken a variety of forms. Twenty-two states (and the District of Columbia) have declined to implement a family cap in the TANF program but have refused to fund nontherapeutic and therapeutic abortions in the Medicaid program.[10] The pronatalist thrust of these regimes is clear: The government uses its economic power to direct women away from abortion and toward motherhood.[11] Two states—Massachusetts and New Jersey—have implemented a family cap while imposing no funding restrictions on therapeutic and nontherapeutic abortions. The antinatalist thrust of these regimes is equally clear: The government uses its economic power to direct poor women toward abortion and away from motherhood.

Finally, a contradiction is produced when states restrict Medicaid funding for all abortions while simultaneously implementing a family cap policy in its TANF program. The pronatalism of the Medicaid abortion funding restriction is inconsistent with the antinatalism of the TANF family cap policy. Interestingly, this contradictory system exists in eleven states.[12] How are we to understand the contradiction in these states? Do these states want to encourage poor women's fertility (through their Medicaid abortion restrictions) or discourage it (through their TANF family cap provisions)?

First, let's remind ourselves that contradictions do not need to be reconciled; they serve their purpose despite their irrationality. Consider cultural theorist Wahneema Lubiano's (1992) examination of Justice Clarence Thomas's confirmation hearings. After Anita Hill accused Thomas of sexually harassing her years earlier when they both were employed at the Equal Employment Opportunity Commission, Senators Orrin Hatch and Strom Thurmond defended Thomas (and Thomas's description of the confirmation hearings as a "high-tech lynching") by calling Hill a "lesbian, spurned woman." Lubiano writes,

> The logic of narratives that demonized Hill didn't seem to require rational defense whether or not such narratives were vulnerable to rational critique. . . . It doesn't matter that no one was ever lynched on behalf of a lesbian, or that being a woman spurned by a man implies heterosexuality. . . . That lesbian and spurned woman cannot be rationally linked together simply means that a debased discourse doesn't care whether the terms of "othering" are logical or not. Any demonic narrative will do in a pinch. . . . [I]t simply depends upon what demon is most effective in making the sense of the world that power requires. (1992, 342)

The contradiction produced by eleven states' simultaneous encouragement and discouragement of poor mothers' fertility through their Medicaid and TANF programs need not be reconciled. It is simply an example of a "debased discourse" that has no goal beyond demonizing poor women. The power of these contradictory antinatalist/pronatalist systems is not that they reduce abortion rates or reduce childbirth rates. Their power is that they demean and disparage poor women through constructing their fertility as a social problem while leaving wealthier women's fertility to be constructed in contradistinction to that of their poor counterparts. As these regimes schizophrenically declare that something—anything—needs to be done about poor women's capacity to reproduce, wealthier women's fertility goes unproblematized; in fact, it is valued and venerated.

Second, a state that implements a family cap policy while refusing to cover abortion in its Medicaid program only implements a contradictory system if the state's goal is either to increase or decrease childbirth rates among indigent women. If the state's goal in erecting the legal landscape is simply to ensure its presence in poor women's reproductive lives, then there is no contradiction. If the state seeks to be a regulatory force in poor women's reproductive decision making—constantly surveilling and always there—then the ostensibly contradictory regime is, in reality, a perfectly consistent one. If the goal of the regime is to produce state omnipresence, then it succeeds wildly—irrespective of whether it has any effect at all on abortion or childbirth rates.

Justifications for Reproductive Privacy Rights

We now examine justifications for reproductive privacy rights. The objective here is to determine the reason why poor mothers have been deprived of these rights, either in the moderate or strong sense. The examination reveals that, as is the case with family privacy rights and informational privacy rights, the moral construction of poverty underlies the justifications.

Reproductive Privacy Rights as Safeguards Against Totalitarianism

Legal theorist Jed Rubenfeld (1989) has offered a compelling description of reproductive privacy rights as mechanisms that nations use to prevent their democratic governments from transforming into totalitarian states. He writes that, with any government, there exists the danger of

> a particular kind of creeping totalitarianism, an unarmed *occupation* of individuals' lives. This is the danger of which Foucault as well as the right to privacy is warning us: a society standardized and normalized, in which lives are too substantially or too rigidly directed. That is the threat posed by state power in our century. (Rubenfeld 1989, 784)

He argues that the purpose of privacy rights, reproductive and otherwise, is to limit the government's ability to determine the form and content of individuals' lives. He identifies abortion rights as paradigmatic in this regard due to the fact that they prevent the government from compelling motherhood—an all-consuming status, occupation, and identity:

> Anti-abortion laws produce motherhood: they take diverse women with every variety of career, life-plan, and so on, and make mothers of them all. To be sure, motherhood is no unitary phenomenon that is experienced alike by all women. Nonetheless, it is difficult to imagine a state-enforced rule whose ramifications within the actual, everyday life of the actor are more far-reaching. For a period of months and quite possibly years, forced motherhood shapes women's occupations and preoccupations in the minutest detail; it creates a perceived identity for women and confines them to it; and it gathers up a multiplicity of approaches to the problem of being a woman and reduces them all to the single norm of motherhood. (Rubenfeld 1989, 788)

For the scores of indigent women in the country for whom it is impossible to raise the money to pay for abortion services, Medicaid abortion funding restrictions compel motherhood. They make childbearing mandatory and, consequently, are "a totalitarian intervention into a women's life" (1989, 791).

We then must ask ourselves this question: If we value reproductive privacy rights because we think that they prevent our government from becoming a totalitarian one, and if we think that having a non-totalitarian government is a good thing, why would we effectively or actually deprive a segment of our population of these rights and allow our government to become totalitarian? There are at least two answers to this question.

First, consider that Rubenfeld describes the right to privacy as "the fundamental freedom not to have one's life too totally determined by a progressively more normalizing state" (1989, 784). To the extent that those empowered to interpret the Constitution deny poor women the right to privacy and, in so doing, allow their lives to be determined by a progressively more normalizing state, it may be due to the belief that these women's lives *ought* to be governed by a *normalizing* state. These are women who, after all, have flouted the exalted norm of economic independence. These are women who ought to be normalized, steeped in the majority's norms, and brought in from the margins where they currently exist.

The second answer to the question of why we, as a society, tolerate effectively or actually depriving poor women of reproductive privacy rights may be found in the recognition that, while the government that is produced by denying poor women reproductive privacy rights is totalitarian, it is only totalitarian *to some*. That is, those who have interpreted the Constitution to allow the state to occupy poor women's lives do not loathe totalitarianism in the abstract. They only loathe it when it applies to them and people like them. Totalitarianism can be tolerated—and, indeed, welcomed and supported—when it is directing *other* people's lives. If "democracy must impose limits on the extent of control and direction that the state exercises over the day-to-day conduct of individual lives" (Rubenfeld 1989, 805), then it is enough that the state remains a democratic one to those who enjoy power and privilege in this country That it is undemocratic to the disempowered and the unprivileged is of no significant consequence.

One final note: Consider Rubenfeld's argument that by making childbearing mandatory, "all will be, by the act of reproduction itself, involuntarily drafted into the service of the state, the first requirement of which is the reproduction of its populace" (1989, 791). This insight helps us make sense of family cap policies. That is, the populace that poor mothers reproduce exists at the bottom of society's hierarchies. The children to whom they give birth are those described in the congressional findings that introduce the Personal Responsibility and Work Opportunity Reconciliation Act, which inaugurated TANF: the damaged, dysfunctional, and always implicitly racialized individuals who are predisposed to criminality and/or economic dependence. Essentially, the poor women coerced to reproduce by Medicaid abortion funding restrictions are an undesirable populace. Family cap policies, then, are recognition of that undesirability. Together, family cap policies and Medicaid funding restrictions reflect the state's ambivalence about whether poor women's reproduction can actually be of service to the state.

Reproductive Privacy Rights as Protectors of Autonomy and Personhood

Many scholars have used the language of autonomy and personhood to describe that which reproductive privacy rights protect. For example, constitutional law scholar Erwin Chemerinksy (2007) has discussed the mystification that characterized the earliest days of reproductive privacy jurisprudence—a time when the Court endeavored to protect individuals' autonomy, but did so by referencing their interest in protecting their property. He writes,

> Consider *Griswold v. Connecticut* as an example of this confusion. The right to use contraceptives clearly is about privacy in terms of autonomy: the right of a person to control whether he or she becomes a parent. But Justice Douglas's

opinion never hinted at this autonomy interest and instead focused entirely on concerns over searching the marital bedroom for signs of the use of contraceptives. (2007, 650)

Since the Court's decision in *Griswold*, however, the right of reproductive privacy has been linked explicitly to autonomy. Indeed, at Justice Ginsburg's confirmation hearing, she articulated her belief that the right to determine whether or not one will become a mother is as much a question of equal protection as it is of "individual autonomy" (Siegel 2013, 71).

Legal scholar Laura Stein (1993) has noted that "[n]umerous commentators have refined this 'autonomy' approach, arguing that decisional privacy doctrine should be seen as protecting 'personhood'" (1173). She writes that these scholars have argued that reproductive privacy rights protect personhood because they identify those things, like the decision whether to assume parenthood, that "are so important to our identity as persons[,] as human beings," and protect them from government interference (1173). Indeed, in the course of affirming that women's ability to access abortion enjoys constitutional protection, the plurality opinion in *Planned Parenthood v. Casey* (505 U.S. 833 (1992)) gives a nod to reproductive privacy rights as protective of personhood, noting that the abortion right allows women the ability to define their "own concept of existence, of meaning, of the universe, and of the mystery of human life," and that "[b]eliefs about these matters could not define the attributes of *personhood* were they formed under compulsion of the State" (852).

The idea is that the decision about whether to become a parent is fundamental to who a person is and who a person wants to be. Indeed, it is self-constituting: While the individual makes the decision, the decision simultaneously creates the individual who makes it. This creation of self is an act of autonomy, an act by which the individual controls the type of person she will become. Reproductive privacy rights protect autonomy because they secure for the individual a space within which she can exert this control. And they protect personhood because, in the securing of that space, individuals can create themselves as the persons they want to be. Thus, autonomy and personhood are intimately intertwined. As legal theorist Dorothy Roberts (1991) formulates the relationship, denying women the ability to step into or avoid motherhood without coercion "violates a woman's personhood by denying her autonomy over the self-defining decision of whether she will bring another being into the world" (1467). Why, then, have poor mothers been effectively or actually deprived of reproductive privacy rights, rendering them unable to be autonomous persons?

Could it be that a society tolerating a Constitution that imposes no limit on the government's ability to impel poor women toward or away from motherhood has given undue significance to—indeed, has fetishized—the fact that these women are reliant on the state for basic necessities? Their poverty and their consequent turn to the state for assistance make them not "autonomous" in a capacity that has always been celebrated and venerated within societal discourse: They are not *economically* autonomous.

Thus, could it be that those who very well could have interpreted the Constitution to bestow reproductive privacy rights on poor women, but who declined to do so, are merely reflecting the judgments of a society that believes that these women are already lacking autonomy in a very foundational sense? Accordingly, to deny an indigent woman the ability to be autonomous with respect to whether she will become a mother may be thought to be of no great moment. Her lack of autonomy in constituting and defining herself simply complements her lack of autonomy in supporting herself financially (Roberts 1991).

Sex Equality

Many theorists have argued that abortion rights are essential to sex equality. Constitutional law scholar Reva Siegel has made this argument quite extensively, and convincingly, in her scholarship. Her excavation of nineteenth-century campaigns to criminalize abortion reveals the relationship between women's inability to access abortion and the enforcement of traditional gender roles. She documents how abortion opponents during that era explicitly argued that abortion was dangerous and ought to be criminalized because it allowed women an exit from the status of wife and mother. Siegel (1992) writes, "The doctors who advocated criminalizing abortion quite openly argued that regulating women's reproductive conduct was necessary, not merely to protect potential life, but also to ensure women's performance of marital and maternal obligations" (291).

While the arguments against abortion have shifted over time, and while it is rare to hear abortion opponents make the case that the procedure should be illegal because women ought to be forced to perform traditional gender roles, the relationship between access to abortion and the ability to reject these gender roles has remained unchanged. It is for this reason that many advocates for abortion rights have asserted that using the rhetoric of privacy to protect abortion access mischaracterizes what is at stake. What is actually at stake, they contend, is sex equality—equal citizenship. Siegel (2005) has been a vocal proponent of this view, arguing that laws criminalizing abortion violate equal citizenship principles because they compel women to perform the work of motherhood in a society still organized around the understanding that those who bear and rear children do not engage in the labor that society most highly values and centrally associates with citizenship (Siegel 2005).[13]

Moreover, the understanding that abortion rights implicate sex equality has come to be reflected in Court opinions over the years. While the Court made no mention of sex equality concerns in its first recognition of the abortion right in *Roe v. Wade,* these concerns appeared in the Court's reconstitution of that right in *Casey.* Nineteen years after *Roe* identified the abortion right as hailing from a line of cases using the language of privacy to shield activities concerning the family and contraception from government regulation, the *Casey* plurality opinion noted that "the ability of women to participate equally in the economic and social life of the Nation has been facilitated by their ability to control their reproductive lives" (Planned Parenthood of Southeastern Pennsylvania v. Casey, 505 U.S. 833, 856 (1992)).

A similar observation of the relationship between abortion access and sex equality was made in *Gonzales v. Carhart* (550 U.S. 124 (2007)), albeit in a dissenting opinion. Justice Ginsburg, joined by three other dissenting justices, wrote that "legal challenges to undue restrictions on abortion procedures do not seek to vindicate some generalized notion of privacy; rather, they center on a woman's autonomy to determine her life's course, and thus to enjoy equal citizenship stature" (172).

If abortion access enables a woman to define the shape and content of her womanhood, what does it mean that poor women do not have this access? Essentially, what is the meaning of Medicaid abortion funding restrictions for sex equality? The answer, clearly, is that these restrictions force *sex inequality* onto poor women. The answer is that wealthier women have been given the space to determine what their womanhood will mean, while the state determines the meaning of womanhood for poor women. Wealthier women have the ability to decide when and whether they will engage in gendered-female caretaking labor or, alternately, the gendered-male labor in the public sphere that society has associated historically with full citizenship; meanwhile, this decision has been wrested from poor women, and they are compelled to do unremunerated, unfavored caretaking labor.

When considered in this light, we see the complexity of the injustice. I have argued in this book that when wealthier women enjoy effective privacy rights that their poorer counterparts lack, it produces a disturbing equality problem. This problem concerns poor women's inequality vis-à-vis other women. However, abortion rights as a sex equality matter reveals another dimension of inequality. When poor women do not share the access to abortion that wealthier women enjoy, they are not only left unequal to other women, but *they are also left unequal to men*. Thus, wealthier women can use their abortion rights to achieve sex equality and equal citizenship with men, while poor women are left to be men's inferiors. They are forced to assume the subordinate roles that wealthier women have fought for ages to occupy on their own terms.

But, what of family caps—policies that encourage abortion and, in so doing, discourage women from assuming traditional gender roles? Do family cap policies reflect the belief that poor women *ought* to achieve sex equality with men? The answer is no. Family cap policies are only triggered after poor women are already mothers, after they already have been performing traditional gender roles. Further, if family cap policies were intended to inspire or persuade poor women to achieve equal citizenship with men, then they would come with the means that would allow women to be mothers *and* contributors to public life; they would be implemented alongside, at the very least, programs that provide poor mothers access to childcare and educational opportunities.

This, of course, is not what has taken place. Family cap policies are what happen when the state retracts. They are what happen when the state demonstrates its lack of commitment to the well-being and full development of poor mothers, poor people, and poor families. As such, they cannot be understood as a tool that the state wields to encourage poor women to "participate equally in the economic and social life of the Nation" (Planned Parenthood of Southeastern Pennsylvania v. Casey 1992, 857).

Siegel's ruminations on laws restricting abortion provide an alternative lens through which we can understand family caps. Siegel (1992) writes that "if restrictions on abortion are analyzed in a social framework, they present questions concerning the regulation of motherhood, and, thus, value judgments concerning women's roles" (265). Essentially, laws restricting abortion reflect the belief that the other roles that become difficult (or, without proper support, impossible) for women to assume when they are mothers are simply not as valuable for women to perform. They reflect a conviction that the only valuable role a woman can play is that of mother. Indeed, they proclaim that women are only valued and valuable when they are reproducing and raising children. If laws that make abortion inaccessible can be interpreted in this manner, how should we interpret laws that encourage women to have abortions, like family cap policies? It would seem like these laws ought to be interpreted to reflect the sense that some women—poor women—are not valued and are not valuable when they are reproducing and raising children. They reveal the certainty that some women cannot and should not assume traditional gender roles. Some women are not good mothers. Some women are not good women.

Consider as well Siegel's analysis of the values underlying nineteenth-century arguments against abortion. She writes,

> At the same time that doctors asserted professional authority over a wife's reproductive conduct, they insisted upon the public character of that conduct. A wife had a duty to bear children which she owed, not to her husband, but to the community: It was "a duty [she] tacitly promised the State." Laws against abortion and contraception were necessary to protect the *public's* interest in procreation. Synthesizing religious, medical, and common law authority in neo-Malthusian terms, the doctors argued that the institution of marriage was of the utmost public regulatory concern because it was responsible for the production of populations, and in the production of populations lay the welfare of the state. (1992, 296–97)

Family cap policies also reflect an understanding of reproductive conduct as a public regulatory concern. As was true in the nineteenth century, reproduction today also has a public character. However, where abortion restrictions reflect the assumption that it was in the public interest for some women (i.e., white women whose dependency had been privatized by the institution of marriage) to procreate, family cap policies reflect the assumption that it is in the public interest for some women (poor women who are assumed to be unmarried and whose dependency has not been privatized) to avoid procreation. If reproduction is responsible for the production of populations, then family cap policies enact the conviction that it is better for the community and the nation when some populations are not produced. And where childbearing and childrearing by middle-class white women are thought to protect the health, prosperity, and longevity of the state, childbearing and childrearing by the poor is thought to threaten those very same things.

Reproductive Privacy Rights as Defenders of
a Realm of Moral Decision Making

Finally, the value of reproductive privacy and reproductive privacy rights is often spoken about in the abstract language of dignity. For example, McClain (1994) has argued that the law has come to use the mechanism of the fundamental privacy right to allow women reproductive privacy with respect to their fertility, and "the existence of a fundamental right signals that . . . [the] range of possible choices are protected out of respect for human dignity" (1069). But, what exactly is the substance of the indignity when women are denied their fundamental right to reproductive privacy and are coerced into or away from motherhood?

McClain (1996) answers by noting that the decision whether to carry an unintended pregnancy to term or to terminate it raises profound moral questions. These are questions of unparalleled profundity; they concern the "mysteries of one's existence and the meaning of reproduction in one's life" (366). Decisions about the trajectory one will allow one's fertility to take call upon women to interrogate and engage with questions of what is good and bad, right and wrong, imperative or insignificant. Women must look to, or create, their own moral compasses, and they must follow the direction in which they point.

Thus, denying women the ability to make these decisions is a crushing indignity because it denies that they are individuals—persons—with a moral capacity. It denies that they are morally competent beings with consciences. Reproductive privacy rights, then, "recogniz[e] the moral capacity of the rightholder by affording her room to exercise moral responsibility in making decisions or engaging in protected conduct" (McClain 1994, 1074).

Dworkin's views on the nature of reproductive decision making are in accord with those of McClain. Dworkin (1993) notes that reproductive decision making calls forth questions about the "sanctity of life[,] . . . a highly controversial, contestable value" (151). He explains that "[m]any political decisions, including economic ones, have serious and special impact on some individuals. Procreative decisions are fundamental in a different way; the moral issues on which they hinge are religious in the broad sense . . . , touching the ultimate purpose and value of human life itself" (158).

Dworkin argues that governments have two options when dealing with the moral issues involved with reproductive decision making, especially the decision to terminate a pregnancy: Governments can either let individuals consult their consciences and determine what their ethical principles dictate, or governments can determine the answer to the moral questions themselves and then compel their subjects to live their lives accordingly. Dworkin (1993) labels these two options "responsibility" and "conformity," respectively, and he argues that the options

> are not only different but antagonistic. If we aim at responsibility, we must leave citizens free in the end to decide as they think right, because that is what moral responsibility entails. But if we aim at conformity, we demand instead that citizens act in a way that might be contrary to their own moral convictions; this discourages rather than encourages them to develop their own sense of when and why life is sacred. (1993, 150–51)

Dworkin concludes that we, as a nation, have chosen to respect the moral issues involved in reproductive decision making by expecting and demanding responsibility from individuals, not conformity. Instead of allowing the government to determine when and whether a woman will become a mother, we have given that authority to individual women. As such, we expect and demand that women wrestle with the moral questions inherent in deciding whether to become pregnant, whether to carry a pregnancy to term, and whether to have an abortion. Further, reproductive privacy rights are the mechanisms for securing for individual women the space to wrestle with these questions. They are the means that we, as a nation, have chosen for enabling women to be morally responsible.

So, if that is what reproductive privacy rights are all about—if they assume an individual's capacity for moral reasoning and provide individuals with a space within which they can decide how best to answer for themselves profound moral questions—then we see clearly why poor women have been effectively or actually denied these rights. We do not trust poor women's capacity for moral reasoning. We do not believe that that they will competently wrestle with the moral issues that reproductive decision making raises. We are not confident that they understand the moral significance of choosing motherhood or eschewing it—of carrying a fetus to term or terminating it before birth. In a society that largely attributes poverty to the personal shortcomings of individuals and that presumes that poor people suffer from behavioral and ethical deficiencies, we doubt that an indigent woman has the moral capacity to assess competently the moral issues pregnancy and motherhood necessarily implicate. Ours is a society that has been convinced that poor women have children not for all the respectable reasons that wealthier women have children, but rather because they are interested solely in increasing the amount of money that they will receive from the government. Will poor women—women who supposedly view their procreative capacities as lucrative commodities—undertake the difficult moral reasoning that McClain and Dworkin describe as inherently implicated in reproductive decision making? The answer given by the Court, lawmakers, and society generally is a resounding no.

In her defense of procreative liberty, feminist legal theorist Robin West writes that reproductive freedom, and the privacy rights that enable and protect that freedom, should rest on the "demonstrated capacity of pregnant women to decide whether to carry a fetus to term or to abort responsibly" (1990, 82–83). But, what of those women who have not demonstrated a capacity to decide such questions responsibly? What of those women whose poverty has been taken to demonstrate that they are, in fact, *irresponsible*? It makes sense to refuse those women reproductive freedom. It makes sense to deny those women reproductive privacy rights.

West (1990) writes that

> [u]nlike the homicidal decision to take another's life, the decision to abort is more often than not a morally responsible decision. The abortion decision typically rests not on a desire to destroy fetal life but on a responsible and moral desire to ensure that a new life will be borne only if it will be nurtured and loved. (83)

Here, West speaks in terms of likelihood; she argues that, "more often than not" and "typically," women will step into or avoid motherhood after determining that it is the morally responsible thing to do. However, in speaking in terms of likelihood, West acknowledges, albeit implicitly, that there are those who will fail to be morally responsible when making decisions about motherhood.

West alludes to exceptions to the rule. In a society where individualist explanations of poverty are dominant, and poverty is thought to provide exacting insight into the impoverished persons' moral character, poor women are those exceptions. Accordingly, while we can assume that wealthier women will make morally responsible decisions around motherhood, we cannot make the same assumptions for poor women. Thus, wealthier women are bestowed with reproductive privacy rights, and poor women are effectively or actually denied them. McClain (1994) is clear on this point. She writes, "American history reveals that characterizing groups of people as irresponsible (characterizing African-Americans as childlike and ignorant) has served to justify denying them rights" (1075). Similarly, assuming the moral irresponsibility of poor women has justified effectively or actually denying them reproductive privacy rights.

McClain's (1994) exploration of opposition to rights and rights-talk launched by self-styled "communitarians" is instructive here. She writes that the communitarian critique of rights

> manifests a lack of trust in people as moral agents exercising freedom of conscience, capable of behaving with integrity, and living pursuant to genuinely held convictions. The communitarians frankly fear that individual conscience is too weak without the strong reinforcement of the moral voices of others. In that sense, they resemble those critics of liberalism . . . who charge that people are not good enough for liberalism and fault it for its apparent fatally flawed assumption . . . that autonomous individuals can freely choose, or will, their moral life. (1994, 1070)

This chapter, and the book generally, propose that this passage describes the state of poor women's privacy rights. It perfectly explains their deprivation, in either the moderate or strong sense. We, as a society, do not trust poor women and poor mothers. We are convinced that their consciences are too weak or are underdeveloped. We believe that poor women and poor mothers are not good enough for liberalism—that, if they are left to their own devices, they will not lead a moral life. Hence, state intervention, coercion, and regulation.

It is worth noting McClain's argument that liberalism "makes assumptions about the possession of capacities for responsibility, maturity, and judgment and does not premise rights on a case-by-case inquiry into the demonstration of such capacities" (1994, 1069). Poor women have been effectively or actually denied reproductive privacy rights because those empowered to bestow and deny those rights have made assumptions about their *dispossession* of capacities for responsibility, maturity, and judgment. Until we change those assumptions—until we reject individualist explanations of poverty—poor women and mothers will continue to be deprived of privacy rights.

Conclusion

The preceding chapters have developed and supported a simple, albeit controversial, thesis: Poor mothers have been deprived of family, informational, and reproductive privacy rights. In these chapters I have shown that those who are empowered to interpret the Constitution have construed the document so as to endow wealthier women with rights that protect their families from regulation by the state, that prevent their most intimate and personal information from being collected by the state and disclosed to third parties, and that provide them with a space wherein they can decide whether or not to become mothers without the government using its immense power to influence their decisions. Simultaneously, the Constitution has been construed to deny poor mothers (and poor women facing the question of whether to become mothers) those same rights.

I invite you to understand this book's thesis—that poor mothers have been deprived of family, informational, and reproductive privacy rights—in one of two ways. One version, the moderate claim, takes the statement that poor mothers have been deprived of privacy rights to assert that poor mothers have been deprived of *effective* privacy rights. The other version, the strong claim (which I strongly encourage you to accept), takes the statement that poor mothers have been deprived of privacy rights to assert that poor mothers actually *do not* possess privacy rights; they are not bearers of the right to privacy.

Prevailing discourses about poverty explain both the moderate and the strong claim. These discourses necessarily inform the Court's decisions. Indeed, to suppose otherwise is to subscribe to a formalism that even modern-day formalists would reject. It is to believe that the relevant constitutional text—providing simply, yet vaguely, that no state shall "deprive any person of life, liberty, or property without due process of law[,] nor deny to any person within its jurisdiction the equal protection of the laws"—yields just one meaning. It is to believe that a jurist does nothing more than divine that single meaning and apply it to the controversy before her.

This book denies that this quaint rendering of the judicial method competently describes what the justices have done when they have interpreted the Constitution as imposing substantial limits on state power in wealthier mothers' lives while not limiting state power in poor mothers' lives. Instead, I argue that the social and cultural milieu in which the Constitution and its interpreters are embedded explain how we have arrived at a present wherein wealthier mothers' rights are effective constraints on the government and poor mothers' ostensible rights constrain nothing.

Since the dawn of the nation, many have embraced the moral construction of poverty. According to this narrative, we can safely presume that a poor person has problematic values and behavioral flaws, as these personal deficiencies—and not structural conditions—are that which cause individuals to be poor. Privacy rights are recognized and protected because they are thought to yield specific values. Due to the belief that privacy rights will not yield these values when individuals who are behaviorally and ethically deficient bear them, poor mothers effectively (consistent with the moderate claim) or actually (consistent with the strong claim) have been denied these rights.

If the moderate claim competently describes our legal present, then the struggle is to give poor mothers' privacy rights some teeth. However, if the strong claim competently describes our legal present, then the struggle is not for the Court to strengthen poor mother's existing privacy rights, but rather for the Court to give poor mothers privacy rights in the first place. Framed in this way, the best guides for how to triumph in this struggle are not those historical moments when groups agitated for more robust protections of the rights that they already bore, but rather times when disenfranchised groups fought for and were granted rights previously denied to them altogether. Thus, the subsequent sections examine the circumstances that led black people and LGBT people to go from being deprived of a set of rights—the right to vote and the right to marry, respectively—to bearing those rights.

Looking to these precedents for guidance, we can see that these disenfranchised groups were successful in winning the rights that had been denied to them largely because they shifted, or took advantage of shifts, in cultural discourses. Thus, if history is a teacher, poor mothers will only be granted privacy rights when cultural discourses around poverty shift as well.[1]

Although those skeptical of the strong claim will derive a different insight from the experiences of black people with voting rights and LGBT people with the right to marry, what is of paramount importance is that *both the moderate and the strong claim agree that poor mothers will only enjoy the privacy rights that wealthier mothers enjoy when we have unseated the moral construction of poverty from its present discursive throne.* It is only in a transformed culture[2]—a culture in which it is not radical, or even progressive, to believe that poverty is best explained by looking to macro forces well outside of the control of individuals—that the Constitution will be interpreted to bestow equal privacy rights to poor and wealthier mothers.

The famed (and oft-quoted) jurist Oliver Wendell Holmes (1881) was correct when he said, "The felt necessities of the time, the prevalent moral and political theories, intuitions of public policy, avowed or unconscious, even the prejudices which judges share with their fellow-men, have had a good deal more to do than the syllogism in determining the rules by which men should be governed" (1). A syllogism has not led to poor mothers' deprivation of a meaningful privacy right. And a syllogism will not lead to their enfranchisement. Rather, an interpretation of the Constitution that bestows poor mothers with the privacy rights that have been bestowed on wealthier mothers will only be the product of changed "moral and political theories" and transformed "intuitions of public policy"—when judges and their "fellow-men" have rid themselves of old prejudices concerning the immorality of poverty. Such an interpretation will only be a product of a changed culture.

Popular constitutionalism—which proposes that "the people themselves" ought to influence what the Constitution is interpreted to mean (Kramer 2004)—is not just a normative approach; it also has some descriptive accuracy.[3] The people themselves currently are not confident that poor mothers will put privacy to beneficial uses. This suspicion has shaped the meaning of the Constitution. When this suspicion has given way to an appreciation of poor mothers as worthy of our respect instead of our disdain, then the Constitution will be interpreted to mean something else.[4]

To argue that culture has shaped the meaning of the Constitution is not to argue that the Court cannot be a countermajoritarian institution—that it cannot act in opposition to and in derogation of the majority's sensibilities and desires. Consider this compilation of odes to the judiciary as a counter-majoritarian force:

> Justice Black once stated the conventional wisdom in particularly ringing terms: Courts stand "as havens of refuge for those who might otherwise suffer because they are helpless, weak, outnumbered, or because they are the non-conforming victims of prejudice and public excitement." In his famous concurring opinion in *Whitney v. California*, Justice Louis Brandeis similarly opined that one function of judicial review is to protect against "the occasional tyrannies of governing majorities." Like-minded scholars have written that without judicial review "there would be little hope for rights or for equality," that courts "restrain the majority's worst excesses," and that judicial review "advances the cause of peaceful change" by preventing the "oppression of individuals and minorities" that might encourage resort to the right of revolution. (Klarman 2005a, 440)

Certainly, the judiciary is capable, in theory, of being a countermajoritarian institution. And Justice Black, Justice Brandeis, and others are right to praise its theoretical capacity to act as such. However, it has not been a "haven of refuge" for poor mothers, protecting them against the "tyrannies of governing majorities." Instead, the jurisprudence that the Court has constructed reflects the majority's sense that it is sometimes pointless, at times counterproductive, and at other times dangerous to cede to poor mothers a space free from government regulation. The Court's jurisprudence reflects the majority's sense that poor mothers are not to be trusted with their children, their families, their intimate information, their fertility, and their lives. Miming the majority's distrust of poor mothers, the Court has constructed a jurisprudence of distrust.

It is unlikely that five justices are going to wake up one morning in the not-so-distant future, read the text of the Fourteenth Amendment, and determine that the jurisprudence that this book has discussed at length—a jurisprudence that authorizes the state to be an omnipresent regulatory force in poor mothers' lives—was wrongly decided. A majority of the Court is not going to discover from precedents and other legal sources that poor women ought to be trusted with their bodies and their children and, in light of this revelation, revise the doctrine accordingly. Instead, if we are to witness legal change in this arena, it will be because society has changed. The catalyst for that change may be a social movement. Or it may be a war. Or it may be a recession. Or it may be a combination of all three. Or it may be none of the three. However, what is true is that poor mothers will not enjoy privacy rights in any meaningful sense until the culture at large believes that they are worthy of these rights and can be trusted with them. The moral construction of poverty needs to be unsettled in order to make that happen.

A note before continuing: There are two mechanisms by which cultural change effects a legal change in the form of a recognition of a new right, the expansion of the class of rightsbearers, or the redefinition of the contours of an existing right. The first mechanism involves a formal change to the law—that is, an amendment to the constitutional text or the passage of a statute. The second mechanism involves a judicial reinterpretation of a seemingly stable legal text. The circumstance of black people's enfranchisement involves the first mechanism: Cultural shifts led to the adoption of the Fifteenth Amendment and then, a century later, to the passage of the Voting Rights Act of 1965. The circumstance of marriage equality involves the second mechanism: Cultural shifts led to a judicial reinterpretation of the Due Process Clause to include LGBT people in the class of bearers of the right to marry.

If poor mothers are to win effective (consistent with the moderate claim) or actual (consistent with the strong claim) constitutional privacy rights, it will likely be achieved through the second mechanism; that is, the Court will have to reinterpret the Due Process Clause to ascribe (effective) privacy rights to poor mothers in view of changing cultural assumptions about poverty (and race and gender). Beyond this basic recognition, however, this Conclusion does not pay much attention to any differences in the two dynamics of legal trans-formation. The precise mechanism by which law changes in response to culture is largely irrelevant here. What is most important to the ensuing analysis is the simple fact of the *indispensability of cultural change* to legal change in either of the two forms.

Black People and Voting Rights

The story of how black people won the right to vote has very little to do with the demands of constitutional text or legal precedents. Rather, the story is a convoluted one, and it begins with a nation whose mores had shifted just enough to accommodate a constitutional amendment that purported to en-franchise a group whose humanity had been debated since the nation's dawn. Proponents of the strong claim will understand the second part of the story—the part of the story involving the years that preceded the passage of the Vot-ing Rights Act—as one about how this group was informally disenfranchised of their formally bestowed voting rights through legal tactics that the Court blessed as consistent with the demands of the Constitution. Devotees of the moderate claim will understand this part of the story differently, conceptualizing black people's inability to vote after their formal enfranchisement as evidence of nothing more than a judicially sanctioned violation of voting rights. Whether read through the lens of the moderate claim or the strong claim, the story ends with the group agitating and acquiring effective rights. We will start at the beginning, with the ratification of the Fifteenth Amendment.

Black people, both enslaved and free, had fought for Union forces in the Civil War. The defeat of the Confederacy and the maintenance of the United States of America as an undivided nation was, in part, owed to black people's loyalty and willingness to sacrifice their lives for the cause. This undeniable fact created the conditions for a social and cultural reimagining of the political role that black men could and should play in the newly restored country. The congressional record is full of paeans—some more maudlin than others—about the worthiness of black men of the franchise, as demonstrated by their service to the Union during the Civil War. To make the case that black people were worthy of voting rights, Senator Ferry from Connecticut referenced a battle in which 19 black Union soldiers were killed and 121 were wounded:

> The dead lie side by side with their white comrades on the shores of the James; the old pine trees there sing the same requiem over both, and the brave souls of both have gone where all merely external earthly distinctions are forgotten forever. But what shall I say, what shall my colleague say, of those one hundred and twenty-one wounded? Shattered and maimed they went home to the State that sent them forth and to the people for whom they had shed their blood. Let my colleague go home, if he can, and look those scarred veterans in the face and tell them that it is doing no wrong to deprive them of all share in that Government for which they have made this horrible self-sacrifice. (*Congressional Globe* 1869, 858)

Thus, war created the conditions of possibility for a cultural shift—a shift in which black men could be perceived as capable and deserving of the ability to participate in the political life of the nation through the right to vote.[5]

However, a changed culture is only a partial explanation of how black men came to be enfranchised. The explanation is incomplete if one ignores the fact that it was politically advantageous to the Republican Party to enfranchise recently freed black men in the South. "Citizenship" and "voting rights" are not synonymous. Accordingly, although the Fourteenth Amendment had made black people citizens, the ability to participate in the government did not necessarily follow from that citizenship.

Without the Fifteenth Amendment, the question of whether to permit black men to vote would have been left to white men in the southern states— white men whose power had been radically diminished and who coveted a return to the slaveocracy that had been dismantled just recently. (Of course, there were white men in the South who had been loyal to the Union and whose politics more closely aligned with the Republican Party than with the Democratic Party. But, these men were in the minority, and there were not enough of them to outvote those who wanted to see a slave-owning South rise again.)

Thus, in order for the Republican Party to maintain its control over the recently treasonous South and to secure its dominance in the nation's politics generally, the Constitution had to be amended to prohibit southern states from denying black men the ability to vote. One Republican senator explained the political situation that his party faced as follows:

> Congress had attempted the work of reconstruction through the constitutional amendment by leaving the suffrage with the white men, and by leaving with the white people of the South the question as to when the colored people should exercise the right of suffrage, if ever, but when it was found that those white men were as rebellious as ever, that they hated this Government more bitterly than ever; when it was found that they persecuted the loyal men, both white and black, in their midst; when it was found that northern men who had gone down there were driven out by social tyranny, by a thousand annoyances, by the insecurity of life and property, then it became apparent to all men of intelligence that reconstruction could not take place upon the basis of the white population, and something else must be done. Now, sir, what was there left to do? Either we must hold these people continually by military power, or we must use such machinery upon such a new basis as would enable loyal republican State governments to be raised up; and in the last resort, . . . [w]hatever dangers we apprehend from the introduction of the right of suffrage of seven hundred thousand men, just emerged from slavery, were put aside in the presence of a greater danger. . . . (*The American Annual Cyclopaedia and Register of Important Events of the Year* 1869, 156)

Black men came to be bestowed with the right to vote—that is, they came to be included in the category of persons who are ascribed the right to vote— because a cultural shift intersected with a political climate that was amenable to the recognition of black men as bearers of voting rights. As Reconstruction historian C. Vann Woodward (1969) describes it,

> [I]t is undoubtedly true that some of the Radicals were motivated almost entirely by their idealism and their genuine concern for the rights and welfare of the freedmen. What is doubtful is that these were the effective or primary motives, or that they took priority over the pragmatic and materialistic motives of party advantage and sectional economic interests. It is clear at any rate that, until the latter were aroused and marshaled, the former made little progress. (522)

The Fifteenth Amendment was adopted in order to inscribe this politico-cultural shift into a legal text.

We know, of course, that the Fifteenth Amendment ultimately was an unsuccessful mechanism for actually enabling black men to access the polls in the South. We know that after federal troops left the South and Reconstruction came to an end, those committed to maintaining black people in a position of political, economic, and social subservience accomplished what the strong claim calls the "informal disenfranchisement" of black men. The year 1890 "marked the beginning of systemic efforts by southern states to disenfranchise black voters legally. . . . Democrats chose to solidify their hold on the South by modifying the voting laws in ways that would exclude African Americans without overtly violating the Fifteenth Amendment" (Keyssar 2009, 88).

There were many mechanisms with which the southern states achieved black male disenfranchisement: residency requirements, which prohibited persons from voting if they had not resided in a jurisdiction for a prescribed period of time prior to an election; literacy tests, which required potential voters to prove that they could read and understand difficult texts; poll taxes, which required potential voters to pay a fee in order to be eligible to cast a vote; the white primary, which explicitly restricted voting in primaries to white males; and criminal disenfranchisement laws, which prohibited people who had been convicted of even minor crimes from voting (Keyysar 2009).

Importantly, the Court sanctioned all of these mechanisms of black disenfranchisement, finding in a series of cases that each was consistent with the Fifteenth Amendment (Klarman 2005b). Essentially, as long as a law did not discriminate on the basis of race on its face, then the Court considered the Fifteenth Amendment's requirements to be satisfied.[6] The results of the Court's decisions are, as historian Alexander Keyssar (2009) notes, "well known": "[T]he African-American population remained largely disenfranchised until the 1960s" (92).

Readers sympathetic to the moderate claim will understand black people as bearers of weak voting rights that were consistently violated. Readers sympathetic to the strong claim will understand black people as having been *informally disenfranchised*: They formally possessed a right, yet they were unable to exercise that right because laws that the Court had found to be constitutional made it impossible to do so.

And we might explain black men's deprivation, in either the moderate or strong sense, of their voting rights in terms similar to those that this book contends explain poor mothers' deprivation of their privacy rights. That is, the present culture, as steeped in individualist explanations of poverty as it is, is one that imagines that privacy rights will be worthless, at best, or dangerous, at worst, when poor mothers wield them. The jurisprudence has come to reflect this culture, with the case law (effectively or actually) depriving poor mothers of the privacy rights that may have been formally bestowed on them.

Similarly, the law—the Fifteenth Amendment that purported to produce equality in political participation between white men and black men—did not reflect the cultural discourses about black men and black people that were circulating during this time. It might have reflected cultural discourses sometimes found in the North, a region that was willing, sometimes, to countenance black men's political equality. But, it certainly did not reflect the discourses that were most prevalent in the South. Because of this failure of reflection, this law, the Fifteenth Amendment, was rejected there. Over time, the North lost its will to impose its values and norms on the South. When the federal government withdrew from the South, thus ending Reconstruction, black people were essentially stripped—informally disenfranchised—of the right that the amendment formally bestowed.

It was not until almost a century later, with the passage of the Voting Rights Act of 1965, that black people were actually able to participate in the political life of the nation through the vote. Accordingly, those who are interested in seeing poor mothers bear meaningful privacy rights might find instructive an exploration of the origins of the Voting Rights Act, which enabled black men and, eventually, black people to bear meaningful voting rights.

The act, which Justice Ruth Bader Ginsburg has described as "one of the most consequential, efficacious, and amply justified exercises of federal legislative power in our Nation's history" (Shelby County, Ala. v. Holder, 133 S.Ct. 2612, 2634 (2013)), was passed in response to the revolutionary demands that black people and their allies made during the civil rights movement in the

1950s and 1960s. Congress passed the act to eliminate racial discrimination in voting, "'an insidious and pervasive evil . . . '" (2618, quoted in South Carolina v. Katzenbach, 383 U.S. 301, 309 (1966)). The Voting Rights Act explicitly proscribed the variety of mechanisms that states had used to disenfranchise black voters—mechanisms, it is important to remember, that the Court had found to be consistent with the Constitution. Moreover, it required that those jurisdictions that had a documented history of racial discrimination in voting acquire prior clearance from the attorney general or from a panel of three judges for any changes that they endeavored to make to their voting laws. It was only after the passage of the act that black people were able to access the polls in significant numbers.

As the Voting Rights Act was a product of the civil rights movement, it is important to appreciate the cultural and political climate that produced this formidable social movement and that enabled it to be effective. Most historians of the civil rights movement note the significance of World War II and observe that it created the ideological terrain on which the South's disenfranchisement and subjugation of black people could be understood as ironic and unjust (Klarman 2007). The philosophy with which the U.S. government justified its participation in World War II was one that exalted democracy and declaimed the evils of fascism. The absurdity that a sweeping swath of the country was the antithesis of a democracy and a hotbed of fascism did not escape the nation's leaders:

> President Franklin D. Roosevelt urged Americans to "refut[e] at home the very theories which we are fighting abroad." Secretary of the Navy Frank Knox declared, "An army fighting allegedly for democracy should be the last place in which to practice undemocratic segregation." (Klarman 2007, 131)

Other institutions noted the irony as well, with one leading black newspaper writing that "our war is not against Hitler in Europe, but against the Hitlers in America" (Klarman 2007, 131).

While other nations were likely interested in the injustices taking place in the United States prior to the advent of World War II, the Axis powers against which the United States and the other Allies were fighting took an increased interest in these injustices after the conflict began. Writes legal historian Michael Klarman (2007), "Within forty-eight hours of the lynching of Cleo Wright—a black man—in Sikeston, Missouri, in 1942, Axis radio broadcast the details of his murder around the world" (131). Because racial inequality now had international significance, the national government was incentivized to address it. And it did just that, making lynching a crime that fell within federal jurisdiction.

The violent conflict of World War II was followed by the nonviolent conflict of the Cold War. The struggle between Russia and the United States for ideological dominance kept U.S. racial injustices within the international consciousness. Or, to be more precise, *Russia* kept southern practices of white supremacy within the international consciousness. The State Department calculated that almost half of the anti-American literature that Russia produced and distributed during this time concerned racial violence and inequality in the South (Klarman 2007, 133). Moreover, it made it quite difficult for the United States to criticize some of the antidemocratic moves that Russia made when the South was making those same moves. For example, "In 1946 Soviet Foreign Minister V. M. Molotov asked Secretary of State Jimmy Byrnes how Americans could justify pressing the Soviets to conduct free elections in Poland when America did not guarantee them in South Carolina or Georgia" (Klarman 2007, 133–34).

The fact that the world was closely observing the nation inspired scores of people within the United States to turn a self-reflective, critical eye on the country's own affairs. And that self-reflection revealed just how ugly, ignoble, and inconsistent with the nation's ideals the country's racial practices were. We might describe this as a shift in norms and values—a shift in culture. The national culture transformed from one that considered the racial practices of the South to be consistent with the values that the country claimed to embrace and embody to one that found the South's racial practices to be irreconcilable with the country's values. Indeed, the culture transformed from one that could tolerate the racial apartheid and hierarchy of the South to one that found the same intolerable.

As the culture changed, the Court's interpretation of the Constitution changed. In *Smith v. Allwright* (321 U.S. 649), decided in 1944, the Court invalidated the white primary, reversing a unanimous decision that was handed down just nine years before upholding that very technique of racial exclusion. In *Shelley v. Kraemer* (334 U.S. 1), decided in 1948, the Court found unconstitutional the racially restrictive covenant, a timeworn mechanism for ensuring that residential neighborhoods remained free of racial minority homeowners. The Court's holding flew in the face of precedent and the decisions of nineteen state supreme courts, which had come to the opposite conclusion.

In *Sweatt v. Painter* (339 U.S. 629), decided in 1950, the Court held that Texas violated the Constitution when it attempted to keep the University of Texas Law School an all-white institution by sending a qualified black applicant to a separate law school for "Negroes." In reaching this decision, the Court foreshadowed the holding at which it would arrive in *Brown v. Board* just four years later. To explain, after noting the inferiority of the physical plant of the proposed black law school, the *Sweatt* Court went on to observe that the already established white law school

> possesses to a far greater degree those qualities which are incapable of objective measurement but which make for greatness in a law school. Such qualities, to name but a few, include reputation of the faculty, experience of the administration, position and influence of the alumni, standing in the community, traditions and prestige. (Sweatt v. Painter 1950, 634)

If such intangible factors must be considered when calculating equality—if unmeasurable characteristics are the stuff of inequality—then it is difficult to imagine how separate institutions for the races could ever be equal. Thus, the *Sweatt* Court foreshadowed the Court's decision in *Brown* by implying that *Plessy v. Ferguson*'s idea of "separate but equal" facilities for the races was a circumstance that would be impossible to achieve in reality.

It is undisputed that the *Brown* decision, handed down four years after *Sweatt*, was in no way foreordained. As Klarman (2007) notes, "When the law is clear, judges will generally follow it. And in 1954, the law—as understood by most of the justices—was reasonably clear. Neither the text of the Fourteenth Amendment nor its original understanding condemned segregation; precedent and custom strongly supported it" (2007, 152). Nevertheless, the Court found, in a unanimous decision no less, that it was unconstitutional for the law to command children to go to racially segregated schools:

> As the justices deliberated over Brown, they expressed astonishment at—and approval of—the extent of the recent changes in racial mores. Minton detected "a different world today" with regard to race. Frankfurter remarked that "the pace of progress has surprised even those most eager in its promotion." Jackson, declaring that "Negro progress . . . has been spectacular," concluded that segregation "has outlived whatever justification it may have had." Justice Frankfurter later conceded that had the issue arisen in the 1940s, he would have voted to uphold school segregation because "public opinion had not then crystallized against it." (Klarman 2007, 152)

In this way, "[t]he Justices in *Brown* did not think that they were creating a movement for racial reform; they understood that they were working with, not against, historical forces" (Klarman 2005a, 443). Essentially, the justices were consciously molding the law so that it would mirror the culture.

Thus, *Brown* is a story of the law reflecting culture. But the fallout from *Brown* suggests that the law did not reflect the *entirety* of American culture. In other words, the nation's culture was not (and is not) homogeneous. Indeed, to identify it as a "culture" denies the heterogeneity that constitutes it. Accordingly, while *Brown* may have mimed the rapidly shifting racial mores of most of the country, it did not reflect the racial mores of large portions of the South. Nevertheless, it is important to recognize, simply, that mores were significant to the justices who decided the case. It is important to recognize that culture goes a long way toward explaining how the Court in *Brown* arrived at a holding that was not unambiguously supported by the constitutional text, its intention, its meaning, nor past Court decisions.

The heterogeneity of culture made it impossible for *Brown* to be accepted serenely and uncontroversially. Indeed, the South violently rebelled against it and other laws that attempted to impose "foreign" racial norms on the region. The civil rights movement was a product of the South's revolt during this time. The more that the South attempted to entrench its racial norms, the more that activists organized themselves and rebelled against that entrenchment.

In the 1950s and 1960s, the country—and the world—watched as racist defenders of segregation revealed that white supremacy was a vicious, malicious, repulsive thing. The nation watched as southerners attempted to prevent the desegregation of their schools by subjecting "quiet, resolute Negro children" to "jeers and violence and sadism" (Klarman 2007, 162). And the nation witnessed the spectacular demonstration of racist violence that took place on March 7, 1965, "Bloody Sunday." On that day, unarmed men, women, and children who had organized to demand the voting rights that the Fifteenth Amendment had promised almost a century prior attempted to cross the Edmund Pettus Bridge in Selma, Alabama. They were met with unrestrained violence in the form of police officers on horseback, tear gas, nightsticks, and whips. Bloody Sunday accelerated the discursive shift that was already occurring within the nation. Moreover, the shift was accompanied by the insistence that it be embalmed within the law:

> Most Americans were horrified. *Time* reported that "[r]arely in history has public opinion reacted so spontaneously and with such fury." Huge sympathy demonstrations took place across the nation, and hundreds of clergymen flocked to Selma to show their solidarity with Martin Luther King Jr. and his comrades.

> Citizens demanded remedial action from their congressional representatives, scores of whom condemned the violence and endorsed voting rights legislation. On March 15, 1965, President Johnson proposed such legislation before a joint session of Congress. Seventy million Americans watched on television as the president beseeched them to "overcome this crippling legacy of bigotry and injustice" and declared his faith that "we shall overcome." That summer the Voting Rights Act became law. (Klarman 2007, 178)

Keyssar (2009) writes that the "Voting Rights Act of 1965 was indeed a milestone in American political history. A curious milestone, to be sure, since the essence of the act was simply an effort to enforce the Fifteenth Amendment, which had been law for almost a century" (212). This encourages us to ask whether black people enjoyed the right to be free from racial discrimination in voting access prior to the passage of the act. If one answers this question in the affirmative, as would skeptics of the strong claim, one would have to acknowledge that black people enjoyed a right to be free from racial discrimination in voting access that did not actually provide them with freedom from racial discrimination in voting access. And one would have to acknowledge the curiosity that the Court—which provided official interpretations of the boundaries of this right—believed that practices denying black people freedom from racial discrimination in voting access did not infringe the right.

The strong claim invites us to resolve this curiosity by concluding that, even though the Fifteenth Amendment formally enfranchised black people, black people nevertheless lacked voting rights, as they had been informally disenfranchised of them. We might be more honest with ourselves—and more faithful to the experiences of black people on the ground—if we conclude that black people failed to enjoy a right to vote (or a right to be free from racial discrimination in voting access) prior to the passage of the Voting Rights Act. The strong claim asserts that formal rights do not necessarily lead to enfranchisement. Informal disenfranchisement can strip individuals of the rights that they have been formally endowed.

Whether one accepts the strong claim or the moderate claim, the story of how black people came to possess actual voting rights—rights that do not exist in theory alone but actually have material effects that enable the rightsbearer to do the very thing that the right is intended to allow him to do—is a tortuous one involving a dialectical relationship between law and culture. Yet, it is also one in which culture, and politics, jumpstart the dialectic. The engine behind the Fifteenth Amendment was a war. Because of black people's service during the Civil War, they were re-envisioned within the cultural imagination. Moreover, political circumstance made it expedient for the Republican Party to preserve that new vision in the law. Thus, culture and politics explain how black people won the right to vote.

And culture and politics explain how black people lost this right to vote, effectively or actually. When the North lost the political will to enforce its norms and mores on the South—withdrawing from the region at the end of Reconstruction—the South was able to implement its own distinct set of racial norms and mores in law. Thus, the law became saturated with poll taxes and grandfather clauses and residency requirements and literacy tests and white primaries—the stuff of informal disenfranchisement, according to the strong claim (or the stuff of judicially sanctioned rights violation, according to the moderate claim).

And culture and politics explain how black people regained in the mid–twentieth century the right that had been (effectively or actually) stripped from them. A world war and international scrutiny encouraged the country to view the southern system of racial inequality through a democratic ideological lens. It was apparent that the practices of a significant portion of the country were inconsistent with that ideology. The federal law changed to accommodate that ideology. The South reacted violently against that accommodation. The national culture shifted more dramatically in response to the South's response. And eventually that dramatic shift was reflected in the Voting Rights Act—which the strong claim understands as finally conferring voting rights to black people, undoing the informal disenfranchisement that had been accomplished. (Of course, the content of the rights that the act confers depends on courts and agencies, whose interpretations of the statute are driven, again, by heterogeneous cultural and political forces.)

The Court's role in this story is one of echo, in that the Court echoed an existing cultural sense. And, given the heterogeneity of culture, there are always several cultural senses that the Court might reflect in any particular decision. However, in the case of black people's voting rights, the Court reflected the most ascendant one. That is, the Court's decisions echoed the dominant culture out of which those decisions sprang and onto which those decisions would act. As Klarman (2007) summarizes it, "In the late 1890s, when most of the nation supported white supremacy, the Court rejected constitutional challenges to racial segregation and black disfranchisement. By the time the justices had become more racially progressive, so had much of the nation" (8).[7]

This exploration of black people's experience with the right to vote may provide lessons to those of us who are interested in poor mothers' experiences with state power. The story of how black people came to be conferred with actual and meaningful voting rights is a complex one involving wars and social movements and politics and law. It is a story about how wars and social movements and politics and law changed the culture. It was because of cultural change that black people came to be meaningfully enfranchised. Similarly, I propose in this book that it will be because of cultural change that poor women come to bear meaningful privacy rights.

Sexual Minorities and Marriage Rights

The history of how lesbians and gay men have won a constitutional right to marry deserves consideration because, like the history of how black people won the right to vote, it is one that has very little to do with the constitutional text and everything to do with a transformation in cultural discourses. Unlike the history of black people's enfranchisement, however, the story of lesbians and gay men's acquisition of a constitutional right to marry is succinct.

In fact, this succinctness is remarkable. Indeed, in just a couple of decades, LGBT people have gone from being social pariahs to being valued, and legally protected, members of the body politic. Just fifty years ago, the mores of the country with respect to sexual minorities, as a general matter, were quite different than they are today. Indeed, during this time, sexual attraction to a person of the same sex was considered a symptom of mental illness, and those who would indulge that attraction were considered sick, pathological, dangerous, and in need of containment (D'Emilio 1983). As one would expect, the laws reflected those mores; for example, sodomy was criminalized in many states (Cain 1993). This criminalization was blessed by the Supreme Court in 1986; in its decision in *Bowers v. Hardwick*, the Court held that the Constitution did not impart LGBT individuals with a right that protected them from criminal punishment for having sex.[8]

The criminalization of their sexual expression enabled sexual minorities, as a whole, to be conceptualized and treated as presumptive criminals (Cain 1993). Their ostensible criminality justified their exclusion from housing, jobs, the military, and other spaces that are basic to citizenship. Moreover, because law enforcement presumed that the places in which sexual minorities gathered were places within which crimes would be committed, the bars and clubs that sexual minorities frequented were treated as crime sites (Cain 1993). Police raids of these spaces were a constant, and LGBT people experienced harassment by law enforcement as an ordinary fact of life.

Although there was a predictability to police harassment, sexual minorities did not find it unobjectionable. Quite the contrary, LGBT persons found the police practices that identified and reinscribed them as excluded members of the body politic as wholly intolerable and unjust. Eventually, they rebelled. Most historians and LGBT activists recognize June 27, 1969, as the beginning of the gay rights movement. That evening, the New York Police Department did what they had done on so many past evenings: It raided a gay bar. However, on this particular day, the patrons of this particular bar, the Stonewall Inn, rebelled. Three days of protest, demonstration, and rioting ensued in New York City. These protests inspired more protests in other parts of the country, thus making an event that might have only had temporary regional significance into one with lasting national import (Cain 1993).

The Stonewall rebellion is meaningful because it marked the beginning of a period wherein the country's norms and values with respect to sexual minorities shifted. Differently stated, Stonewall launched the cultural change that, invariably, is a precondition for legal change. This is not to say that sexual minorities had not attempted to transform social mores regarding sexuality and gender identity prior to that night.[9] However, earlier attempts to change mores regarding sexual minorities had not been effective, in large part because society was not amenable to transformation at those times. But, Stonewall occurred within a context of massive cultural change, generally. Indeed, legal scholar Patricia Cain cautions against viewing Stonewall "in isolation from other radical movements of the 1960s":

> Martin Luther King preached nonviolent opposition to the racist power structure and led civil rights marches to protest the inequality between black and white Americans. Student radicals in Berkeley challenged the authorities in charge of the University of California by claiming their free speech rights. Students exercised these rights by protesting the war in Viet Nam. Students for a Democratic Society was formed in the early 1960s in Michigan and launched a new left political movement. The second wave of feminism began in the early 1960s, and by the late 1960s had spawned several radical organizations. In 1968, protesters at the Democratic convention in Chicago were beaten by police officers. It was within this broader context of resistance and public challenges to governmental authority that the Stonewall riots began. (Cain 1993, 1580)

The events that Cain itemizes—the events that constituted the environment within which Stonewall occurred—were efforts to transform cultural discourses respecting race, sex and gender, and the legitimacy of the Vietnam War. As the nation was being incited to evaluate critically its norms and values in the 1960s, it was more receptive to interrogating its norms and values regarding sexual minorities—an interrogation that the Stonewall riots inspired and upon which it insisted.

Cain describes the scores of post-Stonewall lawsuits in which sexual minorities fought to retain their positions in the military and other government jobs, fought to have their student organizations recognized by the universities in which they were enrolled, and fought to be naturalized as U.S. citizens. (In these naturalization suits, lesbians and gay men refuted the claim that their sexual orientation denoted a lack of "good moral character," a trait that the naturalization statute requires of prospective citizens.) And, of course, sexual minorities challenged laws criminalizing sodomy. It is important to recognize that both the cause and the effect of this litigation were rapidly shifting norms around sexual orientation and gender identity. Sexual minorities demanded that the law facilitate and protect their presence within society because society had begun increasingly to accept them. And the dialectic between law and society turned.

Many analysts of LGBT rights identify popular culture as an agent in the transformation of the nation from one in which the only safe place for sexual minorities was the closet to our more inclusive present. Writes journalist Mark Barabak (2012),

> Popular culture and its shaper, the mass media, have also played a crucial role in changing attitudes, much as news accounts helped advance the cause of the black civil rights movement. Only this time it wasn't images of fire hoses and police dogs turned on innocents but the sympathetic portrayal of gay and lesbian characters in prime time, in what has become a TV staple. (Barabak 2012)

Analyses of the role of popular culture in the evolution of society's mores regarding sexual minorities invariably cite the celebrity Ellen DeGeneres and the television show *Will & Grace*. In 1997, when the television show that bore DeGeneres's name was hugely popular and highly watched, she came out on Oprah Winfrey's equally popular and highly watched talk show. Legal theorist Kris Franklin (2001) describes DeGeneres's coming out as "a watershed in the way the traditional mainstream media conceived of lesbians and gay men as simultaneously culturally meaningful and not intimidating (that is, 'just like everyone else')" (60). Eventually, when DeGeneres's fictional character came out on her titular television show, 46 million people watched the episode (Kelley 2014).

Meanwhile, *Will & Grace* concerned the quirky trials and tribulations of a successful gay lawyer named Will and his straight female best friend and roommate, Grace. The television show was the highest rated sitcom among 18- to 49-year-olds for four years out of its eight-year run and frequently has been credited with helping to familiarize the public with sexual minorities and, in so doing, facilitate their acceptance into the body politic. Indeed, former Vice President Joe Biden once claimed that *Will & Grace* "probably did more to educate the public [about sexual minorities] than almost anything anybody has ever done so far" (Barbaro 2012).

Interpersonal interaction is equally essential to changing social mores regarding sexual minorities. Writes legal scholar William Eskridge (2013), "It is a cliché, but a valid truth, that a person's homophobia is ameliorated by knowing and working with a lesbian or gay person" (314). The idea is that if a sexual minority is one's colleague at work, or one's neighbor, or one's sibling, or one's child, one is less likely to conceptualize sexual minorities as an abstract (and therefore, detestable) Other and more likely to conceptualize them as concrete individuals with whom empathy is possible—concrete individuals that deserve the same rights, liberties, and privileges within law that those in the sexual majority enjoy. As society became more accepting of LGBT individuals, sexual minorities were less likely to hide their identities as sexual minorities, therefore decreasing the possibility that those in the sexual majority could work and live with a lesbian or gay person and be none the wiser.

There is the oft-told story of Justice Powell saying that at the time that the Court was deciding *Bowers v. Hardwick*, he did not know any lesbians or gay men personally and that he may have voted to strike down the Georgia statute criminalizing sodomy if he could call a sexual minority an acquaintance. However, Justice Powell *did* know a gay man personally at the time that the Court decided *Bowers*. One of his law clerks was gay. This clerk had not made his sexual orientation known to his jurist boss (Liptak 2013). As popular culture made the larger culture one in which it was *safe*—physically, emotionally, socially, and economically—for LGBT people to come out of the closet, it decreased the likelihood that a story of the kind that is told about Justice Powell and his clerk would recur.

It is important not to detach the law from the narrative that this chapter tells about popular culture facilitating the transformation in social norms and values regarding sexual minorities. It is certainly true that popular culture made society more accepting of sexual minorities, which encouraged sexual minorities to challenge laws that did not reflect that acceptance. However, it is also true that sexual minorities' challenging laws that treated them as second-class citizens had the effect of transforming popular culture. Consider Eskridge's refutation of the backlash thesis—which, before the sweeping triumph of the marriage equality movement made the thesis appear misguided, posited that litigation harms sexual minorities in their struggle for marriage equality. Eskridge (2013) writes that

> the leading backlash theorists concede that the United States today is more accepting of LGBT persons and supportive of gay marriage than it was at the turn of the millennium, but they claim that "these changes are not primarily the result of litigation. Rather, they are the result of a changing culture." Yet the changing culture is itself a product of social movement litigation . . . (315)

Journalist Ginia Bellafante's (2006) work supports Eskridge's understanding insofar as she illustrates the complex role that litigation has played in shifting public opinion regarding sexual minorities. Her reporting of LGBT individuals coming out of the closet in Kansas in 2006, after the state amended its constitution to prohibit same-sex marriage, complicates the narrative that backlash thesis proponents have told regarding constitutional litigation for LGBT rights. For example, political scientist and legal theorist Gerald Rosenberg (1991) once argued that sexual minorities' court victories would be regrettable ultimately insofar as they tend to inspire those who are opposed to LGBT rights to nullify those victories in the legislature or through amendments to state constitutions. He concluded that conservative responses to progressive decisions in the judiciary made the legal terrain much more hostile to LGBT persons; indeed, he argued that the resulting environment was more hostile than the one that preceded the victories in court.

However, Bellafante has shown how conservative hostility to progressive court rulings actually roused some sexual minorities to come out of the closet and to identify publicly as LGBT persons. This, in turn, enabled those who may have been unsympathetic, or antagonistic, to sexual minorities and their rights to realize that they knew—and possibly already loved—a lesbian or a gay person. This familiarity, this interpersonal interaction, is the engine behind the shift in public opinion about sexual minorities.

Bellafante (2006) writes that after Kansas responded to judicial decisions supporting LGBT rights by amending its constitution to prohibit same-sex marriage, "[a]n energized culture of coming out has emerged, apparently in reaction to what many see as the anti-gay climate that led to the marriage ban." She writes of a woman named Cyd Slayton who, at the age of 54, still had not come out as gay to her mother, family members, and work colleagues. Even when she began to fight the passage of the constitutional amendment, she still did not come out. However, the vicious rhetoric that those campaigning for the amendment used ultimately encouraged her to identify publicly as a lesbian. She opines, "[T]he venom and zealous campaigns to portray us as sinners has been a blessing, a catalyst for many more of us to share our stories." Sharing their stories allowed others to empathize with them, relate to them, and connect with them. Bellafante writes,

> Ms. Slayton found that the more she opened herself up, the more she found solace. The day after the marriage amendment passed, her handyman, a Rush Limbaugh fan who came to install her air conditioner, expressed his sympathies. "He came upstairs and said 'I'm just so sorry, Cyd, I know how hard you worked on this,'" she said. "He put his arm around me and it was just about as touching a thing that happened around this whole issue." (2006)

Slayton's story is the stuff of discursive transformation—the small, interpersonal collisions that change individual minds and that, collectively, move a society from one in which sexual minorities are pariahs to one in which they enjoy the same rights and privileges as straight, cisgender persons.

In 2003, the Court handed down its decision in *Lawrence v. Texas* (539 U.S. 558 (2003)), explicitly overturning its seventeen-year-old decision in *Bowers v. Hardwick* and holding that the Constitution prohibits states from criminalizing sodomy. Of course, neither the text of the Constitution nor the original meaning or intent of the Fourteenth Amendment had changed in the years that separated *Bowers* and *Lawrence*. What had changed, however, was the cultural conscience respecting LGBT people. "In the seventeen years between *Bowers* and *Lawrence*, public opinion went from *opposing* the legalization of homosexual relations by fifty-five percent to thirty-three percent to *supporting* legalization by sixty percent to thirty-five percent" (Klarman 2005a, 443). Those figures make a strong case that the Court's interpretation of the Constitution, in some important sense, parallels the dominant culture from which those interpretations emerge.

On June 26, 2015, the Court handed down its decision in *Obergefell v. Hodges* (135 S.Ct. 2584 (2015)), holding that the fundamental right to marry that the Constitution has long been interpreted to recognize is one that belongs not just to individuals seeking to marry persons of a different sex, but also to individuals seeking to marry persons of the same sex. Many had predicted *Obergefell*. And this was not simply because the logic of the Court's decision in *U.S. v. Windsor*, in which it struck down the Defense of Marriage Act and the federal government's refusal to recognize the marriages into which sexual minorities had entered under state law, seemed to lead to the inexorable conclusion that the right to marry protected by the Constitution also belonged to individuals in love with persons of the same sex. The result in *Obergefell* was predictable, and predicted, because the national culture at the time the Court decided the case was one that was rapidly coming to accept LGBT persons as equal citizens.[10] The decision, while historic and worthy of celebration, simply embedded a widely shared social norm into constitutional law.

Klarman (2005a) had forecast the result in *Obergefell*, calculating that "[i]f public opinion on that issue becomes more tolerant . . . , then the Court is likely to . . . invalidate bans on same-sex marriage. The critical development . . . will have been changes in public opinion, not the inexorable doctrinal logic of the earlier decision[s]" (452). He predicted that once there was an evolution in social norms and values, then "a majority of Supreme Court Justices [would] likely deem marriage equality a constitutional right. That is simply how constitutional law works in the United States" (Klarman 2013, 160). *Obergefell* seems to vindicate his theory of constitutional law.

Lessons for Poor Mothers

If that is how constitutional law works in the United States, then those interested in seeing poor mothers bear the privacy rights that their counterparts with class privilege bear ought to be interested in the evolution of social norms and values regarding poverty and motherhood. Again, my objective in this book is to advance the claim that poor mothers have been deprived of effective (consistent with the moderate claim) or actual (consistent with the strong claim) privacy rights because the moral construction of poverty counsels that privacy rights will not yield the values that they are designed to generate when poor mothers bear them. I contend that poor mothers will only bear the privacy rights that wealthier people bear when immorality is disarticulated from poverty and mothering while poor.

But, we have to ask how likely it is that our national culture will transform from one that blames poverty on the impoverished into one that understands that structural forces beyond individual control cause poverty. Political scientist Evelyn Brodkin (1993) has asked a similar question, noting that

> although the moral construction of the poor is not static, neither is it highly mutable. From the British Poor Laws of the 16th century to American welfare policies of the late 20th century, poverty has persistently represented a debased social status. . . . In light of this history, what are the prospects for a radical reconstruction, one that removes the moral stigma of poverty by recognizing its causes to be largely beyond the agency of the poor? (669)

If this radical reconstruction of culture is to occur, it seems undeniable that it will have to be prompted by something of historic proportions—war, violent conflict within the nation's borders, international scrutiny that incites us to evaluate whether our practices are consistent with our ideologies, and so on. Interestingly, Brodkin observes that historic upheavals in the *economy* have great potential for radically reconstructing discourses around poverty. She writes, "[d]ramatic events can reshape social consciousness, as did the Great Depression, creating a window for the formation of a limited American welfare state" (669).

Indeed, the Great Recession, which most economists identify as beginning in December 2007 and ending in June 2009, was an extraordinary opportunity for structural explanations of poverty to gain cultural salience (Center on Budget and Policy Priorities 2016). During the Great Recession, the worst economic downturn that the country has experienced since the Great Depression of 1929–33 (Taylor et al. 2010), millions of "regular" Americans had brushes with poverty—experiencing joblessness, home foreclosures, the evaporation of assets, and the disappearance of the private safety nets that they had built to shield themselves from the vulnerabilities that accompany financial misfortune. Each of these features of the Great Recession is well documented.

Unemployment levels were historically, and vividly, high during the Great Recession. The unemployment rate peaked at 10 percent, and the rate of persons either unemployed or underemployed was 16.6 percent (Taylor et al. 2010). While these figures are shocking in their magnitude, they fail to indicate the masses of workers who suffered financially during the Great Recession years. First, a third of the adults in the labor force (32 percent) had been unemployed at some time during the recession (Taylor et al. 2010). Moreover, while many other workers managed to keep their jobs, they were forced to take a pay cut, to have their hours reduced, to take an unpaid leave, or to become part-time workers. In all, the Pew Research Center reports that the recession negatively affected more than half of the labor force—55 percent of all workers (Taylor et al. 2010).

Further, the unemployment that many workers endured during this recession was unlike the bouts of unemployment that workers experienced during other economic downturns. Namely, this recession caused the typical worker to be unemployed for 23.2 weeks—almost six months. Prior to this recession, the longest average length of unemployment was 12.3 weeks, which was reported during the economic downturn of the early 1980s. As such, this time around, workers were unemployed for almost double the length of time that they were unemployed in previous recessions (Taylor et al. 2010).

With respect to home foreclosures, one of the signature features of the Great Recession was the foreclosure crisis, in which banks repossessed millions of homes owned by people who, consistent with the received wisdom, believed that owning a home was a smart, safe investment—an uncomplicated touchstone of the American dream. As of 2011, 7.6 million homes had been foreclosed. It is projected that another 7.4 million will be foreclosed in 2016 (Chiu 2011).

Importantly, the foreclosure crisis did not only affect the poor. It is true that, at the beginning of the recession, foreclosures were concentrated in poorer neighborhoods, occurring after low-income, subprime borrowers defaulted on their loans. However, foreclosures eventually found their way outside of economically depressed areas, affecting borrowers who had enjoyed some degree of class privilege (Jordan 2011). So, those who were not poor were compelled to endure an experience that only the poor had previously endured.

With respect to the evaporation of assets, the Pew Research Center reports that during the first year of the Great Recession, "mean household wealth fell by more than in any year since WWII" (Taylor et al. 2010)—an expected outcome given that the implosion of the housing market and the crash of the stock market, two primary sources of household wealth, were the two principal factors that triggered the recession. Indeed, according to the Federal Housing Finance Agency's House Price Index, home prices decreased by 4 percent from 2007 to 2009, and they continued to fall another 7 percent from 2009 to 2010. Moreover, the S&P 500 index dropped 51 percent during this same time period. The result was that Americans' wealth shrunk dramatically "because for most households home equity and stocks and bonds add up to the lion's share of wealth" (Taylor et al. 2010).

As one should expect, the Great Recession did not affect Americans equally. Indeed, those most negatively affected were those who had been most negatively affected by the system of privilege that flows along racial lines. With respect to unemployment, black and Latinx persons experienced disproportionate job losses. With respect to home foreclosures, black and Latinx homeowners, who were more frequently the holders of subprime mortgages, experienced a disproportionate share of foreclosures. Moreover, with respect to the evaporation of assets, there is evidence that the recession affected the wealth of Latinx and black persons more than their white counterparts. One research body documents that the wealth of Latinx persons decreased 52 percent, and black persons decreased 30 percent; meanwhile, the wealth of white persons decreased 9 percent (Taylor et al. 2010).

Nevertheless, race privilege could not immunize those who possess it from the financial pressures that the Great Recession brought. As one commentator said of the foreclosure crisis: "As the foreclosure crisis broadens to include more areas of the country, all sorts of homeowners are falling into its trap from a wide array of incomes, races and cultures. This epidemic like the mortgages that produced it doesn't discriminate based on race, creed, income, national origin or background" (Chiu 2011). People of all socioeconomic statuses and races were made poor and poorer. And, importantly, people of all socioeconomic statuses and races *felt* poor and poorer. The Pew Research Center reports that a fourth of Americans said that they have just enough money to cover their basic needs, while another 11 percent say that they do not even have enough money for the basics. Even more revealing, when asked to identify themselves as upper class, upper middle class, middle class, lower middle class, and lower class, more Americans (29 percent) placed themselves in the bottom two classes than did before the recession (25 percent). Fifty percent of Americans identified as middle class, down from 53 percent in 2008 (Taylor et al. 2010).

Of paramount importance is that the causes of the recession were no secret. Most were aware that *structural* forces triggered the economic downturn.

The tale of how the recession came to pass usually begins with the packaging of mortgages into securities by financial institutions. At the same time, banks had relaxed their lending practices substantially, giving bigger mortgages to borrowers who had not provided, and could not provide, proof of their ability to make payments on the loans in the ensuing months and years (Irwin 2013). The relaxation of lending standards made more individuals potential homebuyers, and these buyers flooded the housing market. Simple microeconomics teaches that as demand outpaces supply, prices are driven up. Eventually, with homeownership at record levels, housing prices peaked—and then began to fall (Holt 2009). As the value of homes depreciated, homeowners who were unable to make mortgage payments according to the terms of their overly generous loans were unable to refinance their homes or to avoid selling them for a loss. Defaults on mortgages began to occur—first among subprime loans, then among purportedly better quality loans. With defaults occurring in alarming numbers, the value of mortgage-backed securities fell precipitously (Holt 2009). Owners of these securitized investments, including banks, were compelled to restate the value of their assets, taking over $500 billion in write-downs (Onaran 2008). Unable to raise capital, financial institutions teetered on the verge of collapse—until the government gave them billions of dollars in the storied bailouts (Irwin 2013).

Although the average person likely could not give a full account of the story behind the recession, most could recite buzzwords: the housing market, subprime mortgages, the bursting of the housing bubble, the imminent bankruptcy of financial institutions that were too big to fail. Most knew that the effects of the collapse of the housing market and financial institutions reverberated throughout the nation—causing the demand for products and services to decrease, businesses to collapse, and millions to lose their jobs, their incomes, their livelihoods, and their economic independence. Most significantly, most understood that structural forces brought on the downturn. Structural forces brought hardships to individuals. Indeed, it was a rarity to hear anyone explain the privations that the recession brought to individuals in terms of their individual inadequacy.[11]

In sum, the Great Recession—a profoundly structural phenomenon—made poor and poorer tens of millions of "regular" Americans. Significantly, these "regular" Americans (many of them not "poor" or even "near poor" according to official standards) experienced the powerlessness of individuals in the face of macro forces. The Great Recession possibly revealed to more Americans—whose own financial security may have been taken for granted—that individual pathology is not what causes unemployment, diminished and eventual disappearance of assets, and the destruction of personal safety nets designed to maintain economic independence. The economic downturn possibly allowed more Americans to see, and intimately so, that structural forces well outside of the control of the individual can lead to the confluence of circumstances that make people poor. Simply put, the Great Recession was an opportunity for the radical reconstruction of culture. It was an opportunity for more people to understand that immorality and poverty are not systematically related—that the poor are not necessarily immoral Others, but rather are frequently ourselves.

But, we largely failed to capitalize on that opportunity: As Chapter 1 has documented, individualist explanations of poverty are still alive and well. The Great Recession did not inaugurate a cultural transformation—at least not an enduring one.

There have been other moments in history during which discourses around poverty shifted. As noted above, Brodkin identifies the Great Depression as one of those moments. Prior to the most ruinous collapse of the American economy in the nation's history, perceptions concerning the poor and the government programs that would assist them were unfavorable at best and typically hostile. The weight of public opinion was that the government—particularly the federal government—did not have any responsibility to help the indigent. The onus fell on private institutions, like the family or charities, to help those who found themselves in the lowest, most vulnerable tiers of the economic hierarchies that capitalism created (MacLeod et al. 1999). Some historians contend that public opinion was forced to shift after the 1929 stock market crash wreaked havoc on the economy and on individuals struggling to meet their basic needs.

In line with pre-1929 political ideology, the government did very little to provide relief to individuals during the initial years of the Depression (MacLeod et al. 1999). However, the election of FDR to the presidency in 1933 reflected a transformed ideology, as he passed legislation that established the modern welfare state. Most significantly,

> [T]he Depression affected the American public's views toward both the poor and the government's responsibility to provide for those in need. . . . [T]he Depression created a public mindset that help should be available to all on the basis of need, not just for a selected group of individuals with particular needs, such as widows and children. (MacLeod et al. 1999, 177)

Essentially, there was a shift in culture. Prior to the Depression, the most salient cultural discourses were those that identified individuals as the causes of their own poverty. Of course, there were groups of individuals who could not fairly be blamed for their poverty—such as widows and children. But, the rest of the poor were not so excused. The Depression revealed the untruth embedded in these discourses. The scores of men and women who found themselves existing in vivid poverty did not cause their desperate situations. The squalor in which they lived was not a result of their apathy; instead, it was a result of the lack of resources with which to maintain or fix their physical surroundings. Their joblessness was not a result of indolence; instead, it was a result of the lack of opportunities for selling one's labor. That their indigence endured for years was not a result of their lack of gumption—their unwillingness to pull themselves up by their bootstraps. Instead, it was a result of the fact that economies only recover slowly; structures only shift gradually. Simply put, the Great Depression demonstrated that poverty, frequently, is not a phenomenon born of individual moral failings and that the individuals seeking relief from such poverty are not immoral failures.

Or, maybe, it did not. Writes poverty scholar Thomas Ross (1991):

> The Depression, as with all great social dislocations, changed somewhat the way we thought about things. The commonly held assumptions regarding the able-bodied man, unemployed and poor, were obviously affected by the experience of the Depression. Nonetheless, the social stigma attached to the receipt of public assistance remained. Even during times of catastrophic levels of unemployment, we could not shake the idea that there was something wrong about an able-bodied man receiving public assistance. (1506)

In their own thorough history of the Great Depression, scholars of the welfare state Joel Handler and Yeheskel Hesenfeld (1991) conclude that although it was obvious to everyone that, during this time, the poor had been made poor because of a structural upheaval, there remained a sense that the poor were nevertheless properly blamed for their poverty and, consequently, were morally flawed individuals. They write:

> Despite massive unemployment and impressive work and relief measures, traditional attitudes towards relief policy and labor discipline prevailed. It mattered not that the vast number of the unemployed were in no sense marginal members of society and that they were out of work due to global structural dislocations. The failure to support oneself and one's family through work was still considered to be fundamentally an individual moral problem. (90)

Accordingly, if the Great Depression could not change the cultural opinion of the poor as morally defective, we should not be surprised that the Great Recession failed to accomplish the same type of ideological shift, separating poverty from immorality.

Some Concluding Thoughts

While the Great Recession did not have the effect of permanently upsetting individualist explanations of poverty, it remains reasonable to believe that, if these explanations are ever to be undone within cultural discourses, economic upheaval will likely play some role. When economies are shaken, it tends to shatter the sense of financial security that those with class privilege take for granted, revealing that one *cannot be* immunized from financial tragedy. When economies are thrown into chaos, it tends to expose the fact that vulnerability is not just reserved for those possessing certain characteristics; rather, vulnerability is a trait that *everyone* retains. Economic downturns have the potential to make it apparent that economic self-sufficiency, like most everything else, is contingent on forces outside of the individual's control.

Recessions and depressions reveal that there are serious deficiencies in market capitalism. They reveal that it could all come tumbling down at any point in time. And they have the potential to reveal that the people who are victims of these deficiencies are not immoral Others, but are morally similar Selves. On this point, Ross (1991) has written:

> The segregation of the poor and the assertion of their moral deviance are intertwined. Accepting the us/them construct makes the assertion of moral deviance easier to accept, and, reciprocally, the acceptance of the construct of moral deviance reinforces the idea of difference. If we had no conception of difference—if AFDC mothers were not thought of as a category distinct from mothers in general—the assertion of moral deviance would be disturbing because it would be an assertion about us and our families. (1541)

When it is accepted that the poor are not "the poor," but simply are ourselves without class privilege, and when it is accepted that "they" are certainly no different from "us" in terms of their moral characteristics, then our national culture would have undergone a significant transformation. When the culture has shifted in this way—when the moral construction of poverty has been defeated—we may have hope that the Court will construct a jurisprudence to reflect it.

Notes

Introduction

1. This interview was first published in Bridges (2011a). Please note that the copyright in the *[Harvard] Journal of Law and Gender* is held by the president and fellows of Harvard College and that the copyright in the article is held by the author.

2. There is a debate in the philosophical literature about whether privacy is best understood as a state wherein persons are inaccessible to others or whether it is best understood as the degree of control a person has over his or her accessibility. See Anita Allen, *Uneasy Access: Privacy for Women in a Free Society* (1988). Illustrating the stakes of this debate, privacy scholar Helen Nissenbaum (2010) asks, "Does a person stranded on a desert island really have privacy? Has a person who intentionally posts photographs of himself to a Web site such as Flickr lost privacy? Does a person who is forced to wear clothing at a public gathering have more or less privacy?" (71). One will answer these questions differently depending on the definition of privacy that one adopts.

If we understand privacy as inaccessibility, then the right to privacy is the right to be inaccessible to the government. If we understand privacy as control, then the right to privacy is the right to control whether the government has access to us. Ultimately, this book does not need to resolve which of these definitions is better than the other, as poor mothers' privacy is compromised in both senses. That is, poor mothers have no ability to remain inaccessible to the government; nor do they have the ability to control whether or not the government can access them.

3. See *Breedlove v. Suttles*, 302 U.S. 277 (1937) (upholding the poll tax in state elections); *Grovey v. Townsend*, 295 U.S. 45 (1935) (upholding the white primary); *Lassiter v. Northampton Cty. Bd. of Elections*, 360 U.S. 45 (1959) (upholding the literacy test); *Grovey v. Townsend*, 193 U.S. 621 (1904) (upholding residency requirements).

4. Here, I borrow the "conventional terminology" that legal theorist Frederick

Schauer (1993) uses, "pursuant to which rights are either satisfied or infringed, with only unjustified infringements being referred to as violations" (425).

5. In fact, philosopher Joseph Raz (1984) has argued that the absence of a remedy is an expected characteristic of legal rights against the government:

> There are legal rights and duties which cannot be enforced and violation of which does not give rise to action for penalties or remedies. The most important class of such exceptional legal rights and duties is certain rights and duties of or against officials. . . . They are, however, clearly exceptional and in a sense parasitical on rights and duties which are enforceable or which do give rise, when disregarded, to actions for remedies or for sanctions. (3)

6. See Richard A. Primus, *The American Language of Rights* (1999): "Dworkin would not contest that a proposition codified into law would be a right, e.g. that if a legislature enacted a 'right to know statute,' a right to know would then exist in that jurisdiction as provided in the law" (14).

7. Interestingly, the requirement that an applicant possess a good moral character in order to naturalize as a citizen is not merely symbolic—an empty condition that has no real bearing on whether or not a person successfully naturalizes. Far from it, the moral character requirement has become a "powerful exclusionary device. . . . Since 1990, Congress has added hundreds of permanent, irrebuttable statutory bars to a good moral character finding triggered by criminal conduct. Where no statutory bar applies, naturalization examiners may still deny an applicant on character grounds in their discretion" (Lapp 2012, 1593).

Chapter 1

1. Katz (1985) argues that people in the preindustrial United States understood poverty similarly to the way people in preindustrial England understood it. He claims that, in preindustrial England, people conceptualized indigence as a morally agnostic status, writing, "In the seventeenth century, to be poor in the eyes of British law carried essentially the meanings of sympathy and pity we sometimes still give the term (as in 'that poor fellow'): the term 'poor' reflexively signified a moral obligation on the part of society, not the moral character of the denoted people" (254).

However, it is debatable whether being poor has ever been a morally agnostic status. The Elizabethan Poor Laws, which were passed initially in 1601, were premised on the assumption that people were poor because of their own moral shortcomings. Legal scholar William Quigley (1996) observes that a 1695 amendment to the Poor Laws required persons receiving relief to wear a letter "P" on their garments. He writes, "Badging or stigmatizing the poor was a legislative reflection of common moral assumptions about the poor: poverty was the fault of the individual who was poor; if people remained poor it was because of their own bad decisions, laziness or drunkenness; poor people are sinful because they are squandering God-given opportunity" (106). Clearly, the moral construction of poverty was alive and well in preindustrial England.

Further, legal historian Jacobus tenBroek's (1964) scholarship suggests that the moral construction of poverty predates the Elizabethan era. He writes that, during earlier periods in the Tudor years, "[i]dleness was thought to be a result of personal choice rather than economic conditions. Based on personal fault, it was personally correctable if only the will were instilled. Accordingly the Tudors, like their predecessors, unleashed the furies of the criminal law against combined idleness and poverty" (277).

2. Cozzarelli and her coauthors go on to note that many people believe in individualist and structural explanations of poverty simultaneously. They conclude that "[t]his allows those who recognize that structural barriers may make overcoming poverty difficult to also believe that these barriers can be surmounted by sustained personal effort" (2001, 210).

3. While it is true that poor mothers have been situated on both the undeserving and the deserving side of the binary at various points throughout history, it is important to note that, generally speaking, women who conceive and give birth to children outside of marriage have always been considered immoral. As immoral, they have always been conceptualized as undeserving—without regard to whether or not they work and without regard to whether or not other working mothers are conceptualized as undeserving. Legal scholar Linda McClain (1996) has documented the cultural sense that unwed motherhood disturbs the

> important moral principle that having children out-of-wedlock is wrong, independent of any economic arguments against it. It is the deviation from traditional sexuality and a two-parent family structure, along with the absence of an appropriate paternal role, that renders this behavior immoral, irresponsible, and dangerous. (348–49)

Indeed, the idea that "illegitimacy is a moral wrong and that it is morally wrong and morally indefensible that children do not have or know their fathers" is ubiquitous in political and cultural discourses (348–49).

4. Handler and Hasenfeld (1991, 70) reference a 1931 survey documenting that, of those who received benefits from mothers' pension programs, 96 percent of the families were white, 3 percent were African American, and 1 percent were "other."

5. Others have also used the concept of property to explain the value of negative rights to the wealthy and the insufficiency of these same rights to the poor. Judge Richard Posner (1996) has noted that the right to be free from government action is one that is valuable to property holders who, by virtue of their property, are independent of the state and only need the state to act when it is protecting their property interests (4). However, such a negative right against government action is less valuable to the poor. This propertyless group does not need the government to act to protect their property (which they do have). Rather, this group needs the government to act affirmatively to shield them from the vulnerabilities that are part and parcel of lacking property within capitalism.

6. This is to say nothing of the unfairness of distinguishing between positive and negative rights and finding that the Constitution recognizes the latter but not the former. First, the modern reality may be that the government just as frequently demonstrates its power by providing—or not providing—goods and services as it does by affirmatively acting on the bodies and property of persons. Accordingly, when the only restraints on government power are those that limit its actions, it allows to go

unchecked the incredible power that the government has through providing goods and services. As constitutional law scholar Seth Kreimer (1984) observes, "th[e] conception of negative rights as freedom from coercive violence has questionable value in shaping constitutional restraints on a government that more often exerts its power by withholding benefits than by threatening bodily harm" (1295). Moreover, as legal theorist Susan Bandes (1990) notes, the government still acts even when it is not active, given the fact of bureaucratic inertia: "Like a dangerous instrumentality set in motion, when government fails to act, its momentum continues. It keeps collecting taxes; its employees continue to perform their jobs; its directives continue in force. In short, the bureaucracy continues to function" (2283).

7. It is for this reason that Dorothy Roberts (1991) champions retention of the privacy right as a negative right, despite its failure to protect sufficiently all of the interests of poor women. She writes that while negative rights against government intervention into the private sphere might be insufficient for relatively privileged women who may experience this sphere as a site of domination, negative rights are valuable to unprivileged women who may experience the private sphere as a reprieve from a dominating public sphere:

> Women of color . . . often experience the family as the site of solace and resistance against racial oppression. For many women of color, the immediate concern in the area of reproductive rights is not abuse in the private sphere, but abuse of government power. . . . Another telling example is the issue of child custody. The primary concern for white middle-class women with regard to child custody is private custody battles with their husbands following the termination of a marriage. But for women of color, the dominant threat is termination of parental rights by the state. Again, the imminent danger faced by poor women of color comes from the public sphere, not the private. Thus, the protection from government interference that privacy doctrine affords may have a different significance for women of color. (1470–71)

8. Of course, one could formulate the Sixth Amendment as a negative right. One could describe it as *constraining* the state from punishing an individual for a crime in the absence of a jury trial. The ability to formulate the Sixth Amendment as either a positive or negative right demonstrates just how analytically indistinct the two categories of rights are in practice.

9. This proposition is only *mostly* true because history is filled with exceptions to it. Here are just two exceptions: First, the Court that acted conservatively in *Carter v. Carter Coal Company* (298 U.S. 238 (1936)) by striking down a statute that regulated the coal mining industry—a decision that was consistent with the *Lochner* era approach to interpreting the Constitution in a way that largely precluded the government from regulating the market and the economy—was the same Court that acted liberally in upholding the Washington minimum wage law for women in *West Coast Hotel v. Parrish* (300 U.S. 379 (1937)). That is, the justices that decided *Carter* were the same justices that decided *West Coast Hotel*. It was simply that the political inclinations of one justice, Owen Roberts, had switched. Second, the Court that acted liberally in *Goldberg v. Kelly* (397 U.S. 254 (1970)) in holding that the Due Process Clause entitled AFDC beneficiaries

to a hearing before those benefits could be terminated was the same Court that acted conservatively in *Dandridge v. Williams* (397 U.S. 471 (1970)) in holding that states could cap the size of the grants that beneficiaries of AFDC receive. The composition of the Court was the same in both cases.

Further, there is the question of what counts as a "conservative" or "liberal" decision. Consider *Planned Parenthood v. Casey* (505 U.S. 833 (1992)). One could easily describe the decision as conservative insofar as it narrowed the abortion right recognized in *Roe v. Wade* (410 U.S. 113 (1973)) and, in so doing, narrowed women's ability to access abortion services. However, one could just as easily describe the decision as liberal insofar as it upheld the "essential holding" of *Roe* and recognized that the Constitution offers some protection to a woman's interest in terminating a pregnancy. Indeed, the Court might have used *Casey* as an opportunity to strike down *Roe* entirely. Because it did not do just that, one certainly does not misspeak when one describes the decision as liberal.

Chapter 2

1. Martha Fineman (1995) has shown that not all wealthier women are similarly situated in this regard. She argues, quite convincingly, that mothers heading families in which the husband/father is absent are frequently incapable of shielding themselves from government intervention. This is true even when they enjoy some degree of class privilege. She writes:

> There is a presumption with constitutional dimensions that natural families have a right to be free of state intervention and control. . . . These presumptions that cushion traditional families are eroded when single mothers make similar or parallel demands. Single mother families fall outside of prevailing ideological constructs about what (or who) constitutes a complete or real family—they may be thought of as "public" families, not entitled to privacy. (177–78)

Fineman notes that divorced mothers of all socioeconomic statuses are denied privacy because the law can limit their physical movement—denying them mobility absent the state or their ex-husbands' consent. Moreover, she describes the "best interest of the child standard," which guides decisions concerning a child's custody and care, as "elusive and ill-defined," and she notes that it can subject divorced mothers to supervision, intervention, and punishment.

2. This fact calls into question whether the unconstitutional conditions doctrine can be invoked when the government burdens two out of the three areas of privacy that this book discusses: informational privacy and reproductive privacy. With respect to informational privacy, the Court has yet to find that a fundamental constitutional right protects an individual's interest in preventing his personal information from being collected, compiled, and/or disseminated. If the Court will not review direct burdens on informational privacy interests with strict scrutiny, then litigants cannot claim that the unconstitutional conditions doctrine requires that indirect burdens on informational privacy interests should be so reviewed.

Moreover, there are serious questions around whether the abortion right, which is an element of the reproductive privacy right, rises to the level of a "preferred" right.

After *Planned Parenthood of Southeastern Pennsylvania v. Casey* (506 U.S. 833 (1992)) replaced *Roe v. Wade*'s trimester framework with the undue burden standard, the abortion right is a right that is not protected with anything approximating strict scrutiny. Accordingly, it is subject to debate whether a litigant can invoke the unconstitutional conditions doctrine should the government attach a condition to a benefit that burdens her interest in terminating a pregnancy.

3. Interestingly, poor mothers frequently find themselves devoid of privacy by way of child protective services and the foster care system *even when they attempt to receive welfare benefits from the state.* This is because many states have attempted to protect their budgets by removing as many people from their welfare rolls as possible. Loic Wacquant (2009) notes that this technique of "shrinking the charitable state . . . consists [of] multiplying the bureaucratic obstacles and requirements imposed on applicants with the aim of discouraging them or striking them off the recipient rolls (be it only temporarily)" (50). Thus, even when poor mothers attempt to choose the "rock" of being a beneficiary of a welfare program and enduring the privacy deprivations concomitant to that identity, she may find herself thrown to the "hard place" of being a wage laborer, attempting the frequently impossible task of earning a wage that will save her family from the privacy deprivations that result when one is unable to shield one's children from the effects of poverty.

4. Wacquant (2009) defines neoliberalism as an "ideological project and governmental practice mandating submission to the 'free market' and the celebration of 'individual responsibility' in all realms" (1).

5. Criminal procedure scholar Tracey Maclin (1998) discusses studies documenting the disproportionate attention that police departments have given to black motorists. In one, while black drivers represented 15 percent of the drivers who violated traffic laws on one stretch of road, they represented 46.2 percent of the drivers who the police had stopped there. In another, data showed that, of the drivers who were violating the traffic laws, 17.5 percent were black and 74.7 percent were white. Nevertheless, of the drivers who the police had stopped, 72.9 percent were black and 19.7 percent were white; 80.3 percent of the drivers who were searched were black (Maclin 1998, 347, 350).

Chapter 3

1. Family law scholar Naomi Cahn (1999) has identified three types of family privacy: marital privacy, which references the idea that the state ought not to interfere with either the formation of marital relationships or with the workings of those relationships once formed; reproductive privacy, which protects the ability of an individual, single or married, to decide whether or not to bear a child; and parent–child relationship privacy, which protects an individual's ability to raise her child according to her values and as she sees fit. Chapter 3 focuses on this final aspect of family privacy.

2. Philosopher Ruth Gavison (1980) offers this definition of moral autonomy:

Moral autonomy is the reflective and critical acceptance of social norms, with obedience based on an independent moral evaluation of their worth. [It] requires the capacity to make an independent moral judgment, the willingness to exercise it, and the courage to act on the results of this exercise even when the judgment is not a popular one. (449)

3. In fact, racial discourses frequently inform poverty discourses to such an extent that attempting to separate the two analytically is impossible. That is, racial discourses and discourses about poverty invariably constitute one another and are mutually reinforcing. This fact explains the "racializing logic of class attributes," whereby gains and losses in socioeconomic status correspond to gains and losses in racial privilege (Bridges 2011b; Ong 1996).

4. One should be mindful that the investigations that child protective agents make can be quite intrusive. For example, Doriane Coleman (2005) relates an incident in which a social worker investigated a suspected case of child sexual abuse. She writes that after the social worker entered the parent's home without a warrant, "she took photographs of the girl's labia in an open and closed position which she later turned over to her supervisor" (525). The allegations of sexual abuse were never substantiated. When the parent later challenged the propriety of the investigation, the investigator's supervisor "described the visual examination and pictures as appropriate because 'caseworkers are trained to find and document all available evidence during their investigations'" (525).

5. On top of the simple confusion of poverty for neglect, Appell (2001) notes the role that bias could potentially play, writing that because assessments of neglect are highly subjective, child protective authorities may be more inclined to see evidence of poverty as evidence of neglect *because* poor people (and people of color, who are disproportionately represented among the poor) have been maligned in cultural discourses. She writes that evidence suggests that "risk assessors are unconsciously biased to see minority and socioeconomically disadvantaged families as pathological" (773).

6. The thrust of Chasnoff's (1985) study concerned race, however. It found that there was no significant difference in the rates at which black and white pregnant women used illicit drugs: 14 percent of black women and 15 percent of white women in the study had a positive toxicology result. Despite the equal prevalence of substance use and abuse, black women were much more likely to be reported to state health authorities. Of the 133 women who were reported to the state, 48 were white; 85 were black (313). Some commentators offered Chasnoff's study as an explanation for the overrepresentation of *black* families in the child protection system; black parents are more likely to be reported to child welfare authorities not because they abuse or neglect their children at higher rates, but rather because racism leads others to believe that black parents are the proper subjects of state supervision.

As one might expect, Chasnoff's study caused quite a bit of an uproar, and some have rushed to dispute the contention that racial bias explains the difference in the rates at which black and white substance users were reported to state authorities in the study. Legal scholar Elizabeth Bartholet (2009), who has vigorously defended the overrepresentation of black children and families in the child welfare system, contends that the reason black pregnant women who used drugs were more likely to be reported to authorities than their white counterparts is that black women used more "serious" drugs. She notes that black women were more likely to test positive for cocaine, while white women were more likely to test positive for marijuana. She writes, "Although both drugs may be damaging to the fetus if used during pregnancy, cocaine use is more strongly associated with destructive addictive patterns, and parental use of cocaine is more strongly associated with child maltreatment" (916). The problem is that Bartholet provides no insight into how the "addictive patterns" that cocaine abusers exhibit differ from the "addictive patterns" exhibited by marijuana abusers; nor does she provide any empirical support for her claim that "parental use of cocaine is more strongly associated with child maltreatment."

Nevertheless, one can see the intuitive truth of her claim: It comports with our common sense that cocaine is a more hardcore drug than marijuana and, therefore, that cocaine users are more likely to be abusive or neglectful toward their children. However, there are other tropes embedded within our common sense that we might tap, tropes that could lead us to believe that *marijuana users* are more likely to be abusive or neglectful toward their children. Consider the stereotype of the lethargic, apathetic marijuana user—the weed head—who sits on the couch all day playing video games and eating junk food. Contrast this figure with the stereotype of the wired cocaine user—the wolf of Wall Street—who snorts a line of coke before walking into the big meeting and closing the deal.

If we allowed *these* tropes to guide our intuitions concerning pregnant women who use illicit drugs, then it would seem like marijuana users would be apathetic toward their children, while cocaine users would be involved, attentive parents. It would reverse Bartholet's supposition about the drugs that make parents inappropriate or ineffective caregivers. Accordingly, it seems clear that different generalizations inform Bartholet's supposition. She appears to be motivated by the idea of the (implicitly black) crack head and the (implicitly white) suburban mom who smokes a joint every now and again when her kids are upstairs sleeping.

However, Bartholet's explanation for why black pregnant women who use drugs are more likely to be reported to child protective authorities in Chasnoff's study is ultimately undermined by her other claims. For example, when she plays devil's advocate and assumes that black children may be *unjustifiably* represented in disproportionate numbers in the child welfare system, she prefers not to conceptualize this as an over-representation of black families but rather as an underrepresentation of white families. As such, she considers the "racial victims" of the child protective system to be white children. She writes, "Even if we were to assume that black children were somewhat overrepresented compared to actual maltreatment rates, this should be understood as discrimination against white children rather than discrimination against black children" (Bartholet 2009, 920).

This is a disturbing framing of the problem. It is disquieting that Bartholet insists upon centering white people's experiences. Moreover, it is disconcerting that Bartholet eclipses discrimination of black people to construct victims out of white people. Indeed, if we relied on our intuitions—as Bartholet encourages us to do in the context of cocaine versus marijuana usage among pregnant women—they would lead us to feel that *black people* are the victims here. Black parents are subject to coercive and punitive interventions when they engage in problematized behavior; on the other hand, white parents, when they engage in the *same* behavior, are left alone. Essentially, Bartholet invites us to selectively use our intuitions to apologize for a system that brutally dissolves black families while allowing white families to remain intact.

7. If stressful conditions increase the risk that a person will maltreat her child, then it is understandable that the children of immigrant parents are at great risk for child maltreatment, as being an immigrant (especially an undocumented one) is a highly stressful state. The stresses associated with being an immigrant include "language difficulties, separation from family and friends, health problems, financial problems, difficulty finding and keeping a job, homesickness and isolation, fear of deportation, [and] conflicting cultural norms for child-rearing" (DePanfilis 2006, 36).

8. Some studies explain the underreporting of wealthier families presenting possible signs of child maltreatment in hospitals as a consequence of private doctors not wanting to lose paying customers. "Doctors have noted that [poor] women are also more likely than their middle-class counterparts to be reported to government authorities because doctors serving paying clients are less likely to make child abuse reports, unless referrals diminish" (Appell 1997, 584 n.38).

Chapter 4

1. "Informational privacy" could also refer to the scores of statutes that govern the collection, use, and disclosure of personal information (Allen 2011, 156–57). Because the focus of the book is constitutional privacy rights, this chapter will not conduct an investigation of statutory privacy rights. However, it is worth noting that, as with constitutional privacy rights, we should be aware of the possibility that poor mothers have been deprived of these statutory privacy rights, either in the moderate or the strong sense.

2. The challenged law required investigators to confirm that "(1) the applicant has the amount of assets claimed; (2) the applicant has an eligible dependent child; (3) the applicant lives in California; and (4) an 'absent' parent does not live in the residence" (Sanchez v. County of San Diego, 464 F.3d 916 (9th Cir. 2006)).

3. Lack of access to high-speed Internet in one's home may not simply be a symptom of poverty; in some important respects, it may actually help to maintain poverty. Consider that in 80 percent of Fortune 500 companies, the only way to apply for jobs—including low-skill, low-level, low-paying ones—is by submitting a job application online. Consider as well that high-speed Internet access at home improves a student's chances of graduating from high school. Finally, consider that "[c]onsumers can save almost $8,000 a year by using online resources to find discounts on essentials like apartment rentals, clothes, gasoline and food" (Smith 2012). As such, ensuring that the poor have high-quality access to the Internet may be an issue of social justice.

4. The digital divide also exists with respect to the confidence and skill with which the wealthy and the poor engage in networked activities. Because the poor spend less time online, they are less adept at navigating the Internet and distinguishing reputable news sources from less reputable ones (Adler 2014).

5. Analogously, computer scientist Latanya Sweeney (2013) has conducted research in which she discovered that a "greater percentage of ads having 'arrest' in ad text ap-

peared for black identifying first names than for white identifying first names in searches on Reuters.com, on Google.com, and in subsets of the sample" (34). Thus, people of all races lack networked privacy and are exposed to online behavioral advertising. However, that lack and that exposure reiterate the marginalization of racial minorities while reinforcing the racial privilege of white people.

6. Moreover, Nissenbaum (2010) observes that people's experiences of price discrimination are not positive; that is, people prefer equality. They prefer that everyone be charged the same price for a good. The "moral legitimacy of capitalism" may be undermined when prices vary based on ability to pay, urgency of need, or other vulnerabilities. Further, price discrimination may encourage *inefficiency*, where consumers engage in costly efforts to be treated on par—that is, as equals—with others:

> [O]nce it becomes known that different services and prices are triggered by the personal characteristics of buyers, the stage is set for adversarial and resentful engagement where buyers might have to initiate defensive investigations of their own, spending resources to discover prices, services, and products not offered to them. (Nissenbaum 2010, 212)

7. While the decision in *Whalen* suggested that if a right to informational privacy exists, its textual home would be in the Due Process Clause of the Fourteenth Amendment, the decision in *Nixon* implied that the textual home of the hypothetical right might be elsewhere. The *Nixon* Court cited its decision in *Katz v. United States* (389 U.S. 347, 351–53 (1967)) for the proposition that former President Nixon had a "legitimate expectation of privacy" in the materials generated during his presidency—an expectation that likely afforded him constitutional protection. However, *Katz* was a Fourth Amendment case, and the "legitimate" or "reasonable" expectation of privacy inquiry is one that the Court uses to determine whether an investigatory tool used by law enforcement is a "search" within the meaning of the Fourth Amendment. Thus, not only is it an open question whether the right to informational privacy exists, but the textual basis of the right is also undecided. Interestingly, most circuits that have recognized the right have stated that it is based in the Due Process Clause, with a minority contending that its origins are in the Fourth Amendment (Moniodis 2013).

8. Two other facts were also significant to the Court: First, it would have been unduly burdensome to canvass all of the materials in order to prevent the disclosure of sensitive private facts, and second, there are powerfully important governmental interests in collecting and keeping the presidential records.

9. It was also significant to the Court that the background checks demanded by NASA were similar to those used by many private companies as well as the federal civil service. The checks helped to facilitate the employer in its task of composing a "competent, reliable workforce" *National Aeronautics and Space Administration v. Nelson* (562 U.S. 134, 136 (2011)). Because the government also has an interest in a competent, reliable workforce, and because the Court denied that the Constitution demanded that the government use means that were "necessary" or were "the least restrictive" in its pursuit of this workforce, the Court upheld the constitutionality of the background checks (136).

10. However, ever resistant to interpreting the Due Process Clause as a repository of unenumerated rights, and therefore resistant to following the lead suggested in *Whalen*

by finding a right to informational privacy in the Due Process Clause, Scalia argued that any right to prevent the collection of private information was a Fourth Amendment matter:

> [R]espondents challenge the Government's *collection* of their private information. But the Government's collection of private information is regulated by the *Fourth Amendment*, and "[w]here a particular Amendment provides an explicit textual source of constitutional protection against a particular sort of government behavior, that Amendment, not the more generalized notion of substantive due process, must be guide for analyzing these claims." (National Space and Aeronautics Administration v. Nelson 2011, 162)

Scalia went on to argue that the Fourth Amendment did not protect the plaintiffs' interest in prohibiting government collection of their information, stating that the questions asked pursuant to the background check at issue "were not *Fourth Amendment* 'searches' . . . and that the *Fourth Amendment* does not prohibit the Government from asking questions about private information" (162).

11. I met Sia when I was conducting research for *Reproducing Race* (Bridges 2011b).

Chapter 5

1. In arguing that poor women's poverty, and not the law, made abortion inaccessible to poor women, the Court turned a blind eye and a deaf ear to the fact that, in countless ways, the law creates, legitimates, and perpetuates poverty. It instead conceptualized poverty as extralegal—as entirely outside of the law (Johnson 1966).

2. And this is why reasonable people argue that the Court's decision in *Maher v. Roe* is an exercise in sophistry. One can easily frame *Roe v. Wade* as having interpreted the Constitution to prohibit states from passing laws, both criminal and noncriminal, that make it difficult or impossible for women to terminate unwanted pregnancies. Clearly, Connecticut did just that: It passed a law that made it difficult or impossible for some women—poor women—to terminate unwanted pregnancies. It requires quite a bit of casuistry to reframe the issue so that the impediment to abortion is not the Connecticut law but rather is poor women's "indigency."

3. We should pay attention to how the Court's decision in *Harris v. McRae* normalizes the exclusion of abortion from the category of medical procedures that we can expect health insurance plans to cover. That is, *Harris* has effects that go beyond its powerful impacts on material lives: It is *discursively* powerful as well, creating and legitimating discourses that describe abortion as "not standard healthcare." If abortion is not standard healthcare, then there is nothing unusual about its exclusion from health insurance plans that cover standard healthcare. Compare this landscape with an alternative landscape wherein abortion is understood as a normal medical procedure; as a normal medical procedure, its *exclusion* from health insurance plans would be abnormal. The discursive effect of the Hyde Amendment is to impede the development of this alternative landscape.

Further, the Affordable Care Act (ACA) broadened the reach of the Hyde Amendment well beyond Medicaid. The ACA created new platforms upon which the government could extend the logic that abortion care is not a normal medical procedure, but rather is a nonmedical technique that just happens to be performed by members of the medical profession. Under the ACA, individuals with incomes that exceed Medicaid limits, but do not exceed 400 percent of the federal poverty level, received federal subsidies that they could use to purchase private health insurance on health insurance exchanges. However, the ACA made clear that these federal subsidies could not be used to purchase insurance coverage for abortion services. Indeed, in an executive order, President Obama reiterated that the restrictions that the Hyde Amendment imposed on individuals with public insurance—the restrictions that the Court legitimated in *Harris*—would be imposed on individuals with *private insurance* if their private insurance was purchased with the assistance of federal monies (Soohoo 2012). In this way, the Hyde Amendment and its delegitimization of abortion care as a species of simple healthcare reached beyond public insurance and into the realm of private insurance.

Moreover, sixteen states passed laws that prohibit abortion coverage within the *private* health insurance exchanges. (Five of these states had banned private insurance coverage of abortion care prior to the passage of the ACA.) Tellingly, "[t]o date, no state has passed a law either requiring abortion coverage or providing state funds for abortion coverage in an exchange" (Schaler-Haynes et al. 2012, 358). Moreover, of the ten essential health benefits that must be included in a health insurance plan that was sold in an exchange, abortions services were not included (Salganicoff et al. 2014). Thus, the ACA proclaimed that abortion care is not essential to a woman's health and well-being. The ACA's conceptualization of abortion was dramatically at odds with the conceptualization held by many women who have terminated pregnancies that, if carried to term, would have changed their lives in unimaginable and wholly undesired ways.

4. This statement is based on research conducted by my research assistant, who called the Medicaid offices of all fifty states and asked the persons with whom he spoke whether the state's Medicaid program covered elective abortions. He then called Planned Parenthood clinics in the fifty states in order to verify the information that his interlocutors in the Medicaid offices had given him.

5. It is here that it becomes apparent that the "welfare queen" lurks in the interstices of the Court's opinion and—perhaps consciously, perhaps unconsciously—nudges the justices that signed the majority opinion toward that result. The abortion funding cases assert the proposition that, although Medicaid beneficiaries receive public benefits, they nevertheless have access to private resources with which they could purchase expensive medical care. This is the welfare queen: she who avails herself of government beneficence not because she needs it, but simply because it is there.

6. Justice Brennan's conceptualization of how abortion funding restrictions violate poor women's abortion rights is more consistent with the argument that poor women exchange their abortion rights for the Medicaid benefit. Writing in dissent in *Maher* (432 U.S. 464 (1977)), Brennan argues that Connecticut's funding restriction violates poor women's abortion rights because it acts in combination with the state's decision to fund the expenses attendant to childbirth. Brennan contends that these dual funding choices, acting in concert, coerce poor women to carry pregnancies to term. He writes,

"As a practical matter, many indigent women will feel they have no choice but to carry their pregnancies to term because the State will pay for the associated medical services, even though they would have chosen to have abortions if the State had also provided funds for that procedure, or indeed if the State had provided funds for neither procedure" (483). If Brennan is correct, and if poor women could and would terminate their unwanted pregnancies if they did not receive a Medicaid benefit that covered childbirth costs, then one could more believably argue that poor women exchange their abortion rights for a welfare benefit.

But, even Justice Brennan is not entirely convinced that the problem with abortion funding restrictions is the coercive force that it exerts on poor women when it acts in combination with the state's decision to subsidize childbirth. There are moments in his dissent where Justice Brennan articulates his disbelief that poor women would be able to obtain abortions even if the state refused to subsidize any costs attendant to pregnancy. At times, he acknowledges his sense that if the state got out of the health insurance business altogether, leaving poor women with no benefit that would help them access medical goods and services, then their poverty would likely preclude them from accessing safe abortions as well as prenatal care and safe childbirth. He writes, "The stark reality for too many, not just 'some,' indigent pregnant women is that indigency makes access to competent licensed physicians not merely 'difficult,' but 'impossible'" (483). Thus, Justice Brennan realizes that the problem is not so much that states make childbirth an irresistible option to poor women when they fund it and not abortion. Instead, the problem is that indigent women are simply unable to scrape together the $300–$3,000 with which they can pay for an abortion.

7. One might conceptualize prohibitions on Medicaid funding for abortion as an antinatalist policy if one believes, as Senator Orrin Hatch did, that, when faced with the knowledge that their Medicaid health insurance does not cover abortion procedures, poor women will simply exercise "increased self-restraint," be abstinent, and avoid becoming pregnant. Of course, prescribing abstinence as the solution to unintended and unwanted pregnancies is unfair inasmuch as wealthier women are not required to be abstinent in order to avoid pregnancy and bearing children that they do not wish to have (Solinger 2001).

One could also argue that the Medicaid funding restrictions are antinatalist—not because they expect poor women to be abstinent, but rather because they expect poor women to use contraception in order to avoid bearing children that they do not wish to have. However, this position ignores that poverty frequently makes it difficult for many poor women to use effective contraception consistently. Contraception is expensive, and providers who can prescribe it may be difficult to access. Moreover, this position assumes that poor women have control over when, where, and how they have sex; in reality, many poor women actually do not have this control. As Linda McClain (1996) writes, presuming that poor women will respond to policies like Medicaid abortion funding by curbing their fertility assumes that poor women "exercise a high degree of agency in their reproductive lives. Thus, like rational actors, they can and will respond to incentives and disincentives, that is, to carrots and sticks, as well as control their male sexual partners" (384–85). For many women, rich and poor alike, this assumption just does not accord with reality.

8. There are variations on this theme. For example, the Maryland AFDC policy that was challenged in *Dandridge v. Williams* (397 U.S. 471 (1970)) capped the amount of a family's grant only after the family reached a certain size. Accordingly, a family's grant would increase in response to the addition of new family members until the family was composed of six individuals. At that point, the grant became static. Thus, families that included seven or more individuals did not receive grants that covered their standard of need—a standard that Maryland itself had calculated.

9. In addition to the seventeen states that have policies that freeze the size of a family's grant, thereby making the grant indifferent to increases in the family's size, Wisconsin and Idaho give flat grants to indigent families. Thus, for example, a family of seven receives the same amount of benefits as a family of three in these states (Center on Reproductive Rights and Justice 2016).

10. These states are Alabama, Colorado, Idaho, Iowa, Kansas, Kentucky, Louisiana, Maine, Michigan, Missouri, Nebraska, Nevada, New Hampshire, Ohio, Pennsylvania, Rhode Island, South Dakota, Texas, Utah, West Virginia, Wisconsin, and Wyoming.

11. Note that we ought not rush to interpret these states' pronatalism as evidence of a belief that indigent women's children are valuable. Rather, this pronatalism may simply be a product of an abhorrence of abortion. Loathing abortion and valuing children once born are not simultaneous.

12. These states are Arkansas, Delaware, Florida, Georgia, Indiana, Mississippi, North Carolina, North Dakota, South Carolina, Tennessee, and Virginia.

13. Reva Siegel, along with legal theorist Neil Siegel, have also argued that *Casey*'s undue burden standard should be interpreted in light of sex equality values, functioning to strike down those abortion regulations that reproduce women's inequality vis-à-vis men. They write,

> Equality values help to identify the kinds of restrictions on abortion that are unconstitutional under *Casey*'s undue burden test. As the joint opinion applies the test, abortion restrictions that deny women's equality impose an undue burden on women's fundamental right to decide whether to become a mother. Thus, the *Casey* Court upheld a twenty-four-hour waiting period, but struck down a spousal notification provision that was eerily reminiscent of the common law's enforcement of a hierarchical relationship between husband and wife. (Siegel and Siegel 2013, 165)

However, there is something dissatisfying about the narrowness of Siegel and Siegel's view of equality. That is, their equality is only concerned about women's subordination to men. It is unconcerned about women's subordination to other women. If *Casey*'s undue burden standard were interpreted in light of *robustly defined* equality values, then a twenty-four-hour waiting period would not pass muster, as this restriction on abortion access moves abortion out of the reach of the most vulnerable poor women, reinforcing their subordination to wealthier women. The undue burden standard ought to recognize that there are multiple dimensions of equality; it ought to be concerned with more than just *sex* equality.

Conclusion

1. It is likely that the rejection of the moral construction of poverty is a necessary, but not a sufficient, condition for poor mothers to acquire the privacy rights that they do not presently enjoy. In addition to rejecting individualist explanations of poverty, it might also be necessary to simultaneously reject neoliberalism. If neoliberalism denies the relevance of social structures and celebrates "individual responsibility in all realms" (Wacquant 2009, 1), then our system of governmentality will need to purge itself of neoliberalism for poor mothers to be recognized as not responsible for their impoverishment and, therefore, recognized as worthy bearers of privacy rights. Indeed, the discursive rejection of the moral construction of poverty and the dismantling of the neoliberal project may be simultaneous endeavors.

2. Of course, "culture" is an underdefined concept. Legal anthropologist Sally Engle Merry (1998), for one, has made this observation, noting that to construct "a definition for anthropology's core concept has always been difficult, but at no time more so than the present. Culture is everywhere a topic of concern and analysis from cultural studies to literature to all the social sciences[,] . . . suggesting both its significance and its elusiveness as a category of analysis" (579). In this chapter and throughout the book generally, the term "culture" refers to an unbounded system in which meanings are created and disputed (Mezey 2001).

3. Theories about popular constitutionalism come in many varieties—some normative and some descriptive (Kramer 2004; Leonard 2002, 2009; Tushnet 2000). Robert Post and Reva Siegel (2004) tend to offer descriptive theories of popular constitutionalism in their scholarship.

4. This chapter does not intend at all to wade into the debate around the merits and demerits of popular constitutionalism. However, it does accept the proposition that extralegal forces—cultural and social discourses, popular opinion, and so forth—influence the Court's interpretation of the Constitution. Thus, while there may be a descriptive truth, and normative value, to more robust formulations of theories of popular constitutionalism, this chapter simply argues that the narrowest and most uncontroversial rendering of popular constitutionalism has some descriptive accuracy. That is, this chapter accepts a version of popular constitutionalism that even skeptics of the theory could accept. As legal theorists Larry Alexander and Lawrence Solum (2005), who certainly fall into the latter camp, state:

> Public opinion can, does, and should play a role in a complex, interactive process of determining constitutional meaning. We might, for example, accept the notion that the Supreme Court's interpretations of the Constitution are final and authoritative in the technical legal sense, but still recognize that popular constitutional opinion can play a role in shaping the Court's understanding of the Constitution. That role could be direct—the Supreme Court could pay attention to popular criticism of its decisions. Or the role could be indirect—the Court could be influenced by popular disagreement over time as Presidents and Senates select the members of the Court. In either case, "popular constitutionalism" could stand for the notion that the Supreme Court is not an oracle—that its decisions, while authoritative and final in the legal sense, are not in-

fallible and are subject to criticism and ultimately to revision, either by the Court itself or through the process of amendment. . . . If that is popular constitutionalism, then we are all for it. (1626)

5. One might overstate what the Fifteenth Amendment achieved if one claims that it created a constitutional right to vote. Instead, a more accurate description is that the Fifteenth Amendment bestowed to all male members of the body politic a right to be free from racial discrimination in voting access.

6. In the case of the white primary, which was clearly a facially discriminatory practice, the Court reasoned that the Fifteenth Amendment prohibited *state governments* from discriminating on the basis of race. The Democratic Party, which held the primaries, was a private actor. Thus, the Court held that it was unconstrained by the Fifteenth Amendment and could discriminate on the basis of race with impunity (Klarman 2005b).

7. If the Court's holdings are aptly understood as thermometers with which we can read the temperature of the national culture, then, anthropologically speaking, the Court's decision to strike down the heart of the Voting Rights Act in *Shelby County v. Holder* (133 S.Ct. 2612 (2013)) is an interesting moment on which to reflect. In *Shelby County*, the Court declared that Section 4(b) of the VRA was unconstitutional. This section contains the formula for determining which districts must get clearance from federal authorities prior to making changes to their voting laws. The districts that 4(b) identified were those "regions of the country with the most aggravated records of rank discrimination against minority voting rights" (2633). Yet, the Court struck down the provision, thus enabling districts to bring out of its cage the Hydra that is the variety of ever-shifting laws that function to disenfranchise racial minorities. If the Court's decisions are echoes of culture, then perhaps we might hear in *Shelby County* a culture that has grown weary of making the sustained effort required to confer racial minorities with the rights that the Constitution has promised. We might even hear a culture that is comfortable with racial inequality—that believes that the obvious and undeniable racial stratification within the nation is not at all inconsistent with the commitments to justice, liberty, and equality articulated in the country's founding documents. We might hear a culture that is convinced that the present, as rife with disparities and inequities as it is, already comports with the ideologies to which the nation purports to be devoted—democracy, freedom, and so on. In *Shelby County*, we might hear the culture's complacency with inequality.

8. The primary goal of this chapter is to make the case that the Court's interpretation of the Constitution reflects culture. Some have argued, however, that *Bowers v. Hardwick* was decided at a time when the culture was willing to recognize and respect sexual minorities' equal citizenship. For example, Justice Kennedy argues in *Lawrence* that there has been an "emerging awareness that liberty gives substantial protection to adult persons in deciding how to conduct their private lives in matters pertaining to sex" and that "*[t]his emerging recognition should have been apparent when* Bowers *was decided*" (Lawrence v. Texas, 539 U.S. 558, 559, 772 (2003)). If Justice Kennedy is correct, then *Bowers* may actually stand for the proposition that the Court's interpretation of

the Constitution does not reflect, or only imperfectly reflects, dominant social norms and values.

In response, first let me say that it is debatable whether the cultural milieu in which *Bowers* was decided was one that supported sexual minorities' inclusion. Indeed, the Court handed down its decision in *Bowers* while the nation was in the throes of the AIDS epidemic. Remember that some of the hallmarks of the AIDS epidemic in the 1980s were fear; a tragic failure of empathy toward the gay men who were dying of the disease; homophobia; government apathy when the disease predominately affected gay males; and a cruel blame directed toward those who were dying for contracting a disease that would kill them. It would be counterintuitive, then, to describe a society that was willing to watch gay men die by the tens of thousands as one that was inclusive of sexual minorities (Spindelman 2001).

Second, if the culture of the mid-1980s actually was one that did not conceptualize sexual minorities as criminalizable outcasts, and if the Court's decision in *Bowers* represented an interpretation of the Constitution that deviated from dominant public opinion, then one might explain this deviation by looking to the demographics of the Court. That is, the justices were "older, better-educated, and more affluent" than the average person (Klarman 1998, 189–90). That the justices were better educated than the general population actually suggests that they would have struck down the Georgia sodomy law, as those who are highly educated tend to be more progressive in their values than those with less education. However, the fact that they were older than the general population may explain their conservatism on the question of LGBT inclusion. Klarman (2005a) cites a 2003 poll that showed that "respondents aged eighteen to twenty-nine *favor* legalization of 'homosexual relations' by fifty-eight percent to thirty-nine percent, while those aged sixty-five and over *oppose* legalization by sixty-one percent to twenty-four percent" (445). More recently, a Gallup poll shows a similar stratification by age regarding support for gay marriage. In 2014, 78 percent of persons between the ages of 18 and 29 years old supported same-sex marriage, while only 48 percent of persons between the ages of 50 and 64 and 42 percent of persons over the age of 65 indicated their support (McCarthy 2014). If the decision in *Bowers* were out of sync with then-existing culture, then the age of the justices may offer the best explanation.

9. Indeed, the first gay rights organization in the United States, the Society for Human Rights, was founded some seventy-five years before Stonewall. The avowed purpose of the organization was to transform society so that LGBT persons could live freer lives within it (Cain 1993).

10. The result in *Obergefell* was also predictable because Justice Kennedy was known to be sympathetic to gay rights. Cultural change created the conditions in which Kennedy, as well as the four justices that joined his opinion for the Court, *could* decide as they did. It bears noting that although cultural change makes the result in *Obergefell* foreseeable, it did not *dictate* it, as there were four dissenters who did not believe that the Court needed to interpret the Constitution to reflect the cultural momentum of gay rights. Indeed, these four dissenters were committed to the proposition that the Court

ought to interpret the Constitution to reflect the persisting cultural salience of the nation's historical commitment to heterosexual supremacy and LGBT erasure.

11. Of course, these explanations can be heard from time to time. Republican presidential hopeful Herman Cain was quoted in 2011 saying, "Don't blame Wall Street, don't blame the big banks, if you don't have a job and you're not rich, blame yourself!" (Lavender 2011).

Bibliography

Adler, Ben. "News Literacy Declines with Socioeconomic Status." *Columbia Journalism Review*. Published March 6, 2014. http://www.cjr.org/news_literacy/teen_digital _literacy_divide.php

Alexander, Larry, and Lawrence B. Solum. "Popular? Constitutionalism?" *Harvard Law Review* 118 (2005): 1594–1640.

Alexander, Michelle. *The New Jim Crow: Mass Incarceration in the Age of Colorblindness.* New York: New Press, 2010.

Allard, Nicholas W. "Digital Divide: Myth, Reality, Responsibility." *Hastings Communications and Entertainment Law Journal* 24 (2002): 449–75.

Allen, Anita. "Compliance Limited Health Privacy Laws." In *Social Dimensions of Privacy,* edited by Beate Roessler and Dorota Mokrosinska, 261–77. Cambridge: Cambridge University Press, 2015.

———. "Gender and Privacy in Cyberspace." *Stanford Law Review* 52 (2000): 1175–1200.

———. "Legal Rights for Poor Blacks." In *The Underclass Question,* edited by William Lawson, 117–39. Philadelphia: Temple University Press, 1992.

———. "Privacy Law: Positive Theory and Normative Practice." *Harvard Law Review Forum* (2013): 241–51.

———. *Uneasy Access: Privacy for Women in a Free Society.* Totowa: Rowman & Littlefield, 1988.

———. *Unpopular Privacy: What Must We Hide?* New York: Oxford University Press, 2011.

The American Annual Cyclopaedia and Register of Important Events of the Year 1868, vol. 8. New York: D. Appleton and Company, 1869.

Annals of Congress. 16th Congress, 2nd Session.

Appell, Annette Ruth. "Protecting Children or Punishing Mothers: Gender, Race, and Class in the Child Protection System." *South Carolina Law Review* 48 (1997): 577–613.

———. "Virtual Mothers and the Meaning of Parenthood." *University of Michigan Journal of Law Reform* 34 (2001): 683–790.

Appleton, Susan Frelich. "Beyond the Limits of Reproductive Choice: The Contributions of the Abortion-Funding Cases to Fundamental-Rights Analysis and to the Welfare-Rights Thesis." *Columbia Law Review* 81 (1981): 721–58.

———. "Standards for Constitutional Review of Privacy-Invading Welfare Reforms: Distinguishing the Abortion-Funding Cases and Redeeming the Undue-Burden Test." *Vanderbilt Law Review* 49 (1996): 1–70.

Autor, David H. "The Polarization of Job Opportunities in the U.S. Labor Market." *Center for American Progress* and *The Hamilton Project*. Published April 2010. http://economics.mit.edu/files/5554

Bach, Wendy A. "The Hyperregulatory State: Women, Race, Poverty, and Feminism." *Yale Journal of Law and Feminism* 25 (2014): 317–79.

Bailey, Kimberly D. "Watching Me: The War on Crime, Privacy, and the State." *U.C. Davis Law Review* 47 (2014): 1539–89.

Balkin, Jack. "The Constitution in the National Surveillance State." *Minnesota Law Review* 93 (2008): 1–25.

Bandes, Susan. "The Negative Constitution: A Critique." *Michigan Law Review* 88 (1990): 2271–347.

Barabak, Mark Z. "Gays May Have the Fastest of All Civil Rights Movements." *Los Angeles Times*. Published May 20, 2012. *http://articles.latimes.com/2012/may/20/ nation/la-na-gay-rights-movement-20120521*

Barbaro, Michael. "A Scramble as Biden Backs Same-Sex Marriage." *New York Times*. Published May 6, 2012. http://www.nytimes.com/2012/05/07/us/politics/biden -expresses-support-for-same-sex-marriages.html?_r=0

Barclay's Official California Code of Regulations. Title 22, Section 51348. Eagan, MN: West, 2016.

Bartholet, Elizabeth. "The Racial Disproportionality Movement in Child Welfare: False Facts and Dangerous Directions." *Arizona Law Review* 51 (2009): 871–932.

Bellafante, Ginia. "In the Heartland and Out of the Closet." *New York Times*. Published December 28, 2006. http://www.nytimes.com/2006/12/28/garden/28kansas.html ?pagewanted=all

Benforado, Adam, and Jon Hanson. "The Great Attributional Divide: How Divergent Views of Human Behavior Are Shaping Legal Policy." *Emory Law Journal* 57 (2008): 311–408.

Benn, Stanley I. "Privacy, Freedom, and Respect for Persons." In *Philosophical Dimensions of Privacy: An Anthology*, edited by Ferdinand D. Schoeman, 223–44. Cambridge: Cambridge University Press, 1984.

Besharov, Douglas J. "Child Abuse Realities: Over-Reporting and Poverty." *Virginia Journal of Social Policy and the Law* 8 (2000): 165–203.

Bibel, Sara. "CNN's New Day Does Not Rank in Top 50 Cable News Programs Among

Total Viewers During the Third Quarter." *TV by the Numbers*. Published October 1, 2013. http://tvbythenumbers.zap2it.com/2013/10/01/cnns-new-day-does-not-rank-in-top-50-cable-news-programs-among-total-viewers-during-the-third-quarter/

Bloustein, Edward J. *Individual and Group Privacy*. London: Transaction Books, 1978.

———. "Privacy as an Aspect of Human Dignity: An Answer to Dean Prosser." *New York University of Law Review* 39, no. 6 (1964): 962–1007.

Bobbio, Andrea, Luigina Canova, and Anna Maria Manganelli. "Conservative Ideology, Economic Conservatism, and Causal Attributions for Poverty and Wealth." *Current Psychology* 29 (2010): 222–34.

Bodger, Jessica Ansley. "Taking the Sting out of Reporting Requirements: Reproductive Health Clinics and the Constitutional Right to Informational Privacy." *Duke Law Journal* 56 (2006): 583–609.

Braveman, Daan, and Sarah Ramsey. "When Welfare Ends: Removing Children from the Home for Poverty Alone." *Temple Law Review* 70 (1997): 447–70.

Bridges, Khiara M. "Privacy Rights and Public Families." *Harvard Journal of Law and Gender* 34 (2011a): 113–74.

———. *Reproducing Race: An Ethnography of Pregnancy as a Site of Racialization*. Los Angeles: University of California Press, 2011b.

Brill, Julie. "The Internet of Things: Building Trust and Maximizing Benefits Through Consumer Control." *Fordham Law Review* 83 (2014): 205–17.

Brito, Tonya L. "The Welfarization of Family Law." *University of Kansas Law Review* 48 (2000): 229–83.

Brodkin, Evelyn Z. "The Making of an Enemy: How Welfare Policies Construct the Poor." *Law and Social Inquiry* 18 (1993): 647–70.

Brooks, Peter. *Troubling Confessions: Speaking Guilt in Law and Literature*. Chicago: University of Chicago Press, 2001.

Budd, Jordan C. "A Fourth Amendment for the Poor Alone: Subconstitutional Status and the Myth of the Inviolate Home." *Indiana Law Journal* 85 (2010): 355–408.

Buss, Emily. "'Parental' Rights." *Virginia Law Review* 88 (2002): 635–83.

Cahn, Naomi R. "Children's Interests in a Familial Context: Poverty, Foster Care, and Adoption." *Ohio State Law Journal* 60 (1999): 1189–223.

———. "Models of Family Privacy." *George Washington Law Review* 67 (1999): 1225–46.

———. "The Power of Caretaking." *Yale Journal of Law and Feminism* 12 (2000): 177–223.

Cain, Patricia A. "Litigating for Lesbian and Gay Rights: A Legal History." *Virginia Law Review* 79 (1993): 1551–641.

Cammett, Ann. "Deadbeat Dads & Welfare Queens: How Metaphor Shapes Poverty Law." *Boston College Journal of Law and Social Justice* 34 (2014): 233–65.

Center on Budget and Policy Priorities. "Chart Book: The Legacy of the Great Recession." *Center on Budget and Policy Priorities*. Last updated September 29, 2016. http://www.cbpp.org/research/economy/chart-book-the-legacy-of-the-great-recession

———. "State Fact Sheets: How States Have Spent Federal and State Funds Under the TANF Block Grant." *Center on Budget and Policy Priorities.* Last updated October 2, 2015. http://www.cbpp.org/research/family-income-support/state-fact-sheets-how-states-have-spent-federal-and-state-funds-under

Center for Constitutional Rights. "Stop and Frisk: The Human Impact." *Center for Constitutional Rights.* Published July 2012. https://ccrjustice.org/sites/default/files/attach/2015/08/the-human-impact-report.pdf

Center on Reproductive Rights and Justice. "Bringing Families out of 'Cap'tivity: The Path Toward Abolishing Welfare Family Caps." Last updated August 2016. https://www.law.berkeley.edu/wp-content/uploads/2015/04/2016-Caps_FA2.pdf?utm_source=CRRJ+New+Brief+about+Welfare+Family+Caps+on+20th+Anniv.+of+TANF&utm_campaign=CRRJ+Welfare+Family+Caps+Brief+Release&utm_medium=email

Chasnoff, Ira J. "Cocaine Use in Pregnancy." *New England Journal of Medicine* 313 (1985): 666–69.

Chavkin, David F. "'For Their Own Good': Civil Commitment of Alcohol and Drug-Dependent Pregnant Women." *South Dakota Law Review* 37 (1992): 224–88.

Chemerinsky, Erwin. "Rediscovering Brandeis's Right to Privacy." *Brandeis Law Journal* 45 (2007): 643–57.

Chiu, Kevin. "Foreclosures Forecast to Hit 15 Million Homeowners." *Housing Predictor.* Last updated October 6, 2011. http://www.housingpredictor.com/2011/foreclosures-crisis-forecast.html

Citron, Danielle Keats. "Civil Rights in the Information Age." In *The Offensive Internet: Speech, Privacy and Reputation,* edited by Saul Levmore and Martha C. Nussbaum, 31–49. Cambridge, MA: Harvard University Press, 2010.

———. "Privacy Enforcement Pioneers: The Role of State Attorney Generals in the Development of Privacy Law." *Notre Dame Law Review,* forthcoming; University of Maryland Legal Studies Research Paper No. 2016–08. Last updated September 14, 2016. http://papers.ssrn.com/sol3/papers.cfm?abstract_id=2733297

———. "Protecting Sexual Privacy in the Information Age." In *Privacy in the Modern Age: The Search for Solutions,* edited by Marc Rotenberg, Julia Horwitz, and Jeramie Scott, 46–54. New York: New Press, 2015.

Citron, Danielle Keats, and Leslie Meltzer Henry. "Visionary Pragmatism and the Value of Privacy in the Twenty-First Century." *Michigan Law Review* 108 (2010): 1107–126.

Citron, Danielle Keats, and Frank Pasquale. "Network Accessibility for the Domestic Intelligence Apparatus." *Hastings Law Journal* 62 (2011): 1441–94.

Cohen, Julie. *Configuring the Networked Self: Law, Code, and the Play of Everyday Practice.* New Haven, CT: Yale University Press, 2012a.

———. "Examined Lives: Informational Privacy and the Subject as Object." *Stanford Law Review* 52 (2000): 1373–438.

———. "The Inverse Relationship Between Secrecy and Privacy." *Social Research: An International Quarterly* 77 (2010): 883–98.

———. "Irrational Privacy." *Journal of Telecommunications and High Technology Law* 10 (2012b): 241–50.

———. "What Privacy Is For." *Harvard Law Review* 126 (2013): 1904–33.

Coleman, Doriane Lambelet. "Storming the Castle to Save the Children: The Ironic Costs of a Child Welfare Exception to the Fourth Amendment." *William and Mary Law Review* 47 (2005): 413–540.

Congressional Globe. 40th Congress, 3rd Session, including Appendix.

Congressional Record 124, 31 (1978).

Cott, Nancy F. *Public Vows: A History of Marriage and the Nation.* Cambridge, MA: Harvard University Press, 2002.

Cowan, Richard. "U.S. House Speaker Boehner Bemoans Notion 'I Don't Have to Work.'" *Reuters.* Published September 18, 2014. http://www.reuters.com/article /2014/09/18/us-usa-congress-poverty-idUSKBN0HD2OC20140918

Cozzarelli, Catherine, Anna V. Wilkinson, and Michael J. Tagler. "Attitudes Towards the Poor and Attributions for Poverty." *Journal of Social Issues* 57, no. 2 (2001): 207–27.

Crenshaw, Kimberlé W. "From Private Violence to Mass Incarceration: Thinking Intersectionally About Women, Race, and Social Control." *UCLA Law Review* 59 (2012): 1418–72.

Crooms, Lisa A. "Don't Believe the Hype: Black Women, Patriarchy and the New Welfarism." *Howard Law Journal* 38 (1995): 611–29.

Dailey, Anne C. "Constitutional Privacy and the Just Family." *Tulane Law Review* 67 (1993): 955–1031.

Davis, Peggy Cooper. "Contested Images of Family Values: The Role of the State." *Harvard Law Review* 107 (1994): 1348–73.

Delaney, Arthur. "Paul Ryan Laments Inner-City Culture of Not Working." *Huffington Post.* Published March 12, 2014. http://www.huffingtonpost.com/2014/03/12/ paul-ryan-inner-cities_n_4949165.html?

D'Emilio, John. *Sexual Politics, Sexual Communities.* Chicago: University of Chicago Press, 1983.

DePanfilis, Diane. "Child Neglect: A Guide for Prevention, Assessment, and Intervention." *U.S. Department of Health and Human Services, Office on Child Abuse and Neglect.* Published 2006. https://www.childwelfare.gov/pubPDFs/neglect.pdf

Dolgin, Janet L., and Katherine R. Dieterich. "The 'Other' Within: Health Care Reform, Class, and the Politics of Reproduction." *Seattle University Law Review* 35 (2012): 377–425.

Dolinko, David. "Is There a Rationale for the Privilege Against Self-Incrimination." *UCLA Law Review* 33, no. 4 (1985): 1063–148.

Douglass, Frederick. "The Constitution of the United States: Is It Pro-Slavery or Anti-Slavery." Glasgow, Scotland. Published March 26, 1860.

Dworkin, Ronald. *Freedom's Law: The Moral Reading of the American Constitution.* Oxford: Oxford University Press, 1996.

———. *Life's Dominion: An Argument About Abortion, Euthanasia, and Individual Freedom.* New York: Knopf, 1993.

———. *Taking Rights Seriously.* London: Gerald Duckworth, 1977.

Edin, Kathryn, and Laura Lein. *Making Ends Meet: How Single Mothers Survive Welfare and Low-Wage Work.* New York: Russell Sage Foundation, 1997.

Edsall, Thomas Byrne, and Mary D. Edsall. *Chain Reaction: The Impact of Race, Rights, and Taxes on American Politics.* New York: Norton, 1991.

Electronic Privacy Information Center. "The Privacy Act of 1974." *EPIC.org.* Accessed October 5, 2016. https://epic.org/privacy/1974act/

Ellerin, Betty Weinberg. "Women, Children, and Domestic Violence: Current Tensions and Emerging Issues." *Fordham Urban Law Journal* 27 (2000): 565.

Epstein, Richard A. "Unconstitutional Conditions, State Power, and the Limits of Consent." *Harvard Law Review* 102 (1988): 4–104.

Eskridge, Jr., William N. "Backlash Politics: How Constitutional Litigation Has Advanced Marriage Equality in the United States." *Boston University Law Review* 93 (2013): 275–323.

Eubanks, Virginia. "Technologies of Citizenship: Surveillance and Political Learning in the Welfare System." In *Surveillance and Security: Technological Politics and Power in Everyday Life,* edited by Torin Monahan, 89–107. New York: Routledge, 2006.

Fagan, Jeffrey, and Garth Davies. "Street Stops and Broken Windows: *Terry,* Race, and Disorder in New York City." *Fordham Urban Law Journal* 28 (2000): 457–504.

Falk, Gene. "The Temporary Assistance for Needy Families (TANF) Block Grant: Responses to Frequently Asked Questions." Congressional Research Service. Last updated January 6, 2016. http://nationalaglawcenter.org/wp-content/uploads/assets/crs/RL32760.pdf

Family Facts. "Four in 10 Children Are Born to Unwed Mothers." *The Heritage Foundation.* Accessed October 5, 2016. http://www.familyfacts.org/charts/205/four-in-10-children-are-born-to-unwed-mothers

Fang, Hanming, and Andrea Moro. "Theories of Statistical Discrimination and Affirmative Action: A Survey." In *Handbook of Social Economics,* edited by Jess Benhabib, Alberto Bisin, and Matthew O. Jackson, 133–200. San Diego: North-Holland, 2011.

Fellner, Jamie. "Policy and Reform: Race, Drugs, and Law Enforcement in the United States." *Stanford Law and Policy Review* 20 (2009): 257–91.

Fineman, Martha L. A. "Masking Dependency: The Political Role of Family Rhetoric." *Virginia Law Review* 81 (1995): 2181–215.

———. *The Neutered Mother, the Sexual Family, and Other Twentieth Century Tragedies.* New York: Routledge, 1995.

Ford, Jason A., and Khary K. Rigg. "White Claims to Illness and the Race-Based Medicalization of Addiction for Drug-Involved Former Prisoners." *Harvard Journal on Racial and Ethnic Justice* 31 (2014): 105–28.

Foucault, Michael. *Discipline and Punish: The Birth of the Prison.* New York: Vintage Books, 1995.

———. *Power/Knowledge: Selected Interviews and Other Writings, 1972–77.* New York: Pantheon Books, 1990.

Fox News Insider. "'True Poverty Is Being Driven by Personal Behavior': O'Reilly Talks War on Poverty." *Fox News Insider.* Published January 9, 2014. http://insider .foxnews.com/2014/01/09/'true-poverty-being-driven-personal-behavior'-oreilly -takes-war-poverty

Franklin, Kris. "The Rhetorics of Legal Authority Constructing Authoritativeness, the 'Ellen Effect,' and the Example of Sodomy Law." *Rutgers Law Journal* 33 (2001): 49–104.

Gandy, Oscar H. *The Panoptic Sort: A Political Economy of Personal Information.* Boulder, CO: Westview Press, 1993.

Gavison, Ruth. "Privacy and the Limits of Law." *Yale Law Journal* 89 (1980): 421–71.

———. "Too Early for a Requiem: Warren and Brandeis Were Right on Privacy vs. Free Speech," *South Carolina Law Review* 43 (1992): 437–72.

Gellman, Barton, and Laura Poitras. "U.S., British Intelligence Mining Data from Nine U.S. Internet Companies in Broad Secret Program." *Washington Post.* Published June 7, 2013. https://www.washingtonpost.com/investigations/us -intelligence-mining-data-from-nine-us-internet-companies-in-broad-secret -program/2013/06/06/3a0c0da8-cebf-11e2-8845-d970ccb0449z_story.html

Gerstein, Robert S. "The Demise of *Boyd*: Self-Incrimination and Private Papers in the Burger Court." *UCLA Law Review* 27, no. 2 (1979): 343–97.

———. "Privacy and Self-Incrimination." In *Philosophical Dimensions of Privacy: An Anthology,* edited by Ferdinand D. Schoeman, 245–64. Cambridge: Cambridge University Press, 1984.

Gilles, Stephen G. "On Educating Children: A Parentalist Manifesto." *University of Chicago Law Review* 63 (1996): 937–1034.

Gilliom, John. *Overseers of the Poor: Surveillance, Resistance, and the Limits of Privacy.* Chicago: University of Chicago Press, 2001.

Gilman, Michele Estrin. "The Class Differential in Privacy Law." *Brooklyn Law Review* 77 (2012): 1389–445.

———. "Welfare, Privacy, and Feminism." *University of Baltimore Law Forum* 39 (2008): 1–25.

Gray, David, and Danielle Keats Citron. "The Right to Quantitative Privacy." Minnesota Law Review 98 (2013a): 62–144.

———. "A Shattered Looking Glass: The Pitfalls and Potential of the Mosaic Theory of Fourth Amendment Privacy." *North Carolina Journal of Law and Technology* 14 (2013b): 381–429.

Greenwald, Glenn. "NSA Collecting Phone Records of Millions of Verizon Customers Daily." *The Guardian.* Published June 6, 2013. http://www.theguardian.com/ world/2013/jun/06/nsa-phone-records-verizon-court-order

Griffin, William E., and Yaw Oheneba-Sakyi. "Sociodemographic and Political Correlates of University Students' Causal Attributions for Poverty." *Psychological Reports* 73 (1993): 795–800.

Gustafson, Kaaryn S. *Cheating Welfare: Public Assistance and the Criminalization of Poverty.* New York: New York University Press, 2011.

———. "The Criminalization of Poverty." *Journal of Criminal Law and Criminology* 99 (2009): 643–716.

Guttmacher Institute. "State Funding of Abortion Under Medicaid." *Guttmacher Institute.* Last updated October 1, 2016. https://www.guttmacher.org/state-policy/explore/state-funding-abortion-under-medicaid

Hafen, Bruce C. "The Constitutional Status of Marriage, Kinship, and Sexual Privacy; Balancing the Individual and Social Interests." *Michigan Law Review* 81 (1983): 463–574.

Hamburger, Philip. "Unconstitutional Conditions: The Irrelevance of Consent." *Virginia Law Review* 98 (2012): 479–577.

Handler, Joel F., and Yeheskel Hasenfeld. *The Moral Construction of Poverty: Welfare Reform in America.* Los Angeles: Sage Publications, 1991.

Hart, H. L. A. *Definition and Theory in Jurisprudence.* Oxford: Clarendon Press, 1953.

Hill, Robert B. "Synthesis of Research on Disproportionality in Child Welfare: An Update." *Casey-CSSP Alliance for Racial Equity in the Child Welfare System.* Published October 2006. http://www.cssp.org/reform/child-welfare/other-resources/synthesis-of-research-on-disproportionality-robert-hill.pdf

Holmes, Jr., Oliver Wendell. *The Common Law.* Boston: Little, Brown, and Company, 1881.

Holt, Jeff. "A Summary of the Primary Causes of the Housing Bubble and the Resulting Credit Crisis: A Non-Technical Paper." *Journal of Business Inquiry* 8 (2009): 120–29.

Hu, Margaret. "Taxonomy of the Snowden Disclosures." *Washington and Lee Law Review* 72 (2015): 1679–767.

Huda, Parvin R. "Singled Out: A Critique of the Representation of Single Motherhood in Welfare Discourse." *William and Mary Journal of Women and the Law* 7 (2001): 341–81.

Hughes, Charles Evans. "Speech Before the Chamber of Commerce, Elmira, New York, May 3, 1907." Published in *Addresses and Papers of Charles Evans Hughes, Governor of New York, 1906–1908* (1908), 139.

Huisenga, Sarah. "Newt Gingrich: Poor Kids Don't Work 'Unless It's Illegal.'" *CBS News.* Published December 1, 2011. http://www.cbsnews.com/news/newt-gingrich-poor-kids-dont-work-unless-its-illegal

Internet Sharing Environment. "Mission and Vision." *Internet Sharing Environment.* Accessed August 23, 2015. http://www.ise.gov/mission-and-vision

Irwin, Neil. "Everything You Need to Know About JP Morgan's $13 Billion Settlement." *Washington Post.* Published November 19, 2013. https://www.washingtonpost.com/news/wonk/wp/2013/10/21/everything-you-need-to-know-about-jpmorgans-13-billion-settlement/

Johnson, Creola. "Payday Loans: Shrewd Business or Predatory Lending?" *Minnesota Law Review* 87 (2002): 1–149.

Johnson, Jr., Earl. "Law and Poverty." *New York Law Forum* 12, no. 1 (1966): 55–61.

Johnson, Robert. "Kant's Moral Philosophy." *Stanford Encyclopedia of Philosophy.* Last updated July 7, 2016. http://plato.stanford.edu/entries/kant-moral/

Jones, Trina. "Race, Economic Class, and Employment Opportunity." *Law and Contemporary Problems* 72 (2009): 57–87.

Jordan, Sandra D. "Victimization on Main Street: Occupy Wall Street and the Mortgage Fraud Crisis." *Fordham Urban Law Journal* 39 (2011): 485–510.

Kang, Jerry. "Information Privacy in Cyberspace Transactions." *Stanford Law Review* 50 (1998): 1193–294.

Kant, Immanuel. *The Philosophy of Law*. Edinburgh: Clark, 1887.

Katz, Jack. "Caste, Class, and Counsel for the Poor." *American Bar Foundation Research Journal* 1985, no. 2 (1985): 251–92.

Katz, Michael. *The Undeserving Poor: From the War on Poverty to the War on Welfare*. New York: Pantheon Books, 1989.

Kelley, Bradford J. "The Rainbow Sea Change: The Impact of Popular Culture on Homosexual Rights." *Scholar: St. Mary's Law Review on Race and Social Justice* 16 (2014): 283–331.

Keyssar, Alexander. *The Right to Vote: The Contested History of Democracy in the United States*. New York: Basic Books, 2009.

Kindred, Kay P. "God Bless the Child: Poor Children, Parens Patriae, and a State Obligation to Provide Assistance." *Ohio State Law Journal* 57 (1996): 519–41.

Klarman, Michael J. "Brown and Lawrence (and Goodridge)." *Michigan Law Review* 104 (2005a): 431–89.

———. "The Supreme Court and Black Disenfranchisement." In *The Voting Rights Act: Securing the Ballot*, edited by Richard M. Valelly, 37–57. Washington, DC: CQ Press, 2005b.

———. *Unfinished Business*. New York: Oxford University Press, 2007.

———. "What's So Great About Constitutionalism?" *Northwestern University Law Review* 93 (1998): 145–94.

———. "Windsor and Brown: Marriage Equality and Racial Equality." *Harvard Law Review* 127 (2013): 127–60.

Kramer, Larry D. *The People Themselves*. New York: Oxford University Press, 2004.

Kreimer, Seth F. "Allocational Sanctions: The Problem of Negative Rights in a Positive State." *University of Pennsylvania Law Review* 132 (1984): 1293–397.

Krugman, Paul. "The Laziness Dogma." *New York Times*. Published July 13, 2015. http://www.nytimes.com/2015/07/13/opinion/paul-krugman-the-laziness-dogma.html?_r=0

Lapp, Kevin. "Reforming the Good Moral Character Requirement for U.S. Citizenship." *Indiana Law Journal* 87, no. 4 (2012): 1571–637.

Lavender, Paige. "Herman Cain: Occupy Wall Street Protesters Should 'Go Home and Get a Job and a Life.'" *Huffington Post*. Published October 28, 2011. http://www.huffingtonpost.com/2011/10/28/herman-cain-occupy-wall-street_n_1063703.html

"Leading Cases." *Harvard Law Review* 125 (2011): 231–41.

Leonard, Gerald F. *The Invention of Party Politics: Federalism, Popular Sovereignty, and Constitutional Development in Jacksonian Illinois*. Chapel Hill: University of North Carolina Press, 2002.

———. "Law and Politics Reconsidered: A New Constitutional History of Dred Scott." *Law and Social Inquiry* 34 (2009): 747–85.

Liptak, Adam. "Exhibit A for a Major Shift: Justices' Gay Clerks." *New York Times.* Published June 8, 2013. http://www.nytimes.com/2013/06/09/us/exhibit-a-for-a -major-shift-justices-gay-clerks.html?pagewanted=all&_r=0

Llewellyn, Karl N. "Some Realism About Realism—Responding to Dean Pound." *Harvard Law Review* 44 (1931): 1222.

Lubiano, Wahneema. "Black Ladies, Welfare Queens, and State Minstrels: Ideological Wars by Narrative Means." In *Race-ing Justice, En-gendering Power: Essays on Anita Hill, Clarence Thomas, and the Construction of Social Reality*, edited by Toni Morrison, 323–63. New York: Pantheon Books, 1992.

Lyon, David. *Surveillance as Social Sorting: Privacy, Risk, and Digital Discrimination.* New York: Routledge, 2003.

Lyons, David. "The Correlativity of Rights and Duties." *Nous* 4 (1970): 45–55.

———. "Utility and Rights." In *Theories of Rights*, edited by Jeremy Waldron, 110–36. Oxford: Oxford University Press, 1984.

MacCormick, Neil. "Children's Rights: A Test-Case for Theories of Rights." In *Rights*, edited by Carlos Nino, 75–86. New York: New York University Press, 1976.

MacLeod, Laurie, et al. "America's Changing Attitudes Toward Welfare and Welfare Recipients, 1938–1995." *Journal of Sociology and Social Welfare* 26, no. 2 (1999): 175–86.

Maclin, Tracey. "Race and the Fourth Amendment." *Vanderbilt Law Review* 51 (1998): 333–93.

McCarthy, Justin. "Same-Sex Marriage Support Reaches New High at 55%." *Gallup.* Published May 21, 2014. http://www.gallup.com/poll/169640/sex-marriage-sup port-reaches-new-high.aspx

McClain, Linda C. "'Irresponsible' Reproduction." *Hastings Law Journal* 47 (1996): 339–453.

———. "Rights and Irresponsibility." *Duke Law Journal* 43 (1994): 989–1088.

McGrath, Soledad A. "Differential Response in Child Protection Services: Perpetuating the Illusion of Voluntariness." *University of Memphis Law Review* 42 (2012): 629–86.

Mediaite. "Wednesday Cable Ratings: Fox's O'Reilly #1 with 4 Million Total Viewers." *Mediaite.* Published November 6, 2014. http://www.mediaite.com/tv/wednesday -cable-ratings-foxs-oreilly-1-with-4-million-total-viewers/

Meese, Edwin. "Law of the Constitution." *Tulane Law Review* 61 (1986): 979–90.

Merrill, Thomas W. "*Dolan v. City of Tigard*: Constitutional Rights as Public Goods." *Denver University Law Review* 72 (1995): 859–88.

Merry, Sally Engle. "Law, Culture, and Cultural Appropriation." *Yale Journal of Law and the Humanities* 10, no. 2 (1998): 575–603.

Mezey, Naomi. "Law as Culture." *Yale Journal of Law and the Humanities* 13 (2001): 35–67.

Moniodis, Christina P. "Moving from *Nixon* to *NASA*: Privacy's Second Strand—

A Right to Informational Privacy." *Yale Journal of Law and Technology* 15, no. 1 (2013): 139–68.

Moynihan, Daniel Patrick. "The Negro Family: The Case for National Action" (1965). United States Department of Labor. Accessed October 5, 2016. http://liberalarts .utexas.edu/coretexts/_files/resources/texts/1965%20Moynihan%20Report.pdf

Murray, Charles. *Coming Apart: The State of White America, 1960-2010.* New York: Crown Forum, 2012.

National Advocates for Pregnant Women. "Pregnant Women and Drug Use: Charles Condon and South Carolina's Policy of Punishment not Treatment." *National Advocates for Pregnant Women.* Published March 9, 2006. http://advocatesfor pregnantwomen.org/issues/criminal_cases_and_issues/pregnant_women_and_ drug_use.php

Neuborne, Burt. "The Binding Quality of Supreme Court Precedent." *Tulane Law Review* 61 (1986): 991–1002.

Nissenbaum, Helen. *Privacy in Context: Technology, Policy, and the Integrity of Social Life.* Stanford: Stanford University Press, 2010.

Novoa, Ana M. "Count the Brown Faces: Where Is the 'Family' in the Family Law of Child Protective Services." *Scholar: St. Mary's Law Review on Minority Issues* 1 (1999): 5–43.

O'Keefe, Ed. "Jeb Bush: 'People Need to Work Longer Hours' Means They Need Full-Time, Not Part-Time Work." *Washington Post.* Published July 8, 2015. http://www .washingtonpost.com/news/post-politics/wp/2015/07/08/jeb-bush-people-need -to-work-longer-hours-means-they-need-full-time-not-part-time-work

Omi, Michael, and Howard Winant. *Racial Formation in the United States from the 1960s to the 1990s.* New York: Routledge, 1994.

Onaran, Yalman. "Banks' Subprime Losses Top $500 Billion on Writedowns." *Bloomberg.* Published August 12, 2008. http://bazaarmodel.net/phorum/read.php?1,6544

Ong, Aihwa. "Cultural Citizenship as Subject-Making." *Current Anthropology* 37, no. 5 (1996): 737–62.

Otteson, James. "The Unintended Consequences of the Welfare State." *Forbes.* Published April 25, 2011. http://www.forbes.com/2011/04/25/welfare-labor-immoral.html

Padavic, Irene, and Barbara Reskin. *Women and Men at Work.* London: Sage Publications, 2002.

Pelton, Leroy H. "Welfare Discrimination and Child Welfare." *Ohio State Law Journal* 60 (1999): 1479–92.

Peppet, Scott R. "Regulating the Internet of Things: First Steps Toward Managing Discrimination, Privacy, Security and Consent." *Texas Law Review* 93 (2014): 85–167.

Perkins, Jane. "Medicaid: Past Successes and Future Challenges." *Health Matrix: Journal of Law-Medicine* 12 (2002): 7–38.

Pew Research Center. "Most See Inequality Growing, but Partisans Differ over Solutions." *Pew Research Center.* Published January 23, 2014. http://www.people-press .org/2014/01/23/most-see-inequality-growing-but-partisans-differ-over-solutions/

Posner, Richard A. "The Cost of Rights: Implications for Central and Eastern Europe—And for the United States." *Tulsa Law Journal* 32 (1996): 1–19.

Post, Robert, and Reva Siegel. "Popular Constitutionalism, Departmentalism, and Judicial Supremacy." *California Law Review* 92 (2004): 1027–43.

Primus, Richard A. *The American Language of Rights.* Cambridge: Cambridge University Press, 1999.

Quigley, William P. "Five Hundred Years of English Poor Laws, 1349–1834: Regulating the Working and Nonworking Poor." *Akron Law Review* 30 (1996): 73–128.

Raigrodski, Dana. "Reasonableness and Objectivity: A Feminist Discourse of the Fourth Amendment." *Texas Journal of Women and the Law* 17 (2008): 153–226.

Rawls, John. *A Theory of Justice.* Cambridge, MA: President and Fellows of Harvard College, 1971.

Raz, Joseph. "Legal Rights." *Oxford Journal of Legal Studies* 4 (1984): 1–21.

Reynolds, Ashley Nicole. "So You Think a Woman Can't Carry out a Suicide Bombing? Terrorism, Homeland Security, and Gender Profiling: Legal Discrimination for National Security." *William and Mary Journal of Women and the Law* 13 (2007): 667–702.

Richards, David A. J. "The Individual, the Family, and the Constitution: A Jurisprudential Perspective." *New York University Law Review* 55 (1980): 1–62.

Richards, Neil. *Intellectual Privacy: Rethinking Civil Liberties in the Digital Age.* New York: Oxford University Press, 2015.

Richter, Greg. "Bernie Goldberg: Poverty Spreading to 'White America.'" *Newsmax.* Published November 13, 2014. *http://www.newsmax.com/Newsmax-Tv/poverty-race-bernie-goldberg-education/2014/11/13/id/607302/*

Roberts, Dorothy E. "Child Welfare and Civil Rights." *University of Illinois Law Review* 2003 (2003): 171–82.

———. "The Only Good Poor Woman: Unconstitutional Conditions and Welfare." *Denver University Law Review* 72 (1995): 931–48.

———. "Prison, Foster Care, and the Systemic Punishment of Black Mothers." *UCLA Law Review* 59 (2012): 1474–500.

———. "Punishing Drug Addicts Who Have Babies: Women of Color, Equality, and the Right of Privacy." *Harvard Law Review* 104 (1991): 1419–82.

———. "Racism and Patriarchy in the Meaning of Motherhood." *American University Journal of Gender and the Law* 1 (1993a): 1–38.

———. "*Rust v. Sullivan* and the Control of Knowledge." *George Washington Law Review* 61 (1993b): 587–656.

———. *Shattered Bonds.* New York: Basic Books, 2002.

Robertson, John A. "Procreative Liberty in the Era of Genomics." *American Journal of Law and Medicine* 29 (2003): 439–85.

"The Role of Rights in Practical Reasoning." In *Rights, Equality, and Liberty,* edited by Guido Pincione and Haracio Spector, 115–36. Dordrecht: Kluwer Academic Publishers, 2000.

Rosenberg, Gerald N. *The Hollow Hope.* Chicago: University of Chicago Press, 1991.

Rosenbury, Laura A. "Between Home and School." *University of Pennsylvania Law Review* 155 (2007): 833–98.

Ross, Thomas. "The Rhetoric of Poverty: Their Immorality, Our Helplessness." *Georgetown Law Journal* 79 (1991): 1499–547.

Rubenfeld, Jed. "The Right to Privacy." *Harvard Law Review* 102 (1989): 737–807.

Salganicoff, Alina, Adara Beamesderfer, Nisha Kurani, and Laurie Sobel. "Coverage for Abortion Services and the ACA." *Henry J. Kaiser Family Foundation.* Published September 2014. http://files.kff.org/attachment/coverage-for-abortion-services-and -the-aca-issue-brief

Sarat, Austin. "' . . . The Law Is All Over': Power, Resistance, and the Legal Consciousness of the Welfare Poor." *Yale Journal of Law and the Humanities* 2, no. 2 (1990): 343–80.

Schaler-Haynes, Magda, Arina Chesnokova, Cynthia Cox, Marla Feinstein, Amanda Sussex, and Julia Harris. "Abortion Coverage and Health Reform: Restrictions and Options for Exchange-Based Insurance Markets." *University of Pennsylvania Journal of Law and Social Change* 15 (2012): 323–87.

Schauer, Frederick. "A Comment on the Structure of Rights." *Georgia Law Review* 27 (1993): 415–34.

Scheingold, Stuart. *The Politics of Rights: Lawyers, Public Policy and Political Change.* Ann Arbor: University of Michigan Press, 1974.

Schoeman, Ferdinand D. "Privacy: Philosophical Dimensions of the Literature." In *Philosophical Dimensions of Privacy: An Anthology,* edited by Ferdinand D. Schoeman, 1–32. Cambridge: Cambridge University Press, 1984.

Schwartz, Paul M. "Privacy and Democracy in Cyberspace." *Vanderbilt Law Review* 52 (1999): 1609–702.

Sedlak, Andrea J., Jane Mettenburg, Monica Basena, Ian Petta, Karla McPherson, Angela Greene, and Spencer Li. "Fourth National Incidence Study of Child Abuse and Neglect." U.S. Department of Health and Human Services. Published January 2010. http://www.acf.hhs.gov/sites/default/files/opre/nis4_report_exec_summ_ pdf_jan2010.pdf

Shapiro, Scott J. "The 'Hart-Dworkin' Debate: A Short Guide for the Perplexed." In *Ronald Dworkin,* edited by Arthur Ripstein, 22–55. Cambridge: Cambridge University Press, 2007.

Sherk, James. "Creating Opportunity in the Workplace." *The Heritage Foundation.* Published December 16, 2014. http://www.heritage.org/research/reports/2014/12/ creating-opportunity-in-the-workplace#_ftn16

Siegel, Neil S., and Reva B. Siegel. "Equality Arguments for Abortion Rights." *UCLA Law Review Discourse* 60 (2013): 160–70.

Siegel, Reva B. "Concurring." In *What Roe v. Wade Should Have Said,* edited by Jack M. Balkin, 63–85. New York: New York University Press, 2005.

———. "Equality and Choice: Sex Equality Perspectives on Reproductive Rights in the Work of Ruth Bader Ginsburg." *Colombia Journal of Gender and Law* 25 (2013): 63–80.

———. "Reasoning from the Body: A Historical Perspective on Abortion Regulation and Questions of Equal Protection." *Stanford Law Review* 44 (1992): 261–381.

————. "She the People: The Nineteenth Amendment, Sex Equality, Federalism, and the Family." *Harvard Law Review* 115 (2002): 947–1046.

Skocpol, Theda. *Social Policies in the United States.* Princeton, NJ: Princeton University Press, 1995.

Slobogin, Christopher. "The Poverty Exception to the Fourth Amendment." *Florida Law Review* 55 (2003): 391–412.

Smith, Gerry. "Without Internet, Urban Poor Fear Being Left Behind in Digital Age." *Huffington Post.* Last updated March 1, 2012. http://www.huffingtonpost.com /2012/03/01/internet-access-digital-age_n_1285423.html

Smith, Rebekah J. "Family Caps in Welfare Reform: Their Coercive Effects and Damaging Consequences." *Harvard Journal of Law and Gender* 29 (2006): 151–200.

Smith, Robert Ellis. "Sometimes, What Is Public Is Private." *Rhode Island Bar Journal* 59 (2011): 33–38.

Solinger, Rickie. *Beggars and Choosers: How the Politics of Choice Shapes Adoption, Abortion, and Welfare in the United States.* New York: Hill and Wang, 2001.

Solove, Daniel J. "Conceptualizing Privacy." *California Law Review* 90, no. 4 (2002): 1087–156.

————. "A Taxonomy of Privacy." *University of Pennsylvania Law Review* 154, no. 3 (2006): 477–564.

————. *Understanding Privacy.* Cambridge, MA: Harvard University Press, 2008.

Soohoo, Cynthia. "HydeCare for All: The Expansion of Abortion-Funding Restrictions Under Health Care Reform." *CUNY Law Review* 15 (2012): 391–442.

Spindelman, Marc S. "Reorienting Bowers v. Hardwick." *North Carolina Law Review* 79 (2001): 359–491.

Stark, Kirk J., and Eric M. Zolt. "Tax Reform and the American Middle Class." *Pepperdine Law Review* 40 (2013): 1209–34.

Stein, Laura W. "Living with the Risk of Backfire: A Response to the Feminist Critiques of Privacy and Equality." *Minnesota Law Review* 77 (1993): 1153–91.

Strahilevitz, Lior. "Privacy Versus Antidiscrimination." *University of Chicago Law Review* 75 (2008a): 363–81.

————. "Reputation Nation: Law in the Era of Ubiquitous Personal Information." *Northwestern University Law Review* 102 (2008b): 1667–738.

————. "Toward a Positive Theory of Privacy Law." *Harvard Law Review* 126 (2013): 2010–42.

Stuntz, William J. "The Distribution of Fourth Amendment Privacy." *George Washington Law Review* 67 (1999): 1265–89.

————. "The Substantive Origins of Criminal Procedure." *Yale Law Journal* 105 (1995): 393–447.

Sullivan, Kathleen M. "Unconstitutional Conditions." *Harvard Law Review* 102 (1989): 1413–506.

Sunstein, Cass R. "Is There an Unconstitutional Conditions Doctrine?" *San Diego Law Review* 26, no. 2 (1989): 337–46.

———. "Why the Unconstitutional Conditions Doctrine Is an Anachronism (with Particular Reference to Religion, Speech, and Abortion)." *Boston University Law Review* 70 (1990): 593–621.

Sweeney, Latanya. "Discrimination in Online Ad Delivery." *Communications of the Association for Computing Machinery* 56 (2013): 44.

Taibbi, Matt. *The Divide: American Injustice in the Age of the Wealth Gap.* New York: Spiegel & Grau, 2014.

Taylor, Paul, et al. "How the Great Recession Has Changed Life in America." *Pew Research Center.* Published June 30, 2010. http://www.pewsocialtrends.org/2010 /06/30/how-the-great-recession-has-changed-life-in-america/

tenBroek, Jacobus. "California's Dual System of Family Law: Its Origin, Development, and Present Status." *Stanford Law Review* 16 (1964): 257–317.

———. "California's Dual System of Family Law: Its Origin, Development, and Present Status." *Stanford Law Review* 17 (1965): 614–82.

Thomson, Judith Jarvis. "The Right to Privacy." In *Philosophical Dimensions of Privacy: An Anthology,* edited by Ferdinand D. Schoeman, 272–89. Cambridge: Cambridge University Press, 1984.

Turow, Joseph. *Daily You: How the New Advertising Industry Is Defining Your Identity and Your Worth.* New Haven, CT: Yale University Press, 2012.

Tushnet, Mark. *Taking the Constitution Away from the Courts.* Princeton, NJ: Princeton University Press, 2000.

U.S. Environmental Protection Agency. "Children's Environmental Health Disparities: Black and African American Children and Asthma." Last updated April 19, 2016. https://www.epa.gov/children/childrens-environmental-health-disparities -black-and-african-american-children-and-asthma

U.S. Senate, Permanent Subcommittee on Investigations, Committee on Homeland Security and Governmental Affairs. "Federal Support for and Involvement in State and Local Fusion Centers." *Homeland Security and Governmental Affairs.* Published October 3, 2012. https://www.hsgac.senate.gov/subcommittees/investi gations/media/investigative-report-criticizes-counterterrorism-reporting-waste -at-state-and-local-intelligence-fusion-centers

Wacquant, Loic. *Punishing the Poor: The Neoliberal Government of Social Insecurity.* Durham, NC: Duke University Press, 2009.

Waldron, Jeremy. *Liberal Rights: Collected Papers 1981–1991.* New York: Cambridge University Press, 1993.

Wallace, Janet L., and Lisa R. Pruitt. "Judging Parents, Judging Place: Poverty, Rurality, and Termination of Parental Rights." *Missouri Law Review* 77 (2012): 95–147.

Warren, Samuel D., and Louis D. Brandeis. "The Right of Privacy." *Harvard Law Review* 4, no. 5 (1890): 193–220.

Wellman, Carl. "Upholding Legal Rights." *Ethics* 86 (1975): 49–60.

West, Robin L. "Taking Freedom Seriously." *Harvard Law Review Association* 104 (1990): 43–106.

Woodward, C. Vann. "The Political Legacy of Reconstruction." In *Reconstruction*, edited by Kenneth M. Stampp and Leon F. Litwack, 516–33. Baton Rouge: Louisiana State University Press, 1969.

Zickuhr, Kathryn, and Aaron Smith. "Digital Differences." *Pew Research Center.* Published April 13, 2012. http://www.pewinternet.org/2012/04/13/digital-differences/

Index